COLOSSIANNOTES

AN INSPIRATIONAL COMMENTARY
ON PAUL'S EPISTLE TO THE COLOSSIANS

D1559893

COLOSSIAN NOTES

AN INSPIRATIONAL COMMENTARY
ON PAUL'S EPISTLE TO THE COLOSSIANS

GREG HINNANT

CREATION
HOUSE

ColossianNotes by Greg Hinnant
Published by Creation House
A Charisma Media Company
600 Rinehart Road
Lake Mary, Florida 32746
www.charismamedia.com

Eerdmans Publishing, Grand Rapids, MI; located in Logos Digital Software.

Scripture quotations marked YLT are from *Young's Literal Translation*. Public domain.

AUTHOR'S NOTE: Some Scripture quotations have specific words and/or phrases that I am emphasizing. I have added italics to these verses to show that emphasis. Also, in some of the Scripture quotations, with the exception of the Amplified Bible, I have inserted in brackets explanatory text to help with the understanding of certain words and phrases.

Design Director: Justin Evans
Cover design by Nathan Morgan

Visit the author's website: www.greghinnantministries.org.

Library of Congress Cataloging in Publication Data: 2016944689
International Standard Book Number: 978-1-62998-560-2
E-book International Standard Book Number: 978-1-62998-561-9

While the author has made every effort to provide accurate telephone numbers and Internet addresses at the time of publication, neither the publisher nor the author assumes any responsibility for errors or for changes that occur after publication.

First edition

16 17 18 19 20 — 987654321
Printed in the United States of America

To my late, fatherly friend, and the most faithful man I have ever been privileged to know and work with, John J. McHugh Jr.

BIBLE ABBREVIATIONS

AMP: The Amplified Bible

ESV: The English Standard Version

GW: God's Word Translation

ISV: International Standard Version

KJV: The King James (or Authorized) Version

MLB: The Modern Language Bible: The New Berkeley Version in Modern English

Moffatt: The New Testament: A New Translation, by James A. R. Moffatt

NAS: The New American Standard Version

NCV: The New Century Version

NIV: The New International Version

NKJV: The New King James Version

NLT: The New Living Translation

Phillips: The New Testament in Modern English, Rev. Ed., by J. B. Phillips

The Message: The Message: The Bible in Contemporary English (a paraphrase)

WEY: The Weymouth New Testament

Wuest: The New Testament: An Expanded Translation, by K. S. Wuest

YLT: Young's Literal Translation

CONTENTS

CONTENTS

PREFACE

YEARS AGO I received an unmistakably clear call, supported by God's providential working in my life as well as prophecy, to be a New Testament scribe (Matt. 23:34). Simply put, that refers to a professional student, practitioner, and teacher of God's Word, or in today's parlance a Bible scholar and teacher.[1] I complied, God confirmed, and my work continues—with Christian living books, devotional works, educational courses, and now Bible commentaries.

ColossianNotes is my third inspirational commentary, with others coming. This work thoroughly searches Paul's letter to the Colossians giving attention to major themes and minor details, always aspiring to expound what Paul has written in a style and vocabulary that's easily understood by scholars, ministers, laymen, and new converts alike. Besides the obvious historical and grammatical information, I've

---

1. In Christ's day, since Jewish scribes (also "lawyers," Luke 11:45–46) were experts in Mosaic Law, they also served as judges, adjudicating disputes between Jews. They are to be distinguished from non-theological scribes, who were simply copyists of literature or public documents in a largely illiterate ancient world (Esther 3:12), and lawyers, who dealt with matters of Roman law (Titus 3:13).

included historical anecdotes and biblical references to prod you to launch your own studies as your curiosity or God's Spirit leads. If you absorb this work I assure you of one thing: You'll understand what Paul said to his Colossian correspondents in AD 60. But my hope is much more.

My higher aspiration is that the insights presented will stir and move you to walk, work, and worship more closely and consistently with Jesus daily. He is, after all, the heavenly Head who by His Spirit inspired Paul's words to speak not just to the Colossians but also to us. Paul's message is as vital and timely today as when he dictated it. Perhaps it is more so, since we're much nearer the church's heavenly climax Paul envisioned. I also hope this exposition reproduces itself by inspiring many sermons, teachings, and devotionals, or at the least meaningful conversations. I've spent considerable time on the footnotes. If you do the same, I believe you'll find sufficient information and inspiration to make them worthwhile. So don't pass over the footnotes!

Ponder them, with every entry, and pass them on. And as you gather information, may inspiration, motivation, life application, and transformation follow—till He comes who inspired Colossians. *Soli Deo gloria!*

—Greg Hinnant

ACKNOWLEDGEMENTS

I WANT TO GRATEFULLY acknowledge the following individuals for taking time from their busy schedules to peruse this manuscript and offer helpful suggestions and comments:

- BRENDA J. DAVIS: former longtime editor of *SpiritLed Woman* Magazine, former acquisitions editor and marketing coordinator for Creation House Press, freelance writer, and currently a researcher with *The 700 Club*

- DR. ERNST LUTZ: a Swiss citizen (PhD, University of California, Berkeley), was for many years a Senior Agricultural Economist with the World Bank, has authored or edited numerous books in his field, has published Christian pieces in leading magazines, who still travels widely on various assignments in African and Asian countries and is my longtime friend

- DR. CHARLES H. GAULDEN: professor of religion at Southeastern University, author, former pastor, and my fellow instructor with CLST-Global

- KEN KOONTZ: senior pastor of Northgate Church in Salisbury, North Carolina, who serves a network of churches in Israel and is my ministerial brother in Evangel Fellowship International

- DR. MIKE CHAPMAN: longtime pastor of The City Church, Chattanooga, Tennessee, and my fellow instructor with CLST-Global

Thanks so much, and may Christ richly bless you as you pursue your respective vocations and ministries for the King and kingdom!

INTRODUCTION

THE APOSTLE PAUL dictated his Colossian epistle in approximately AD 60 while under house arrest in Rome awaiting trial before Nero (cf. Acts 28:30–31). Epaphras, a Colossian elder, had come to Rome to inform Paul the small but strong and largely Gentile Colossian church was being infiltrated by heretics peddling a toxic blend of philosophical, esoteric, and legalistic errors. The discerning apostle quickly addressed the situation with prayer, revelation, and wisdom—and ink, stylus, and papyrus. And I'm so glad!

By helping them Paul blessed us! Though comparatively speaking a mustard seed epistle (about 1,979 words), Colossians presents a mountainous message. It offers lofty and practical theology, challenges and comforts, commends and warns, and helps us be spiritually enriched, inspired, and ready to "seek those things which are above" while overcoming things below (3:1). Colossians opens numerous key topics—Christ's creatorship, deity, preeminence, headship, and complete sufficiency; our future presentation before Him; His triumph on the cross; the cancellation of Old Testament Law; the dangers of worldly philosophies;

spiritual circumcision; readiness for Christ's return; our relational responsibilities; and others—and leaves unforgettable verses ringing in our ears:

> Christ, in whom are hidden all the treasures of wisdom and knowledge.
>
> —COLOSSIANS 2:2–3

> In him dwelleth all the fullness of the Godhead bodily.
>
> —COLOSSIANS 2:9

> Set your affection on things above, not on things on the earth.
>
> —COLOSSIANS 3:2

> Whatever ye do, do it heartily, as to the Lord, and not unto men.[1]
>
> —COLOSSIANS 3:23

Colosse was located in Phrygia and the Roman province of Asia some one hundred miles east of Ephesus in the Lycus Valley. Colosse, Hierapolis, and Laodicea formed a triad of cities, each less than a day's walk from the others and Hierapolis and Laodicea being larger and richer than Colosse. Before Roman times, however, because Colosse was situated on a primary east–west highway, its trade in wool and other commodities made it the chief city in the area.[2] But this highway was now relocated to Laodicea, and Colosse's importance was declining as Laodicea's affluence and population inclined. Colosse would also experience a devas-

---

1. This is the universal Christian work ethic.

2. Laodicea was not founded until 260 BC.

tating earthquake not long after Paul's epistle arrived (AD 61). Thus, Colosse was a smaller city waning in influence that was nearing sudden disaster, out-trafficked, out-traded, and overlooked by its larger, more prosperous sister cities— but not by God. For it was to the mustard seed church of Colosse, quietly hidden in its day of small things, that God gave the very best ministry available from no less than that Everest of an apostle, Paul.

The Colossians' problems were formidable. They faced an invasion of confusing, toxic heresies stemming primarily if not exclusively from an early form of gnosticism. Throughout this commentary my use of the term *gnostic(s)* refers to this embryonic form, not the more fully developed gnosticism of the next century with which we are better acquainted.

Combining elements of Greek philosophy, mysticism, and mythology, gnostics believed salvation came by one receiving special knowledge (Greek, *gnosis*), and this knowledge was given only to a select group of enlightened persons who had within them a spark of the divine. Being dualistic, gnostics taught there were two gods, one good and the other bad. The good (true) God ruled the higher, eternal, spiritual world from which our souls come and to which they go. The evil god (Demiurge) created this lower, temporal, material world through which our souls pass in life. Thus, everything material is evil. This meant the true God could have no contact with anything material, including our bodies. For this reason gnostics claimed the Incarnation and Atonement were incredible. If Jesus was indeed God, He could not have inhabited a real body but only *appeared* to do so.[3] This

---

3. The apostle John combated the same gnostic error (1 John 4:2–3; 2 John 7).

rendered farcical Jesus' purportedly substitutionary death on the cross and our hope of salvation by grace through faith in His sacrifice. Thus, gnostics invalidated the gospel.

Gnostic belief that material bodies are evil spawned two very different reactions. Some gnostics practiced asceticism, apparently hoping to minimize the body's effects and maximize their spiritual knowledge and consequent oneness with God. Others reasoned if only their spirit affected their relationship to their deity, their bodily acts were irrelevant. Therefore, they lived licentiously.

Additionally, to enable the good God to contact this evil world, gnostics claimed there was a "bridge" (the Pleroma) of angelic and other created intermediaries (aeons), of which Jesus was but one, through which the deity communicated the fullness of saving truth (*gnosis*) with humans.[4] For this salvific intermediary work, these angels were due worship (2:18–19).[5]

---

4. This, of course, flatly contradicted Paul's orthodox teaching on Christ's sole mediatorship (1 Tim. 2:5). Without meaning to be contentious, I must also state the obvious: Roman Catholics' practice of praying to Mary and saints so that they may in turn pray to God for them clearly parallels this gnostic concept of a "bridge" of intermediaries between God and humanity.

5. One source suggests this early gnosticism was linked to astrology, and the ancients associated the bridge of mediating angels with the stars and the influence they supposedly exerted over human lives and events: "These star-gods were held to exercise power over men and women who were victims gripped by a pitiless fate and helpless to break free...But a special way to 'salvation' was promised by seeking fellowship with some angelic power that might raise its protégés above the hopeless round of fate...controlled by the astral deities." See Merrill C. Tenny and Moises Silva, editors, *The Zondervan Encyclopedia of the Bible*, Vol. 1, A–C (Grand Rapids, MI: Zondervan, 2009), 956.

Some heretics were claiming Christians needed Greek philosophies to augment Christ's wisdom. Jewish brothers, perhaps stubborn remnants of the discredited Judaizers (Acts 15:1), were calling the Colossians to return to legalistic observances. Besides these, there were other suitors calling them to aspects of the various mystery religions of the day (cults of Isis, Mithras, Cybele, etc.). Thus, many falsehoods were wooing the Colossians. This courtship may have occurred in one of two ways.

First, Colosse's heretics may have represented a single early sect of gnostics selling their syncretistic faith—combining all the errors above—to the unsuspecting Christians. Second, it's possible these heresies were advocated separately by representatives of different groups of philosophers, gnostics, Jews, ascetics, mystics, and others offering the Colossians a diverse spread of false truth claims.[6] In either case, the threat was syncretistic and Paul's refutation of it complete and convincing, as we will see. And it's still speaking to us today.

Where are our Pauls, ready to refute our generation's errors by lectures or letters? Are we forgetting Colossians' memorable verses or imbedding them in our memories by meditation? Though our city or nation may be waning in influence or our church small and overlooked, are we convinced that God has no more overlooked us than He did the Colossians? Are we eager to devour and apply the epistle God sent them through His exceptional spokesman? Whatever problems and errors challenge us, are we confident God's wisdom hidden

---

6. Though not a large city, Colosse's culture was cosmopolitan. This, plus its location in the prosperous, populous Roman province of Asia, tells us it could easily have been home to people holding such disparate religious views.

in Christ is more than enough to refute or overcome them all? Why do we need this faith?

We are Colosse. Our postmodern world is changing rapidly. America's preeminence is declining as other parts of the world (Europe, China, Russia) are inclining. A catastrophic "earthquake"—the Tribulation, with its earth-dismantling judgments—is not far off, making Paul's call to set our heart on "things above," including Christ's appearing, most timely (Col. 3:1–4). A plethora of neo-gnostics are deceiving millions and wooing Christians to seek their *gnosis*. Though declining now, the New Age movement, with its syncretistic smorgasbord of deities and doctrines from various religious, philosophical, and mystical schools of thought, underpins much of our society's emerging anti-Christian norm.[7] New Age's striking parallels to the Colossian heresies prove that, though everything has changed, nothing has changed! Additionally, the world's major religions will soon begin moving toward merger. By imperceptible increments, fundamental theological distinctions will be downplayed, revised, or ignored to facilitate unity. No coincidence, this will prepare the way for a worldwide religious system that's coming faster than we may think. Thus, first century Colossian syncretism is at our twenty-first-century doorstep.

So, my fellow Colossians, may this commentary help us be ready for what's coming.

---

7. For more on the New Age religious movement, see John Gordon Melton, *Encyclopaedia Brittanica*, Encyclopaedia Brittanica, Inc., s.v. "New Age movement," last modified April 4, 2016, accessed April 20, 2016, at http://www.britannica.com/topic/New-Age-movement.

Chapter One

CHRIST'S PREEMINENCE—AND OUR PRESENTATION

On the eve of disaster in Colosse, Paul sent this inspired message which prepared its believers spiritually for what lay ahead. Among his first chapter's key subjects— thanksgiving, faith, loving all Christians, prayer, the gospel, suffering, intercession, the full teaching of God's Word, the mystery of the church—two stand out: the utter preeminence of Christ and the ultimate presentation of the church in heaven "perfect in Christ Jesus."

Today, on the eve of disaster in our world—the fast approaching end-time judgments—let's study Paul's instruction so we'll be spiritually prepared "when Christ, who is our life, shall appear" to deliver us from the wrath to come.

1

1:1–8 Paul's instructive introduction. Paul began his introduction by claiming he had a sovereign, divine call[1] to
the apostolic ministry (1:1; cf. Rom. 1:1). This quietly reas-
sured them that his words were those of a genuine spiritual
authority, not an impostor, and his revelations truly given by
Christ. On a more personal note he disclosed "Timothy, our
brother," with whom they were probably familiar due to his
ministry in their region, was presently his companion (1:1).
This would have further set them at ease by rendering Paul's
message not only authentic but also embraced by those they
knew and trusted.[2]

After identifying the Colossian Christians as his
addressees, he prays for them, as in all his letters, that God's
"grace" and "peace" ("heart peace," 1:2, AMP) may be freshly
bestowed on his readers by God the Father and His Son,
Jesus (1:2). Habitually given to prayer, Paul began everything he did, including his writing ministry, with humble,
believing petitions for divine assistance.

He then began his message by giving thanks for the
Colossians (1:3) and advising them he continually prayed for
them (1:3, as in 1:9–12). This set a good example for them
and further endeared him to them by revealing the man who
was writing them was no hypocrite but a practitioner of the
things (thanksgiving to God, prayer) he preached!

---

1. On Christ's sovereign, personal call to Paul, see Gal. 1:15–16. On other
disciples, ministers, priests, or prophets called of God, see Mark 3:13–15;
Luke 10:1; Heb. 5:4; Exod. 3:10–12; Jer. 1:4–10; Ezek. 2:3; Amos 7:14–15;
Num. 17:5.

2. Bear in mind during this period there were false apostles and heretical
teachers who challenged Paul's apostleship and teachings (2 Cor. 11:1–15),
some apparently going so far as to forge letters purportedly authored by him
(2 Thess. 2:2).

Next he commends them for their genuine faith (1:4), exemplary wide love (for "all" saints, 1:4), for holding fast to their heavenly hope (of Christ's return and kingdom and their resurrection and rewards, 1:4–5; cf. 1 Pet. 1:3–6), and for having received the "truth of the gospel" and the "grace of God" (1:5–6).[3] These commendations showed his loving approval of their present spiritual walk and hooked their attention with his favor, drawing them to listen attentively to the rest of the letter, which would eventually broach less desirable things such as corrections, warnings, and challenges. And no accident, the mention of the gospel in his opening statement is intended to remind his readers of his and the New Testament's most basic, indispensable, and salvific doctrine: salvation by grace and faith alone (Eph. 2:8–10; Gal. 1:6; 5:4; Rom. 3:24; 5:15, 17).[4]

This gospel, he adds, was bearing God lush kingdom fruit "in all the world," as it had in the Colossians (1:6). Thus, Paul confirmed the fruit of the Spirit[5] was growing in and

---

3. Paul's commendation in 1:4–5 reflects the three most important matters for Christians: "faith, hope, and love" (1 Cor. 13:13). Paul also commended the Thessalonican Christians for evincing these central virtues (1 Thess. 1:3).

4. Grace gives without merit; mercy forbears without merit. "Two words in the Christian vocabulary are often confused: *grace* and *mercy*. God in His grace gives me what I do not deserve. Yet God in His mercy does not give me what I do deserve." See W. W. Wiersbe, *The Bible Exposition Commentary*, Vol. 2 (Wheaton, IL: Victor Books, 1996), Col. 1:6b, note.

5. This rich, diverse, godly spiritual fruit—Christlikeness!—which forms in our lives as the Spirit is fully present and flowing (having His way in us through our consistent trust and obedience), is referred to variously in the New Testament as "fruit of the Spirit," "fruit(s) of righteousness," "good fruits," and "precious fruit" (Gal. 5:22; Eph. 5:9; Phil. 1:11; Heb. 12:11; James 3:17–18; 5:7). Is this fruit increasing on the branch of your life? Abiding close to the Vine is the secret of growing this fruit (John 15:1–8).

showing through their lives and also assured them the faith they trusted in, like their God, was universal, not merely a local or provincial religion or fringe Jewish sect.[6] The gospel was presented to them originally by Epaphras (1:7), who was probably their pastor (or one of their elders) and one of many disciples Paul converted and trained in Ephesus and sent out to evangelize and disciple others throughout the province of Asia (today Asia Minor or western Turkey; see Acts 19:9–10, 26). Paul then praised Epaphras as a "dear fellow servant" (1:7; "co-worker," NLT) of Christ and "faithful minister" to the Colossians, adding it was through Epaphras' glowing report he and Timothy first learned of the Colossians' extraordinary Spirit-inspired love, a Christlike affection for fellow Christians everywhere (1:8). This "love in the Spirit" (1:8) was God's own love, which He planted and grew in their hearts by the work of the Spirit (Rom. 5:5) and which was being perfected as they obeyed Him in their daily tests of mercy and love.

By thus opening his letter with commendations for the Colossians and their founding evangelist–shepherd, Epaphras, Paul unwittingly followed the pattern of ministry

---

6. It would boost the growing faith of the somewhat bypassed Colossians to know that others all over the Roman world were also believing and living and hoping, just as they were, in a miracle-working, messianic, crucified and resurrected divine Carpenter from lowly Nazareth in faraway Galilee. This information may seem unnecessary to us today, with Christianity's universal renown, but at the time (c. AD 60) Christ was largely unknown (Acts 17:18), and Christianity was not an authorized religion in the highly polytheistic Roman world (Acts 16:21). Those who accepted and followed Jesus put themselves at considerable risk of sudden arrest, punishment, and public humiliation for following an illegal and much-maligned religion. Thus, Paul wisely strengthened the Colossians' confidence in the rapidly expanding growth of Christianity, albeit still mostly beneath the Roman radar.

Christ modeled some thirty-five years later for all spiritual leaders. That pattern of *commendation, criticism, and challenge* is established in Christ's posthumous messages to the seven churches of Asia in AD 95 (Rev. 2–3). In both Paul's and Christ's letters their commendations were followed by needed criticisms and motivating challenges aimed at one goal: to cleanse, reorder, and grow these assemblies into spiritual maturity. Paul's introduction is instructive.

Will you learn from it? Will you, like Paul, be utterly God-dependent and begin all your activities or labors with prayer? Will you, pastor (elder, spiritual leader), set a good example by practicing what you preach and by periodically reminding your listeners salvation is by grace alone and Christianity is not a regional or national but a worldwide faith? Will you commend them for growing in the fruit of the Spirit and give them balanced ministry, commending, correcting, and challenging them as needed? And will you, believer, receive such Pauline ministry and not clamor for elementary teachings or faddish or contentious preaching that condemns others while requiring no change and producing no spiritual growth in you? These things will reveal whether Paul's introduction has instructed you.

1:7–8 Paul's providential prompt. When Epaphras initially brought Paul news of the Colossians' strong spiritual condition, Paul must have been overjoyed to hear of their growth and exemplary faith, love, and hope (1:4–8; 2:5–7). But there was more.

Epaphras also reported that trouble was brewing in Colosse! False teachers had infiltrated their assembly with a strange and deadly cocktail of errors springing from Greek philosophy, esoteric religious sects, and Jewish legalists. Paul instantly discerned the seriousness of this threat to the Colossian church. Thank God, Epaphras had done his part in relaying the full report about Colossae's spiritual condition.[7] Now Paul would do his.

Paul surely realized Epaphras' report was providential. Epaphras was a deeply spiritual minister and likely one of Paul's former students in Ephesus (Acts 19:9–10). Knowing Paul trusted Epaphras' spiritual discernment, God sent him to Paul at this crucial time trusting Paul would quickly address the Colossians' errors before they grew. Thus, Epaphras' report was a providential prompt, spurring the apostle to write this corrective epistle.

Here is evidence of Christ, the all-seeing, all-knowing, all-controlling Head of the church at work overseeing and guiding His flock worldwide. As human heads (brains) send inspired prompts (neurological impulses) via their nerves to various parts of their bodies to prompt necessary action, so Christ, our heavenly Head, seeing problems arising among His people, sends prompts via the Spirit to members of His body who are able to deal with those problems—if they're willing. Paul was willing to address the Colossians' pressing problems and faithfully responded to Christ's providential prompt through Epaphras.

---

7. Thus, Paul reaped what he sowed (Gal. 6:7). Just as Paul was careful to tell not part but "all the counsel of God" (Acts 20:27) to those to whom he ministered, God saw to it that others gave him full disclosure of issues he was responsible to oversee and address, in this case, the spiritual condition of the Colossians. Faithfully tell others "everything" you know God wants you to tell them about their spiritual responsibilities or problems, holding back "nothing" (1 Sam. 3:15–18, NAS), and God will faithfully see to it you are told all you need to know when you need to know it (Acts 23:16).

Will you respond? When prompted by news of trouble, sin, discouragement, heresy, compromise, lukewarmness, or failures in another believer or church, will you respond to the Head, who has entrusted you with timely awareness of their problems? Will you in love address those problems— praying,[8] exhorting, visiting, telephoning, e-mailing, writing a letter, or whatever else is within your power—to render saving assistance to your troubled, stumbling fellow believers?

1:2 On the eve of disaster. A powerful earthquake struck Colosse and nearby Laodicea and Hierapolis in AD 61.[9] Laodicea, a very wealthy city (Rev. 3:17), rebuilt itself, turning down an offer from Nero to fund its reconstruction. Hierapolis and Colosse, however, were never fully rebuilt. Its economy wrecked and citizenry, including Christians, partly dispersed by the disaster, Colosse became a small village surviving quietly for several more centuries. This explains why Jesus addressed Laodicea but not Colosse when He dictated messages to the other churches of Asia (Rev. 2–3) approximately thirty-five years later (AD 95): by that time the Colossian church was significantly diminished. Though Paul was a prophet, we have no evidence he knew of this approaching earthquake at the time he wrote the Colossians (c. AD 60).

But the Holy Spirit knew. So when the omniscient Comforter prompted Paul to write the Colossians, He

---

8. Oswald Chambers taught God gives us discernment not for criticism but for intercession. The apostle John's teaching agrees (1 John 5:16).

9. The Roman historian Tacitus states this quake occurred in Nero's seventh year (AD 61), but Eusebius assigns it to his tenth year (AD 64). Whichever date is correct, the fact remains Colosse was devastated by a quake shortly after receiving this epistle from Paul.

inspired him to raise the very subjects and issues that would fully prepare them for the difficult "things to come" (John 16:13). When examining this epistle, therefore, we find Paul not only addressed the heresies troubling them (2:4–23) but also, and most significantly, urged them to "set" their loves and hopes on "things which are above," not on "things on the earth" (Col. 3:1–4).[10] To facilitate this, his letter gave them plenty of heavenly revelations to ponder (1:15–29), a prayer revealing God's heavenly purposes for them (1:9–14), and numerous practical orders which, if obeyed, would deepen and fully develop their heavenly (spiritual) walk with Christ (3:1–4:6). Then nothing, no demon, deceiver, or disaster— even an earthquake!—could separate them from Him. Even if their nearest, dearest, and humanly speaking most vital "things on the earth" (3:2) were rocked, they would stand! Shaken perhaps, but not panicked! Still focused on their heavenly life and Head, Christ! Still preparing for His appearing, the Rapture (3:1–4)!

Let's walk through this entire epistle noting more specifically the things the Spirit through Paul pointed the Colossians to seek, consider, believe, or practice on the eve of disaster.

They should:

- Seek a full knowledge of God's plan (will) (1:9)

- Seek wisdom (good judgment) and spiritual understanding (insight) (1:9)

---

10. While there are many theological peaks in the spiritual mountain range we call Colossians, they all seem to point and lead up to the climactic apex of Colossians 3:1–4.

- Pursue a spiritually and morally worthy life (1:10)

- Practice and become fruitful in good works (1:10)

- Seek more (scriptural and experiential) knowledge of God (1:10)

- Pray for inner strength to endure sufferings patiently and with joy (1:11)

- Give thanks they are redeemed by Christ's blood: forgiven, fellow heirs with the saints, delivered from the power of darkness, and in Christ's (spiritual) kingdom (1:12–13)

- Remember that, unlike this world's material idols, their God is invisible (1:15)

- Believe Jesus is God's exact image and the Creator of everything visible and invisible (1:15–16)

- Believe Jesus created invisible but real spirit "thrones," "dominions," and "principalities" "in heaven [the heavenlies]" for His purposes (1:16; cf. Dan. 10:13, 20)[11]

---

11. Presently these invisible thrones are held by Satan's host of demons who serve the "prince of this world['s]" malicious will (John 16:11), often in collaboration with ungodly human authorities, though Christ sovereignly overrules both by His people's prayers and actions and by His angels whenever necessary to forward His redemptive or prophetic plan or relieve His distressed servants (Exod. 12:30–31, 41–42; Ezra 6:6–12, 22; Acts 12:1–11, esp. vv. 5, 11).

- Believe Jesus also created and sovereignly controls all worldly "thrones," "dominions," and "principalities"[12] "in [on] earth" for His purposes (1:16)

- Believe in the glorious, unrivaled preeminence[13] of Christ in "all things," who alone is Head of the church (1:17–18)

- Believe Jesus has already fully reconciled them to God by His blood (1:20–21)

- Believe Christ eagerly awaits the moment He will "present" them to Himself in heaven, "holy and unblamable" (1:22, 28; cf. Eph. 5:27; Jude 24)

- Accept, and willingly bear, as Paul did, their share of the ongoing sufferings of Christ—not for redemption but for the church's reviving and blessing (Col. 1:24, NCV, NLT)[14]

---

12. "Principalities" (Greek, *archē*) means, "to begin, to rule," describing one who begins something and subsequently rules or leads it. Thus, the word means "rulers, leaders, superiors, principals." See G. Kittel, G. Friedrich, and G. W. Bromiley, *Theological Dictionary of the New Testament*, electronic ed. (Grand Rapids, MI: W.B. Eerdmans, 1985), s.v. "archē."

13. "Preeminence" (Greek, *prōteuō*) means holding absolute "first place," (implicitly) uncontestably and without peers or rivals. Is it possible Satan wishes to rival Jesus' unrivaled preeminence by encouraging the excessive exaltation or veneration of popes, Mary, saints, martyrs—or renowned Protestant preachers!—in Christ's church? Peter, whom many hold incorrectly to be the first pope, was very careful to honor Christ's preeminence (Acts 10:25–26). For "preeminence," see Kittel, Friedrich, and Bromiley, *Theological Dictionary of the New Testament*, s.v. "*prōteuō*."

14. Paul so thoroughly accepted His sufferings he "rejoiced," realizing they enabled Christ to pour more reviving life into the church through his

- Believe and muse the great "mystery" of the Gentile–Jewish church, specifically the wonder of "Christ [living] in" us, imparting "the hope of [living in eternal] glory" (1:26–27)

- Remember effective ministers must sometimes face "great conflict" to bless God's people (2:1)

- Believe a deeply securitizing "full assurance of understanding" awaits them, if they persevere (2:2)

- Rejoice that "all the treasures of wisdom and knowledge" are hidden in Christ—not secular philosophers! Or gnostics! Or other wisdom-peddling heretics (2:3)![15]

---

ministry and kept other Christians from having to suffer as much.

15. From the first century, Christians have struggled to reconcile revelation (biblical) truth with philosophical (secular, reason-based) truth. Clement, Origen, and others of the Alexandrian school, following the lead of the Jewish sage Philo, tried to reconcile Greco-Roman philosophy with Judeo-Christian theology. Realizing the futility, and needlessness, of this, Tertullian famously asked, "What has Athens to do with Jerusalem?" Or, paraphrasing, "Why should we who hold the genuine divine revelation of eternal truth (from the God of Jerusalem) try to reconcile our precious inspired truths with the faulty, uninspired reasonings and speculations of astute but unenlightened secular philosophers (from Athens)?" Two common reasons are: (1) we fear their reproach, and (2) we want them to respect our views of truth—something only conversion to our God and faith can accomplish (cf. 1 Cor. 2:14). Though the struggle between the schools of reason and revelation, often posed as atheism vs. faith, continues, Tertullian had it right. Do we? Don't let postmodern secular humanist philosophers, or New Age or other heretics, wow or cow you. You have in Christ, "the truth" inspired, inerrant, incarnate (John 14:6), the only Source of "all the treasures of wisdom and knowledge" (Col. 2:3). Have you searched and meditated upon the wondrous riches of His Word today?

- Realize God loves and commends all "order"—submission to proper human authority, orderliness of conduct and worship—and live in it (2:5; cf. 1 Cor. 14:33, 40)

- Not only receive but also "walk...in" (live close to) Christ daily (2:6; cf. Gal. 5:16; Zech. 2:7)

- Take measures to "root," "build up," and "establish" their faith (2:7)

- "Abound with thanksgiving" (2:7; 3:15, 17; cf. 1 Thess. 5:18; Eph. 5:20; Heb. 13:15)

- Avoid philosophies or religious traditions or other teachings (purportedly inspired or scientific) that pose as truth but contradict Christ's sayings (2:8, NIV, NCV, NLT; cf. 1 Tim. 6:20)

- Ponder and rejoice in the utter divinity of Christ—in whom the very fullness of the eternal Godhead (Father, Son, Holy Spirit) dwelt bodily (2:9; cf. John 3:34; 1:16; 14:10)

- Rejoice that this, His amazing divine fullness, now in them, makes them spiritually "complete" (full) as they continue abiding in Him (2:10; cf. John 1:16)

- Believe by Christ's salvation they've been raised from spiritual death and circumcised of their old fleshly sins (2:11–13; cf. Rom. 6:1–13)

- Believe by Christ's salvation their record of offenses against the Old Testament Law has been cancelled and the ordinances of the Law abolished or deactivated (2:14; cf. 2 Cor. 3:13; Eph. 2:15)

- Believe after Jesus' resurrection He held a great triumph (victory parade[16]) to openly demonstrate His victory over the devil and all his demonic rulers (2:15)

- Realize Moses' Law is a "shadow" of the New Testament realities they now enjoyed in Christ (2:17), thus the letter of the Law is no longer binding upon them

- Not fear or yield to those demanding they observe Jewish regulations—and condemning them for not doing so (2:16)

- Diligently "hold the Head," Christ, as sole Sovereign of their lives and churches so their spiritual nourishment, growth, unity, and guidance may continue increasing (2:18–19)

- Refuse to venerate angels, worshiping instead only Christ, the Head—or risk losing their

---

16. See my note in Chapter Two on Colossians 2:14–15, "Jesus, our Triumphator—and His triumph!"

rewards (2:18–19; cf. Rev. 19:10; 22:9; 1 Cor. 3:11–15; 2 John 8)

- Refuse to submit to man-made religious rules or ascetic practices which, while appearing wise, humble, and self-disciplining, do not honor God but only harm their bodies and increase their (self-congratulatory) religious pride (2:20–23, ncv, The Message)

- "Set" (and periodically reset) their hearts and minds on heavenly, not worldly, things, and "seek" them diligently, in anticipation of Jesus' "appear[ing]" (3:1–4)

- "Mortify" (deny to death) all illicit sex and greed—or suffer God's anger (3:5–6)

- "Put off" all bad attitudes and speech and steadily "put on" the knowledge, attitudes, and ways (spiritual disciplines) of Christ (3:7–10)

- Remember, unlike the world, the church is classless; all the elect stand equal before Christ—and they should live like it! (3:11; cf. Gal. 3:27–28)[17]

---

17. With various wordings the Bible asserts "God is no respecter of persons" no less than seven times! See Deut. 10:17; 2 Chron. 19:7; Acts 10:34–35; Rom. 2:11; Eph. 6:9; Col. 3:25; 1 Pet. 1:17). Since seven is the biblical number for completion and perfection, God wants us to be completely sure that he is perfectly unbiased in His view and judgments. Am I fawning over Christians of worldly importance or forgetting the needs of those who seem unimportant?

- Diligently and persistently "put on" the vital virtues of "humbleness of mind," "long-suffering,"[18] and "love" (3:12–14)

- Let God's very peace rule their souls and thank Him for it (3:15)

- Let God's Word—the Bible!—"dwell in" them "richly" or fully—frequently reading, studying, discussing, reciting, and pondering it (3:16)[19]

- "Admonish" (exhort or warn) other believers when necessary (3:16)

- Praise and worship the Lord daily in song[20] (3:16)

---

18. This "long-suffering" (Col. 3:12, Greek, *makrothymia*) speaks of an enduring, forbearing patience, especially with people who greatly try us, as the next verse implies (3:13). See J. Lust, E. Eynikel, and K. Hauspie, *A Greek–English Lexicon of the Septuagint: Revised Edition* (Stuttgart: Deutsche Bibelgesellschaft, 2003), s.v. "*makrothymia.*"

19. The twenty-seven books of the New Testament canon would not be officially recognized for three more centuries (AD 367). Meanwhile, when the Colossians met for worship, like other churches of their day (c. AD 60) they typically heard readings, homilies, and songs (psalms) from Old Testament Scriptures, the oral Gospels (recollections of the apostles), and the apostolic letters currently in circulation. The latter were usually read aloud first to their addressees and then copied by hand to share with other churches (Col. 4:16; 1 Tim. 4:13). So while the Colossians didn't have our complete Bible, they had plenty of God's Word to "richly" study, discuss, and share.

20. Paul also recommended the singing of "psalms and hymns and spiritual songs" to the Ephesians (Eph. 5:19). This is an endorsement of today's "blended worship," where praise and worship songs are drawn from the different but acceptable wells (ancient biblical psalms, traditional Christian hymns, and newer popular songs) and offered heavenward with instrumental accompaniment—or without it! (Church worship was a cappella for over a thousand years!) Primarily, these blended songs and styles are offered to please God. Secondarily, they help give worshipers at least one style of

- Do "whatever" they do in Jesus' name, "heartily," and "as to the Lord"—as if He personally asked them to do it (3:17, 23; cf. Eccles. 9:10)

- Faithfully discharge their family obligations to please Christ (and bless their family) (3:18–21)

- Faithfully discharge their occupational duties to please Christ, not men (3:22–23)

- "Fear," or stand in awe of, God, remembering He will reward or punish them for their works without partiality (3:22, 24–25)

- Be fair, if they are employers or supervisors, remembering Christ supervises them (4:1)

- "Continue" to pray, and "watch" for answers to prayer, giving thanks for them (4:2)

- "Continue" to ask for their ministers and themselves "doors of utterance," or opportunities to share Christ and His Word (4:3–4)

- Interact wisely, not naively, with unbelievers (4:5)

- Use their time well—remembering how brief life is (4:5; cf. Ps. 39:4–5)

- Speak to everyone "with [God's] grace [ability and graciousness]" (4:6)

---

worship music they can identify with, which in turn helps incline them to fully and freely enter into the congregation's worship. Personally I find hard rock and rap two styles that fall outside the scope of appropriately reverent praise and worship music—but don't reject Christians who disagree.

- Comfort other believers with loving communications regularly, as Paul did (4:7–8)

- Value, commend, and endorse their faithful
"fellow workers," as Paul did (4:10–11)

- "Always" intercede for fellow believers to "stand
perfect [mature] and complete in [the knowledge and execution of] all the will of God," as
Epaphras did (4:12; cf. Eph. 6:18–20)

- Steadfastly "fulfill" whatever "ministry"
they've "received in the Lord," as Paul charged
Archippus (4:17; cf. 1 Cor. 15:58)

These were the heavenly truths, topics, and eternal things
the Spirit through Paul instructed the Colossians to earnestly seek, ponder, or practice. If attended to, these truths
and duties would leave them prepared for anything. We too
should focus on them. Why?

Our position today parallels that of the Colossians.
Through Scripture God has assured us that, to establish
His Christ-worshiping kingdom, He will quake this Christ-
rejecting world in these last days (Heb. 12:25–29). This spiritual shaking will be threefold.

First, the present American culture, steeped and settled
in shocking sins and shameless defiance of God's holiness,
is unquestionably poised on the brink of a disastrous divine
judgment. And too many American Christians, largely
untaught concerning God's judgments, are spiritually asleep,
or indifferent, toward our nation's true spiritual condition,
God's increasing displeasure, and the certainty and immi-
nency of His reckoning.

Second, the whole world is about to experience its worst and most prolonged disaster, God's final judgment of this increasingly atheistic world, the seven-year Tribulation. It is during this purging of the present social order that God will fully shake everything that can be shaken so only His redemptive work may survive and enter Christ's subsequent thousand-year earthly kingdom (Heb. 12:25–29).

Third, Jesus is about to "rock" the church with increased adversities that are both corrective and character-forming. The "fiery trial[s]" (1 Pet. 1:6–7; 4:12–19) we will face in these last days of the church age will force us to make decisions that favor and thus foster either our spiritual or worldly lives—but not both! The Spirit will search and convict us of wrong motives, desires, and life goals and challenge us to reset our souls on the "things above," as Paul urged the Colossians (Col. 3:1–4). If we continue living in and for "the things on this earth," we'll be badly shaken when God rocks our nation and world with stunning turns of events that damage, diminish, or destroy the things we've unconsciously trusted in as much or more than God: our economy, government, petroleum supply, national hegemony, military superiority, established religious organizations, generally comfortable way of life, and so forth. But this shaking will be a blessing. It will help us finally distinguish between what does and doesn't matter, expediting developmental moral choices long overdue. Why will God deal with Christians so rigorously? It's urgent! "Judgment," or the final divinely enforced restoration to divine order, "must begin at the house of God" (1 Pet. 4:17). In His holy love, Christ will do whatever it takes not to destroy His bride but to awaken her to her immediate need to get ready for His soon-coming appearing (4:18). A. W. Tozer wrote:

> History reveals that times of suffering for the Church have also been times of looking upward. Tribulation has always sobered God's people and encouraged them to look for and yearn after the return of their Lord. Our present preoccupation with this world may be a warning of bitter days to come. God will wean us from the earth some way—the easy way if possible, the hard way if necessary. It is up to us.[21]

Therefore, since our churches, nation, and world are soon to be shaken, our position is similar to that of our Colossian brothers and sisters in AD 60. And like Paul, we don't know exactly what's going to go down in the next year or decade, but we know the Holy Spirit knows. So why not trust the inspired wisdom He sent to prepare the Colossians to also prepare us for our challenging "things to come"? Whatever tomorrow holds, let's hold fast to His wisdom today.

1:1–8 Key links: First-century networking. Paul's introduction, along with his closing (Ch. 4), reveals a network of ministers and churches working in unity, all under Christ's headship and the Holy Spirit's guidance.

Timothy, who was or would soon become pastor of the church at Ephesus, was with Paul in Rome (1:1) and both were interacting with members of the Roman Church daily (Acts 28:30–31). Timothy was supporting Paul (perhaps as his amanuensis, or secretary) as the latter wrote the

---

21. A. W. Tozer, *The Best of A. W. Tozer* (Harrisburg, PA: Christian Publications, 1978), 57.

Colossians, who in turn were founded and probably pastored through the ministry of Epaphras, who it so happens was also with Paul and Timothy and earnestly interceding for the Colossians daily (4:12). Thus, the churches and ministers of Rome, Ephesus, and Colosse are linked by the ministries of Paul, Timothy, and Epaphras.

Paul's letter mentions the churches of Laodicea and Hierapolis. We're very familiar with the Laodiceans thanks to Christ's message to them some thirty-five years later (Rev. 3:14–22). Scripture reveals nothing about the ecclesia at Hierapolis, except that Epaphras ministered there and perhaps, upon returning from Rome to his Colosse–Laodicea–Hierapolis ministry field (or circuit, Col. 4:13), gave the Hierapolians personal insights on Paul's Colossian epistle originally read to them by another (cf. Col. 4:16). Thus, we link two more city-churches to the network.

To this we add the ministry of Onesimus and Philemon, and the church in the latter's home (Philem. 1–2). Philemon was an elder and house church pastor (or host) in Colossae who was converted by Paul probably during his ministry in Ephesus (Philem. 19b) and helped Epaphras found or build the Colossian church. Onesimus was Philemon's runaway slave who fled to Rome, was converted by Paul, served Paul faithfully, and then returned to Philemon, humble apologies and Pauline epistle in hand (Philemon 10–21). In love and wisdom Paul returned Onesimus to Philemon, to be reconciled and assume his new place in the Colossian church and Philemon's service or friendship (perhaps as a freed man, Philem. 16, 21). Thus, another New Testament church and more Christians are linked in.

Then there was Tychicus, one of Paul's companions in Rome. Tychicus was a faithful minister whom Paul entrusted to deliver this letter to Colosse (4:7) and those he authored to Philemon and Ephesus (Eph. 6:21–22). Paul must have enjoyed Tychicus' fellowship immensely, since twice he called him not just his brother but his "beloved brother" (Col. 4:7; Eph. 6:21).

Thus, Paul introduced us to one of his first-century networks: Paul, Timothy, Epaphras, Philemon, Onesimus, Tychicus, and the churches of Rome, Ephesus, Colosse, Laodicea, and Hierapolis. In His eternal plan Christ sovereignly linked these souls and congregations for His kingdom purposes—to evangelize, disciple, launch missions, write corrective and revelatory epistles, share edifying exhortations, facilitate reconciliation, and increase love among Christians. But not without their cooperation! They chose to let Christ rule and His Spirit guide! Also they were willing to befriend and work with other Christians and churches, and not quickly judge each other over petty differences. Once introduced, they decided to come together in the loving friendship and humble ministerial cooperation Christ so repeatedly commanded and earnestly prayed for (John 13:34–35; 17:21–23, 26; cf. Col. 3:12–14; Ps. 133:1–3) rather than let proud, petty judgmentalism or an envious spirit of religious competition divide them.

What might Christ do, and what kingdom-building networks might He establish, if we adopt the humble, loving spirit of Paul and company? Over the last decades we've seen Internet-driven social media link the world, albeit for mostly trivial communication. What might we see in the coming decades if we ask Christ by His Spirit to link us with believers, ministers, and churches of like mind and commitment to further His vital, final work in the church?

> *Lord, please link me to networks created by Your Spirit to bless and build Your people; not good connections but God connections. May Your networking sweep the world in this century as it did the first, enabling us to finish the commissions first-century networks began, to evangelize and disciple the nations before You come. Amen. So be it, Lord.*

1:3 The chief of thanksgiving. Paul opened his letter informing the Colossians he constantly thanked God for them in his prayers: "We give thanks to God…praying always for you, since we heard of your faith…love…hope" (1:3–5). While astute ancient writers typically opened letters with expressions of thanksgiving to various deities, and Paul was undoubtedly rhetorically trained, his thanksgiving was no mere formality. New Testament scholar Craig Keener notes:

> Thanksgivings to God or gods were customary in the openings of ancient letters…[but] Paul's prayer times clearly include many thanksgivings to God; hence this is not merely a conventional expression of thanks for the purposes of the letter.[22]

Indeed Paul's offerings of thanks and exhortations to thanksgiving litter his epistles, as if the man is blessedly obsessed with thanking God and urging others to do the

---

22. C. S. Keener, *The IVP Bible Background Commentary: New Testament* (Downers Grove, IL: InterVarsity Press, 1993), Col. 1:3–13, note.

same. Consider these many examples in which Paul—the unofficial but undisputable chief of thanksgiving—offers or recommends thanksgiving: in this epistle, (Col. 1:3, 12; 2:7; 3:15, 17; 4:2); in other writings or experiences (Acts 27:35; 28:15; Rom. 1:8; 6:17; 7:24–25; 14:6; 1 Cor. 1:4, 14; 14:16–17; 14:18; 15:55–57; 2 Cor. 1:11; 2:14; 8:16; 9:15; Eph. 1:16; 5:4, 20; Phil. 1:3; 1 Thess. 1:2; 2:13; 3:9; 5:18; 2 Thess. 1:3; 2:13; 1 Tim. 1:12; 2:1; 2 Tim. 1:3; Philem. 4; Heb. 13:15, if Pauline). Not content with thanking God, Paul also graciously thanked people for their help, especially when it was extraordinary or sacrificial (Rom. 16:3–4). On such occasions he undoubtedly saw God's providence and grace in their assistance or kindness and simultaneously thanked Him as well.

Perhaps Paul's incessant thanksgiving explains why his bodily tabernacle was so blessed with God's presence, voice, guidance, and power, and why he was so constantly assured of the Lord's faithfulness to him.[23]

What is even more amazing is the adverse conditions in which Paul offered or taught thanksgiving to God: in prisons, storms, shipwrecks, weariness, persecutions, death

---

23. Paul continually offered the "sacrifice of praise" to God (Heb. 13:15). This is the New Testament equivalent of the Old Testament continual burnt offering (Exod. 29:38–46), the divinely promised benefits of which were: God met and spoke with those who complied (29:42); He sanctified (set apart) their tabernacle with His glorious, manifest presence (29:43); He sanctified (approved for use) their ministers for His work (29:44); He lived with them (29:45–46); and thus these benefits caused the people to "know" (enjoy deep assurance) that He was their personal God (29:46). If we, as Paul did, offer our "burnt offering" of praise to God continually (1 Thess. 5:18; Eph. 5:20; Col. 3:17), we too will enjoy divine rendezvous, God's timely voice through His Word, approval and consecration for service, God's presence in our gatherings, and unshakable assurance that the Lord is indeed our very personal God, ready always to provide for, assist, and defend us.

plots, beatings, privation, and yes, also when abounding or honored. No matter what you did to Paul or where you placed him, the man would give thanks constantly to the Lord. If there was no apparent reason to prompt thanksgiving, he would offer it anyway, just because God Himself is so good all the time, desires our thanksgiving, is always blessed by it (1 Thess. 5:18), and reciprocates by blessing the thankful. Why was Paul so focused on thanking God?

Clearly, he recognized it is God's will (1 Thess. 5:18) and wanted to please Him. He also realized the opposite habit, murmuring, stirs God's wrath (1 Cor. 10:10) and wanted to avoid it. Maybe he also wanted to set a good example for the many churches he founded, nurtured, and guided, as he urged Timothy to do (1 Tim. 4:12). Perhaps Paul, who had often been in God's immediate presence, and had heaven on his heart and mind daily (Col. 3:1–4), just couldn't contain himself, so moved was he by God's awesome love, constant grace, persisting good will, and by the marvelous inheritance "laid up" (1:5) for us in New Jerusalem. Perhaps all of the above motivated him. One thing is certain: Paul's ceaseless praise plants him in spirit squarely among the four living beings and twenty-four elders around God's throne who offer Him thanks incessantly (Rev. 4:9–11; 11:17). Which raises another question: Why are we so often unthankful...and unfit for worship around the throne? We don't have to be.

We can follow the chief of thanksgiving. We can remember thanksgiving is God's will and pursue it; and murmuring angers Him, and avoid it! We can determine to set a good example for others. We can meditate often on the eternal realities Paul was so deeply assured of and upon which his affections were irrevocably "set" (Col. 3:2); occasionally reading about the glorious eternal home and company that awaits us is one sure way to do this (Rev. chapters 4–5, 21–22). But let's face facts. We'll never change until we make the cold, stark choice to give the Lord thanks at all times for all things in all moods in all situations with all people all the rest of our days.[24] Then our hearts will ignite and glow with gratitude to God until we become as blessedly obsessed with it as the chief of thanksgiving was.

1:4, 8 Loving *all* Christians. Having been informed by Epaphras of the Colossians' wide love, given and fostered by the Holy Spirit, Paul commended them (1:4, 8). Not exclusively reserved for their local fellowship, their love was lavished upon "all the saints" they met (1:4). This prompts a question: We know we love many, perhaps most Christians, but do we love them "all"?

Most would immediately respond, "Yes!" But perhaps we need to slow down and examine our hearts a little closer. Every offense or grudge we hold blocks us from having or showing God's love toward others. So does pride, the spirit of envy, and prejudice! Theoretically all Christians are one (followers of one God), but actually a plethora of prejudicial walls separate us: denominational dogmas, politics, race, nationality, socioeconomic status, occupation, preferences for

---

24. Thanksgiving depends upon not our circumstances but our choices. Those who choose to be unthankful will find something to complain about no matter how often God favors or blesses them. Conversely, whoever chooses to comply with God's thanksgiving request will find something to thank Him for in even the lowest, cruelest, darkest, most confused valleys of life (Acts 16:22–24, 25). Have you crossed your spiritual Jordan yet, leaving the wilderness of murmuring behind to enter the new, spiritually enriched, stable, promising land of continuous thanksgiving...no matter what?

simplicity or intellectualism in preaching, and many other things. It's a great day when we determine to love "all" believers, including those whom we previously dismissed because they "follow not with us" (Luke 9:49–50)—and those who still dismiss us because we follow not with them!

Ours should be a special love, driven by deep, abiding adoration for Jesus (John 21:15–17) and our heavenly Father (1 John 5:1–2). We should love "all" believers, even when we don't agree with, can't respect, or can't support their opinions or practices in one or more of the non-essential or debatable matters.[25] Remember "love" (1:4, Greek, *agapē*) means we value other Christians (because they are believers, 1 Pet. 2:17) and hold them in high esteem with deep, practically demonstrated respect[26] (especially faithful ministers, 1 Thess. 5:12–13; 1 Tim. 5:17–18). We maintain good will, not malice, toward them, consistently desiring and working for their highest good. We pray for them, address them with dignity, assist them whenever possible, and, if they offend us, we quickly forgive them in our hearts and are ready to reconcile whenever possible.[27] That's humble, Christian love—

---

25. Some of these debatable things are: how we worship, our days of worship, our style of church government, our dress, ministers' vestments, how we celebrate the Lord's Supper, our baptismal practices, and the role of women in pastoral ministry, to name a few.

26. C. Spicq and J. D. Ernest, *Theological Lexicon of the New Testament* (Peabody, MA: Hendrickson Publishers, 1994), s.v. "*agapē*."

27. In Matthew 5:38–48, Jesus' teaching implies when we consistently maintain God's patient, understanding, non-retaliatory love toward even our most impenitent serial offenders (non-Christian and, yes, Christian "enemies" too!) our love and Christlike character will be "perfect, even as your Father, who is in heaven, is perfect" (5:48). Paul's commendation implies the Colossians were progressing rapidly toward this goal (Col. 1:4, 8).

Messianic mercy, the Lord's love, Christlike consideration, *agapē* affection—and the Colossians had it for not some but "all the saints."

Here are seven compelling reasons we should follow their example and walk in love toward every Christian we meet:

1. Jesus expressly ordered us to love "one another," and didn't add, "If they suit you," or, "If they don't have chronic faults" (John 13:34–35).

2. Christ prayed passionately that we would live, work, and worship together in perfect unity (John 17:21, 23) and Paul reminds us "love...is the bond of perfectness" (Col. 3:14).

3. We're all spiritual siblings, in one "household," God's family (Eph. 2:19; cf. 3:15).

4. We will all live together in the same kingdom...forever (Rev. 21–22).

5. Jesus loves all Christians intensely, even if we love them indifferently.

6. We're all saved by God's grace (Eph. 2:89), so none of us deserves to receive Christ's righteousness more than anyone else!

7. If faithful, we all experience degrees of rejection or distress in this world for Christ's sake (Luke 9:23; Phil. 1:29; 2 Tim. 3:12), so we need each other's acceptance and support (Gal. 6:1–3).

Pause to consider which kinds of Christians—and specific individuals!—you don't care for. That's where conscious repentance and change is needed. And immediately, because "The time is come that judgment must begin at the house of God" (1 Pet. 4:17). It's time, then, that we banish all the petty things that separate us unnecessarily—with the exception of the essentials, willful sin and fundamental (salvific) error (1 Cor. 5:9–13; Gal. 1:6–9).[28] If we'll begin lavishing love on "all the saints," our loving God, pleased, will lavish upon us all the joy we can hold. And we'll protect ourselves from excessive satanic assaults.

In the post-exile period, Jerusalem's broken walls left its remnant in a state of increased vulnerability, since their enemies could easily enter the city. Zion's broken walls illustrate churches whose love has broken down. Their unchristlike attitudes (envy, bitterness, unforgiveness, superiority, judgmentalism, prejudice, etc.) create breaches in their spiritual unity through which Satan's agents may easily attack not only them but also their entire assemblies[29]—and spoil our unity, harm souls, misrepresent Christ to others, cause Him reproach, and even delay the Rapture, since Jesus won't appear until the Spirit culminates His maturing, unifying work in the true body of Christ (2 Pet. 3:10–12).[30] Determining to

---

28. It behooves us to remember the old Christian motto, now attributed to the seventeenth-century Lutheran theologian Rupertus Meldenius (c. 1627), that has for centuries inspired many a peacemaker and helped forge many a reconciliation: "In essentials, unity; in nonessentials, liberty; in all things, charity." Church historian Philip Schaff dubbed this, "The watchword of Christian peacemakers." See http://www.ligonier.org/learn/articles/essentials-unity-non-essentials-liberty-all-things/ (accessed March 8, 2016).

29. Thus, Paul warned the Corinthians that their proud, unforgiving spirit and stubborn refusal to receive a penitent brother back into fellowship was giving Satan a spiritual "advantage" against them (2 Cor. 2:9–11; cf. Gal. 6:1–3).

30. In Jesus' high-priestly prayer (John 17)—His blueprint for the church

walk in God's love toward all Christians repairs our "walls," restoring our ability to quickly discern and repel Satan's crafty devices and prevent his divisive, destructive work among us.

Isn't it time we become like the Colossians? Love not many or most but "all" believers? Watch God rebuild the walls of our churches' unity? Hasten Jesus' coming?

1:4–5 Hope-driven faith and love. Paul says the Colossians' outstanding faith and love were prompted by their sure heavenly hope (1:4–5). Several excellent translations highlight this:

> We have heard of your faith in Christ Jesus and your love for all of God's people, which come from your confident hope of what God has reserved for you in heaven.
>
> —COLOSSIANS 1:4–5, NLT

> We have heard about your faith in the Messiah Jesus and the love that you have for all the saints, based on the hope laid up for you in heaven.
>
> —COLOSSIANS 1:4–5, ISV

> You have this faith and love because of your hope.
>
> —COLOSSIANS 1:5, NCV

No surprise here.

---

and instructions to its Builder, the Holy Spirit—He asked for His followers first to be made "perfect in one"(John 17:23); then, after this, that we be translated, or taken to be "with me where I am, that they may behold my glory [in heaven]" (17:24). Are we humbly pursuing Christian unity so we may hasten His coming?

Not just the Colossians but every human being, including you and me, is hope-driven. The natural man fixes his hopes on the prospects of future joys in this world, but the Christian can, and should, look beyond this material realm and fallen social order and plant his motivating aspirations squarely in heaven—supernatural, like nothing in this world, Eden's paradise regained, *heaven!* We should look for "things above," not on Earth, a "better country," a new Earth, a holy populace, a divinely established social order (Col. 3:2; Heb. 11:8–10, 15–16).[31] Hence later in this epistle Paul calls the Colossians to look up and set all their hopes and dreams on heavenly, not earthly ends (3:1–3) and reminds them they'll begin experiencing this wondrous future when Jesus appears (the Rapture) (3:4). Other New Testament texts amen his celestial summons.

Scripture calls Christ's appearing our "blessed hope" (Titus 2:13), suggesting all who have it are specially blessed—and those who don't aren't! It also calls the appearing a purifying hope: "Every man that hath this hope in him purifieth himself" (1 John 3:2–3), suggesting all who hold it will more likely be motivated to walk in purity—and those who don't won't! It further reveals our hope in Christ's appearing: is "one hope," not many, and thus not to be denied, changed, or confused (Eph. 4:4); is a sure, steady, spiritual "anchor" holding our souls in place (near Christ) in this world's turbulent storms (Heb. 6:18–19); is "lively," giving inspiring quickenings that dispel apathy (1 Pet. 1:3–4); imparts "the patience of hope" (1 Thess. 1:3); will fill us with "joy and peace" if we

---

31. Though it wasn't yet revealed when Paul wrote the Colossians (c. AD 60), Christ later disclosed through John (AD 95) many details about our glorious eternal home: New Jerusalem (Rev. 21–22)!

believe it (Rom. 15:13); causes "rejoicing" (Rom. 12:12); and is to be held fast to the end of this church age (1 Pet. 1:13).

Finally, in these last days as never before, our unique hope will mark us as a "peculiar people" (1 Pet. 2:9), sweetly special to God but strangely deceived in the opinions of unspiritual or untaught Christians and unbelievers. Despite the distinction, and to many, oddness, of our claim that Christ will appear to catch us away,[32] both our gospel and its hope will draw many to Christ as they become disillusioned with this world's false hopes and shaken by the strange and ominous "things which are coming on the earth" in these last days of the church age leading up to the tribulation (Luke 21:26). Are we listening to Paul and Scripture?

Together they declare our hope of heaven strengthens our faith and love, motivates purity, increases God's blessing upon us, and much more. Its fulfillment begins when Jesus appears. Don't be hopeless! Keep "the hope which is laid up for you in heaven" (1:5) clear, strong, and growing, well fed by God's Word, watered by meditation, promoted in preaching, and stirred in song.

1:4–7 Prayer-driven growth. After commending the Colossians for their hope-driven faith and love, Paul noted

---

32. I freely acknowledge the utter unreasonableness, to the unenlightened rationalistic mind, of the Rapture—the sudden catching away of millions of believers worldwide to rendezvous with Jesus in the sky, thence to be escorted by Him to heaven (1 Thess. 4:14–18)—yet affirm it without hesitation, apology, or retraction. Equally as unbelievable to the faithless are the creation; Deluge; Red Sea parting; resurrection of Christ; conception of Isaac; survival of Israel; bodily translations of Enoch, Elijah, and Christ; and innumerable other biblical revelations or miracles. The faithful stand firm on these words from the living Word: "I will come again, and receive you unto myself, that where I am, there ye may be also" (John 14:3)!

Epaphras was their "faithful minister" (1:7). Thus, it appears Epaphras not only evangelized but also pastored them, or at least served as a teaching elder (cf. 1 Tim. 5:17–18).

Later in this letter Paul lauded Epaphras' exemplary intercession for the Colossians, describing it as not sporadic and apathetic but constant and impassioned, "always laboring fervently for you in prayers…[with] a great zeal" (4:12–13). So it appears Epaphras ministered to the Colossians by word and intercession, frequently and fervently.

This is directly in line with the original church's first leadership decision, in which the apostles decided to focus their efforts on "prayer and on the ministry of the word"—and not occasionally but "continually" (Acts 6:4). Did Epaphras consciously pattern his pastoral or teaching ministry after the apostles' dictum, aiming to empower the Word spoken through intercession in the Spirit? We don't know, but if so it certainly reveals one reason why the Colossians experienced commendable spiritual growth. It also challenges us.

Every minister and congregant needs to remember we build churches with not only our sermons, teachings, counsels, donations, life examples, administrative decisions, and good works ("helps," 1 Cor. 12:28) but also by our intercessions. And intercession is and will remain the highest ministry, to which Christ is presently ceaselessly committed (Heb. 7:25) and which on Earth He and the leaders and members of the early church practiced diligently—with remarkable results (Mark 6:46, 51; Luke 22:31–32; Acts 12:1–11; 2 Cor. 1:8–11). Like Epaphras, Paul prayed steadfastly for the Galatians to become "fully developed" in Christ (Gal. 4:19, NLT). More recently the eighteenth-century New England pastor Jonathan Edwards often prayed hours before delivering his sermons. Consequently, though Edwards calmly read his messages aloud without charismatic flamboyance (unlike his contemporary, George Whitefield), the Spirit of God moved charismatically, powerfully reviving, inspiring, and changing his listeners. Prayer-driven spiritual and numerical growth followed in his congregation. And in his community. And nation!

Whether a minister or congregant, will you steadily give yourself to the great work of "prayer and the ministry of the Word" (Acts 6:4) and expect the same prayer-driven growth that occurred in Colosse and New England to reoccur in your life, church, community, and nation?

1:5–6 The gospel. Paul referred to "the truth of the gospel" (1:5), and the "grace of God" (1:6), which had spread around the Mediterranean world, bearing God "fruit" in many lives (1:6). The Colossians fully understood him. Do we?

Literally, "gospel" (Greek, *euangelion*) means "good tidings; good news."[33] This good news states simply that instead of judging and destroying our fallen race, God has mercifully made a way to save us from sin and judgment through His Son, Jesus—if we'll receive Him! That's glad tidings indeed to anyone troubled by their besetting sins and their consequences, and especially for those struggling, as Luther and countless others have, to try to save themselves by religious rites or good works.

More broadly, the gospel reports Jesus paid the penalty for our sins on the cross to save us from eternal punishment

---

33. Lust, Eynikel, and Hauspie, *A Greek–English Lexicon of the Septuagint: Revised Edition*, s.v. "*euangelion*."

and reconcile us to God to live in union with Him in this life and the next...forever! The requirements are simple: As Jesus taught, we "repent" and "believe the gospel" (Mark 1:15)—firmly turning our minds and lives from sin as we know it and trusting the truthfulness of the gospel message with all our hearts (Acts 8:37). This gospel faith always produces gospel confessions (Rom. 10:9–10). We openly say we believe Jesus was crucified for our sins and resurrected for our justification by faith through grace alone (Rom. 10:8–10; Eph. 2:8–9), and He has personally saved us. And when probed, we assert unapologetically He is the only true Savior, Lord, and Way to God (Acts 4:12; John 14:6; Rom. 10:11).

Paul also spoke to the Colossians of "the hope" this gospel brings (1:5, 23). Briefly, this hopefulness eagerly anticipates Jesus' return, as He promised (John 14:1–3), and our subsequent sweet, unending life with Him (1 Thess. 4:17b–18; 5:9–11). New Testament hope expects Him to appear and catch away all closely abiding believers, living and deceased, to, with Him, enjoy our incorruptible, undefiled "inheritance"— the many rich blessings He has "laid up" for us from the foundation of the world, including rewards for our good works in Christ (Col. 1:5, 23; 1 Pet. 1:3–7; 1 Cor. 3:12–14; 2 Cor. 5:10)—in God's kingdom. This will occur in three phases: first in heaven after the Rapture (Rev. 4–5), then on this Earth in the Millennium (20:6), and finally on the new Earth...forever (21:1–22:5)! No other hope compares.

This "truth of the gospel," therefore, contains these key elements:

- Repentance of sin

- Faith in Christ as God's only appointed Savior, Lord, and Way, leading to personal conversion (John 3:1–8, 16; 14:6)

- Justification, including the forgiveness of sins and granting of God's righteousness by grace through faith

- The hope of Jesus' appearing, and our translation or resurrection to live forever with Him (1 Thess. 4:13–18)

- Our eternal inheritance, or common divine legacy as God's children

- Rewards for our individual good works in Christ (Matt. 25:21, 23; Luke 19:17)

- God's glorious kingdom, on this Earth and the next (Matt. 6:10)

- Eternal life, beginning now as we learn to walk closely with Christ in this world (John 17:3)

Officially, gospel history originated with John the Baptist, whose ministry laid the foundation for "the beginning of the gospel" (Mark 1:1, see vv. 1–4).[34] Jesus then emerged the first to preach the "gospel of the kingdom" (Matt. 4:23; 9:35).[35]

---

34. There is also a "beginning of the gospel" in individuals, families, cities, and nations. It occurs the moment the gospel, however presented, is first received (Phil. 4:15).

35. Though, as Paul taught, God preached a limited form of the gospel to Abraham, informing him that He would save the Gentiles through faith,

He did so liberally to: poor and lowly crowds (11:5); high and mighty religious leaders (Luke 20:1); His own people, the "lost sheep" of Israel (Matt. 15:24); their bitter religious enemies, the Samaritans (John 4:39–42); and Greeks, Phoenicians, and other Gentile seekers (John 12:20–22; Matt. 15:21–28).[36] But that wasn't all.

During Jesus' ministry He sent first the twelve and then seventy others to preach His gospel throughout Israel, and their preaching, like that of Paul and other early Christians, was authorized by signs of God's compassionate healing and delivering power (Luke 9:1–6; 10:1–12, 17–20; Heb. 2:3–4; 1 Thess. 1:5; Acts 6:8). Jesus prophesied His future followers would continue His work by sowing gospel seeds in "all nations" before this age ends (Matt. 24:14; Mark 13:10). For this wide task He commissioned not just leaders but every believer to share His gospel by personal or official evangelism with people everywhere so all would have opportunity to receive Him (Mark 16:15; Matt. 28:18–20; Acts 1:8; John 3:16).[37]

---

which He did in Christ (Gal. 3:6–9; cf. Gen. 12:3).

36. Jesus' limited ministry to Gentile seekers was a hint of His intention to save Gentiles as well as Jews on equal ground, but many deeply prejudiced Jewish Christians were slow to catch on. Are there any people groups or individuals—criminals, Muslims, communists, atheists, social liberals, illegal aliens, street people, occultists, homosexuals—with whom we would not willingly share the gospel of God's grace, given the opportunity? See Jonah 4:1–2.

37. In the early church not only apostles and deacons but ordinary Christians preached the gospel (Acts 8:4, 25; 14:7), sometimes with surprisingly significant results. The thriving church in Antioch, for instance, was founded by God through anonymous lay evangelists whose ministries were unknown to and unauthorized by the apostolic leadership—yet seen, approved, and abundantly blessed by God (Acts 11:20–21, 23)!

Those who do so will find, as Paul did, that presenting the "truth of the gospel" (1:5) always stirs "great conflict" (Col. 2:1). The gospel produces not only advocates inspired to spread it but also "enemies" eager to stop it, or at least hinder by causing "much contention" for its advocates (Rom. 11:28; 1 Thess. 2:2). Thus, we should daily seek the Spirit's fullest anointing for strength to bear our "afflictions," including if necessary "bonds," for presenting gospel truth (Luke 4:18, 32; Acts 1:8; 2 Tim. 1:8; Philem. 13). To continue faithfully proclaiming the gospel, we will sometimes have to make great sacrifices, dying to our dearest personal aspirations, relationships, and possessions (Matt. 20:22–23; Mark 10:29). But Christ will always repay us with sweet consolations in His time and way (Mark 8:35; 10:30–31). Let's review more gospel facts.

Though a simple message, and despised by atheistic intellectuals, followers of other faiths, hardened sinners, and even some professing but unconverted Christians, the gospel remains the "power of God" sufficient to change anyone, anywhere, anytime into a child of God (Rom. 1:16). So we must never be "ashamed of the gospel" (1:16). God's children are spiritually "begotten," or born again, by the gospel and in no other way (1 Cor. 4:15). It's a "beautiful" thing to God when He sees us sharing the good news with the lost (Rom. 10:15), especially so when we endure arduous journeys, emotional anguish, or bodily infirmities to do so (Gal. 4:13). For this reason angels watch with interest whenever and wherever it's preached (1 Pet. 1:12).

While Christ constantly opens "doors of utterance[s]" (Col. 4:3) for us to share the gospel (2 Cor. 2:12), Satan ceaselessly tries to blind sinners' minds with a cloud cover of unbelief so they won't receive its rays of saving truth (2 Cor. 4:3–4). To confuse them he promotes false gospels ("another gospel," Gal. 1:6) that twist the truths in God's Word into false teachings typically proposing salvation by God's grace plus our works.[38] We should never receive, aid, or pray blessings upon those preaching false gospels (2 John 9–10) because they're under God's double curse (Gal. 1:8–9) for spreading eternal damnation in the guise of eternal salvation.[39] Thus, as custodians of God's eternal truth, all of us, especially ministers, must zealously preserve the original and authoritative "truth of the gospel" (Gal. 2:5), speaking out when its purity is threatened by erring leaders (2:14) or heretics (Jude 3).

While ministers' financial misdeeds misrepresent and hinder the gospel (1 Cor. 9:12), Christ has nevertheless decreed that those who preach His gospel be supported by it (9:14). Yet His and Paul's examples also encourage ministers to preach it "without charge" whenever possible (9:18).

This gospel is called a "mystery" only because it was not fully revealed before this age (Eph. 6:19; cf. Col. 1:26–27; 4:3).[40] We have "fellowship," or union and mutual interest,

---

38. Paul says such teachings "pervert" (lit., twist) the gospel of Christ (Gal. 1:7).

39. It is our duty to identify, denounce, and reject false gospels and errant ways to God and have no fellowship with their proponents (Eph. 5:11), yet we should also pray for their repentance, binding their message and influence in our cities and loosing those under their influence (Matt. 18:18–20). While standing against them, however, we should never in any way harass or harm them in excessive and misguided zeal for the Prince of Peace. He alone will ultimately judge all men and messages (John 5:22; 1 Cor. 4:5).

40. As stated, Old Testament writings hinted God would save the Gentiles (Gen. 12:3). Yet it wasn't until He disclosed to Paul His intention to

with other believers in the gospel (Phil. 1:5). Our consistent behavior should recommend the gospel to others (Phil. 1:27), making it beautiful in their eyes (Titus 2:9–10). Though primarily facilitating salvation, the gospel also prophesies that not just Christians but all people will ultimately give account to the Savior (Rom. 2:16). In the Great Tribulation, when Antichrist is worshiped worldwide and only God's "two witnesses" speak publicly for Christ, angels will proclaim the "everlasting gospel" from the sky in God's passionate, last-ditch effort to turn sinners to Him (Rev. 11:3; 14:6–7). While most will ignore this plea, surprisingly some will heed it, receive Christ, and join others helping His remnant of persecuted, believing, Jewish brethren (Matt. 25:34–40; Rev. 12:16).

The apostle Paul considered his life "separated unto the gospel" (Rom. 1:1) and his overarching mission "to testify the gospel of the grace of God" (Acts 20:24). As an apostle (special messenger) he was at times called by Christ to share the gospel with kings, governors, and nations (Acts 9:15; 16:10; 23:11; 27:24). But Paul was always humbly "ready to preach the gospel" (Rom. 1:15) to anyone and in any conditions (Acts 21:40–22:22) and urged us to do the same (Eph. 6:15). He remained committed to the "confirmation," "defense," and "furtherance" of the true gospel until his last day (Phil. 1:7, 12, 17; 2 Tim. 4:6–8). We should too.

Let us, then, ponder these precious gospel truths. And then let us practice, preach, preserve, and proliferate them,

---

save Gentiles and Jews on equal grounds, by grace and faith alone, that the gospel was fully understood.

planting them in hearts everywhere in these last days—until our last day.

1:7 A powerful Pauline plug. Paul puts in a good word for Epaphras, citing his close unity with him in ministry: "Our dear fellow servant" (1:7). His words imply sweet friendship and oneness of purpose and vision, and also his opinion that Epaphras is a "faithful" minister of Christ: "He is a faithful and well-loved minister of Christ, and has your well-being at heart" (1:7, PHILLIPS). Or, he is "faithful to your interests" (MOFFATT). While Paul told the Corinthians he didn't need ministerial endorsements, or "epistles of commendation" (2 Cor. 3:1),[41] he didn't mind writing them for others, as his plug for Epaphras' ministry proves.

While we know precious little about Epaphras, this Pauline endorsement should convince us that he was indeed an excellent, committed elder (pastor, teacher, or deacon), evangelist (1:6–7), messenger, and zealous intercessor for at least three city-wide churches (4:12–13). Thus, he lived up to his name, which means "commended" for being "charming" or "lovely."[42] We may assume the reading of this epistle to

---

41. He went on to say all the endorsement he wanted or needed was the Holy Spirit's powerful work accompanying his ministry, transforming believers' hearts and lives into Christ's image: "Ye are our epistle [of commendation], written in our hearts, known and read of all men...the epistle of Christ [Christlikeness] ministered by us" (2 Cor. 3:2–3). Here's an endorsement every minister should humbly and prayerfully seek.

42. For this syncretized definition, see S. Smith and J. Cornwall, *The Exhaustive Dictionary of Bible Names* (North Brunswick, NJ: Bridge-Logos Publishers, 1998), s.v. "Epaphras." Also see: C. Brand, C. Draper, A. England, S. Bond, E. R. Clendenen, T. C. Butler, and B. Latta, editors, *Holman Illustrated Bible Dictionary* (Nashville, TN: Holman Bible Publishers, 2003), s.v. "Epaphras."

the believers in Colosse, Laodicea, and Hierapolis, where Epaphras apparently ministered regularly, encouraged them to love him and respect the biblical truths he shared with them even more (Col. 4:13, 16; 1 Thess. 5:12–13; Heb. 13:7).

For examples of other Spirit-led and effective ministerial endorsements in Scripture, see:

- Jesus' endorsement of John the Baptist's unique prophetic calling and work (Luke 7:24–28) and its immediate results (7:29)

- Peter's magnanimous endorsement of Paul's epistles as "scripture[s]" (2 Pet. 3:15–16)

- John's endorsement of Demetrius' character and leadership (3 John 11–12)

- Paul's praise for Timothy's selfless, Christ-centered ministry (Phil. 2:19–23)

- Paul's commendation of John Mark's ministry of helps (2 Tim. 4:11b).

- Luke's and Paul's endorsements of Apollos (Acts 18:24–28; 1 Cor. 3:5–8)

- Ezekiel's implicit (and God's explicit) endorsement of Daniel's godliness and wisdom (Ezek. 14:14, 20; 28:3)[43]

---

43. Though not a ministerial endorsement, the queen mother of Babylon's recommendation of Daniel was timely, glowing, and most effective (Dan. 5:10–12).

- Barnabas' two endorsements of Paul's calling
  and ministry, in Jerusalem (Acts 9:27–28) and
  years later in Antioch (11:25–26)

In nearer times, the pre-Tribulation, pre-Millennial end-time view many Christians (including this author) hold today was systematized by John N. Darby in the nineteenth century. Its wide and enduring acceptance, however, was initially facilitated by the hearty endorsements of famous evangelist Dwight L. Moody and prolific Bible publisher C. I. Scofield. Indeed, "A man's gift maketh room for him, and bringeth him before great men" (Prov. 18:16). Oh the power of one high-profile, God-inspired endorsement of a God-gifted servant of Christ!

Today a well-known minister's plug of a little-known minister goes a long way in establishing congregations' confidence in the latter's ministry. It helps him (or her) get his foot in the door of the church, conference, or denomination—and many hearts. The rest is up to the Spirit's confirmation of his gift and message and the integrity of his sustained, faithful, love-driven ministry to Christ's sheep. Epaphras, as his name prophesied, was "commended" because he was gifted, faithful, diligent, love-driven, and thus commendable. Are we?

1:3, 9–14 A powerful Pauline prayer. To prompt more spiritual thinking and intercessions from the Colossians Paul disclosed the petitions he and his ministry team were ceaselessly praying for them. This affords us a glimpse of his exemplary prayer life and samples of the inspired petitions he prayed for all the churches he oversaw.

Specifically, he prayed "always" (1:3) for the Colossians that they might:

- Be "FILLED [FULL] WITH THE KNOWLEDGE
  OF HIS [GOD'S] WILL" (PLAN) (1:9). "Filled"
  (Greek, *plēroō*) means to "fill to the full" or be
  "completely full," as a ship with all holds filled
  and fully manned, and thus ready for voyage[44]
  (cf. Eph. 3:19). So Paul wanted them to not
  partially or mostly but fully grasp God's plan
  for the world, church, their lives, and their
  ministries; or, possess "complete knowledge" of
  it (NLT); or, "acquire a thorough understanding
  of the ways in which God works" (THE
  MESSAGE); or, enjoy "the advanced and perfect
  experiential knowledge of His will" (Col. 1:9,
  WUEST).[45] Thus, "filled full" of God-knowledge
  they could set sail to carry and share Christ
  across the sea of humanity. To be thus "filled
  full" with divine knowledge requires the fullness of the Holy Spirit, seeking God, studying

---

44. Kittel, Friedrich, and Bromiley, *Theological Dictionary of the New Testament,* s.v. *"plēroō."*

45. At the time heretics were offering the Colossians an early form of gnosticism which claimed to impart secret knowledge only accessible to those specially enlightened, and alleged this knowledge alone saved people. But Christ, through Paul's inspired prayer, wanted to give them (and us) the full measure of the vast riches of true divine knowledge, the prime tenet of which declares by grace alone we are saved through faith alone in Christ alone, who is the lone Way to God (Eph. 2:8; John 14:6). Truly, "It's not what we know that brings salvation but whom we know." (Quote extracted from *Life Application Study Bible* [Wheaton, IL: Tyndale House, 2004], Col. 1:4–5, note, 2027.)

Scripture, a life of steadfast obedience, and considerable time walking with God through the trials of life, as well as a willingness to discover and obey God's guidance in every situation.[46]

- HAVE "ALL WISDOM AND SPIRITUAL UNDER-STANDING" (1:9). Wisdom is good judgment, the ability to choose wisely or apply knowledge correctly to the spontaneous situations of life. "Understanding" is insight, the ability to see through the visible and obvious and discern the underlying reality. Thus, Paul wanted them to have "comprehensive insight into the ways and purposes of God" (AMP), or "every kind of wisdom and intelligence that is spiritual" (WUEST). He later asserted such replete divine wisdom and insight are "hidden" only in Christ (2:3), not in worldly philosophies or other religions (including Christless, Pharisaic Judaism), however intellectual, angelic, or ascetic their teachers and teachings (2:8–23).

- "WALK WORTHY OF THE LORD" (1:10). This is the end of being "filled full" of

---

46. George Mueller, a master of the life of faith and divine guidance, listed six steps to discovering God's will: (1) Have no will of your own; (2) Don't decide God's will merely by your impressions or feelings; (3) Seek His will in connection with His written Word; (4) See how God is working in your circumstances; (5) Pray for God to reveal His will; (6) After doing these things, patiently reflect and, if you continue to have peace, proceed. For the full version, see George Mueller, *Answers to Prayer* (Chicago: Moody Press, 1984), "How to Ascertain the Will of God," 6.

God-knowledge, wisdom, and insight.[47]
"Walk" describes our characteristic lifestyle
or how we usually live. Our walk becomes
"worthy," or like the worthy One, Christ, when
we determine to please Him by living what
we're learning (Matt. 7:25–28; James 1:22–25;
2 Tim. 2:15; 1 Thess. 4:1; Gal. 1:10; Phil. 4:9).
The next phrase describes the sole motive that
produces a worthy life: "To please Him in all
respects" (1:10, NAS). So Paul prayed, "Live the
kind of life that honors and pleases the Lord
in every way" (Col. 1:10, NCV); or, "Give him
entire satisfaction" (MOFFATT). Such worthy
living—close to Jesus, prayerful, devoted, biblical, upright, dutiful—imparts assurance one
will be taken in the Rapture (Luke 21:34–36;
Matt. 24:42–51)[48] and is also (as the KJV reads)
pleasing "unto all" reasonable unbelievers,
shining the saving, attracting light of Christ in
their sin-darkened, hopeless lives (Matt. 5:14–
16; Titus 2:9–10).

- "BE FRUITFUL IN EVERY GOOD WORK" (1:10).
  Paul asks that all the Colossians' works may in

---

47. However spiritual, profound, or revelatory, "All Bible truths are practical…If we are growing in knowledge [spiritual intelligence], we should
also be growing in grace [practical obedience] (2 Peter 3:18)." For quote see
W. W. Wiersbe, *The Bible Exposition Commentary*, Vol. 2, Col. 1:10, note.

48. Remember, Enoch is a type of the "rapturable" church, and the primary
reason he was taken to heaven before the Deluge, stated twice for emphasis,
was "Enoch walked with God…Enoch walked with God" (Gen. 5:22, 24).
Then one day, "He was not; for God took him" (5:24). So it will be with us
if we "walk worthy" with Christ (Col. 1:10).

some way bear kingdom fruit. May ours also! Our good deeds reveal our King's compassion, our hard work His ethics, and our upright- ness His righteousness. Our sharing of the gospel draws the lost into His kingdom. Our vocational labors earn financial fruit—tithes and offerings to support His kingdom works, churches, and missions. Our sharing of God's Word strengthens, blesses, teaches, and corrects its citizens. And our most basic "work," our abiding, daily faith-walk with the King (John 6:28–29), produces lush "fruit of the Spirit," or Christlikeness of character, that beautifies His kingdom with more of His image (Gal. 5:22–23).

- EVER "INCREASE" IN KNOWING GOD (1:10). By prayerful, systematic Bible study we discover more about God's character, ways, judgments, and mercies. By seeking and most importantly obeying Him, we grow in the experiential knowledge of Him, becoming taught of His Spirit, more familiar with His inner voice and intimate signs, and more aware of His provi- dential hand correcting, chastening, or blessing us (Isa. 50:4; John 6:45). Thus, we come to know God personally as well as biblically (John 7:17). Paul prays this "knowing" will con- tinue growing "with fuller, deeper, and clearer insight" forever (Col. 1:10, AMP; cf. John 17:3). It's our duty then to steadily seek more God- truths—accurate, useful, and timely biblical information—and obey it so we can continue knowing God more, intellectually and intimately. There is no end to knowing God—unless we make it by neglecting to seek or obey Him.

- BE "STRENGTHENED WITH ALL MIGHT" BY GOD'S POWER (1:11). Paul prayed the Colossians, no longer relying merely on their human strength, would be fortified with every aspect of the Holy Spirit's divine strength, or "strength of every kind" (1:11, WEY). This would give them: a strong spirit; Spirit-enhanced physical strength, as needed (Deut. 33:25); strength for steadfastness in duty; confidence in fearful situations; authority to influence others for Christ with their words (Matt. 7:28–29); miraculous power, for those so gifted;[49] and gifts of the Spirit (1 Cor. 12:1–11). But he particularly requested divine empowerment for patient endurance in long, demanding trials and sufferings; or, "perseverance and forbearance" (AMP) with the difficult people and situations God was using to test their mettle[50]—and

---

49. The word Paul uses for God's glorious "power" is the Greek *dynamis*, meaning "divine strength, ability, miraculous power" (Acts 1:8; 6:8; 10:38). See J. Swanson, *Dictionary of Biblical Languages With Semantic Domains: Greek (New Testament)*, electronic ed. (Oak Harbor: Logos Research Systems, Inc., 1997), s.v. "*dynamis*."

50. The word Paul uses for "long-suffering" (Greek, *macrothymia*) means "forbearance, patience towards people," thus referring to chronically difficult people being the cause of much of our protracted sufferings. For definition, see Lust, Eynikel, and Hauspie, *A Greek–English Lexicon of the Septuagint: Revised Edition*, s.v. "*macrothymia*."

"with joyfulness" not grumbling or sullenness. Only a divinely empowered life can endure grievous long-suffering joyfully.

- EVER BE "GIVING THANKS" TO THE HEAV-ENLY FATHER (1:12). Paul prayed the Colossians would thank God the Father as constantly as he did (1:3; 1 Thess. 5:18; Eph. 5:20; Col. 3:17). Why? He has delivered us from the "power of darkness,"[51] redeemed us by Jesus' blood, trans-lated us into His kingdom, and "qualified" (NKJV) us to share in the indescribably fabu-lous "inheritance of the saints"[52] in the next life (1:12–14). That's a lot to give thanks for, so let's give thanks for it a lot.

---

51. How wonderful! The light of Christ's truth has freed us forever from the power, hold, and control of Satan's dark demonic hosts and their anti-God, faith-destroying lies (John 8:44; 2 Cor. 4:4; Eph. 6:11–12; 1 Tim. 4:1; 1 John 4:1). False religions, atheism, naturalism, humanism, liberalism, Dar-winism, the false promise of satisfaction in sin and self-centered living—we're released from the powerful, oppressive grip of all these dark lies and free to walk in Spirit-led, faith-nourished, loving, joyful fellowship with Jesus. Have you thanked your Father for this lately (1:12)?

52. This heritage is New Jerusalem and everything and everyone in it. Our central Blessing will be God—indescribably precious, sweet fellow-ship with the Father, Son, and Holy Spirit...forever! Second, we'll have rich, wide fellowship with all the elect and the angels! Third, we'll receive many delightful blessings (abilities, tasks, authority, positions, etc.) as per-sonal rewards for our works in Christ in this life. Fourth, we'll enjoy the entire new material creation (new heavens and Earth, Rev. 21:1) and all its unimaginable visual and tangible splendors "in light," or the light of the presence (Rev. 21:22–24; 1:16c). One commentator notes that while Israel received an earthly inheritance, the Promised Land of Canaan, the church (and every Christian) has received a heavenly inheritance, New Jerusalem (Rev. 21–22). On this last point see Jack W. Hayford, general editor, *The Spirit-Filled Life Bible* (Nashville: Thomas Nelson Publishers, 1991), 1813.

Like Paul's other New Testament prayers, this one is powerful. It's inclusion in Scripture means it's inspired—breathed out by the Spirit, breathed in by Paul, and then inscribed in his epistle (2 Tim. 3:16–17; 2 Pet. 1:20–21). Thus, its real origin and writer was not Paul but Christ; Christ the Head (Col. 1:18) prompted these thoughts to Paul by His Spirit. Inspiration also means it has multiple applications; it's for the historic Colossian Christians and also for all of us today. The same is true of all Paul's prayers in Scripture (2 Cor. 13:7–9; Gal. 4:19; Eph. 1:15–20; 3:14–19; 6:18–20; Phil. 1:9–11; Col. 1:9–14; 2 Thess. 1:11–12), including his brief but key prayers for our "grace and peace" with which he begins and ends his epistles (Col. 1:2; 4:18; cf. Rom. 1:7; 16:24; 1 Cor. 1:3; 16:23). Now that we know the power of Paul's prayer, there's only one path of practical response.

Let's ponder this powerful Pauline prayer. And practice it. And preach it. And most importantly, pray it for Christians everywhere!

1:9 The incessant Intercessor. Paul said he did not cease to pray for the Colossians (1:9; cf. 1:3). He said the same to many other churches and individuals (Rom. 1:9; Eph. 1:15–16; Phil. 1:3–5; Col. 1:3; 1:9; 1 Thess. 1:2; 3:9–10; 2 Thess. 1:11; 2 Tim. 1:3; Philem. 4). These scriptures prove constant prayer was Paul's modus operandi. They also reveal that he practiced what he preached, not only calling for but also conducting prayer "always" (Eph. 6:18) and "without ceasing" (1 Thess. 5:17). His prayers were as often for saints as for sinners: "Praying always with all prayer and supplication in the Spirit...with all perseverance...for all saints" (Eph. 6:18).[53]

---

53. Do we wrongly assume that because sinners are converted or converts

An incessant intercessor, Paul prayed with structure and spontaneity—at prayer times and all times—even when suffering galling injustice and painful abuse (Acts 16:24–25).

Thus, he mirrored the most eminent incessant Intercessor, Christ, who prayed much more frequently than we imagine during His earthly ministry, publicly for the sick and afflicted[54] and privately for His and His disciples' needs,[55] and who in this age "ever liveth to make intercession for us" in heaven (Heb. 7:25).

Others also mirrored our heavenly Intercessor. For instance:

- Anna, the aged Jewish prophetess who prayed and fasted constantly (Luke 2:36–37)

- Epaphras, who was with Paul when he wrote Colossians (Col. 4:12)

- The Jerusalem church, whose dynamic intercessors met in the home of Mary, mother of John Mark (Acts 12:5, 12)

---

are growing they need no more prayer? Paul didn't. He realized God wants all Christians to grow continuously and that thriving Christians are Satan's favorite targets. Thus, all Christians need intercession as much as sinners. "He heard that they were good, and he prayed that they might be better…Where there is spiritual life there is still need of spiritual strength." For quote see Matthew Henry, *Commentary in One Volume* (Grand Rapids, MI: Zondervan Publishing, 1961), 1869–1870.

54. Jesus was touching and praying for the sick hours every day in public meetings (Mark 1:32–34) and also responding to private requests for healing prayer (Mark 5:22–24). As His ministers, it's time we take time for intercession.

55. See Mark 1:35; 6:46; Luke 5:16 (NIV); 6:12; 22:32; 22:41–42; John 17:1–26.

- The leaders of the fledgling Antioch church (13:1–2)

- Many first-century Christian widows who, said Paul, prayed "day and night" (1 Tim. 5:5)

- Moses, whose nonstop intercessory stand lifted Israel to victory over the Amalekites (Exod. 17:8–13)

- Daniel, who offered thanksgiving and intercession three times daily (Dan. 6:10)

- Elijah, who on Carmel (and probably for the previous three and a half years) prayed persistently for Israel's restoration (1 Kings 18:41–46)

- The Moravians, who prayed for missions 24-7 for a hundred years[56]

- Jonathan Edwards, who prayed for hours before delivering his sermons

- The intercessors in Charles H. Spurgeon's Metropolitan Tabernacle, who prayed selflessly in the basement while he preached powerfully in the pulpit

---

56. Under the leadership of Nicholas von Zinzendorf in Herrnhut ("the Lord's Watch"), Saxony, each adult Moravian intercessor manned a one-hour prayer shift in their unceasing prayer watch. Soon the Moravian youth followed suit! Is it any wonder that this remarkable commitment to utter God-dependency through prayer produced a Spirit-led mission work that impacted continents, influenced John Wesley's salvation, and inspired William Carey, the "father of modern missions"? What new God-wonders will follow if we commit to extraordinary prayer watches?

- Charles G. Finney's prayer teams, who, led by "Father" Daniel Nash, interceded for weeks before his powerful evangelistic campaigns

- Jeremy Lanphier and the participants in the lay-led, noonday prayer meetings that swept many American cities in 1857–1858, sparking the Third Great Awakening[57]

- William Seymour, whose commitment to praying first five and then seven hours daily spawned the Azusa Street Pentecostal Revival[58]

Besides these high-profile examples, thousands of anonymous individuals and prayer groups have given themselves to intercessory prayer with remarkable results following in their families, churches, cities, and nations. This challenges the best of us.

We may already be habitual, committed intercessors, praying often for others with whom we live, work, or interact (cf. Job 1:4–5). But are we willing to pray even more? Willing to pray during our free time slots daily or nightly? This will require taking time from nonessential activities or interests. Will we give it? The truth is many Christians, even ministers, won't commit to increased prayer.[59] Every church des-

---

57. For more information on how the Third Great Awakening was sparked by prayer, see http://www.cslewisinstitute.org/webfm_send/577 (accessed September 25, 2015).

58. See Eddie Hyatt, *The Azusa Street Revival* (Lake Mary, FL: Charisma House, 2006), 20.

59. Let every pastor honestly compare the time he spends in intercession for his flock and other souls to that given to his favorite avocation or entertainment, and he (or she) may be surprised and embarrassed.

perately needs a band of intercessors committed to the ways and teachings of the incessant Intercessor—if it's serious about bearing eternal kingdom fruit. Let's join these hidden, faithful prayer bands, as Paul did, and watch in awe as the incessant Intercessor responds to our incessant intercessions by touching those for whom we pray in wonderful new ways!

1:11–12 Suffering strength. As stated earlier, Paul asked the Lord to give the Colossians strength to endure long, difficult adversities with joy and thanksgiving. Or simply, suffering strength—the strength to suffer well. How odd!

We also want God's strength, but for other things, such as to succeed in our worldly vocations, professions, or interests. It never occurs to us that we need a mighty baptism of the Spirit and His divine power to, well, *suffer!* That is, to successfully endure whatever unpleasantness God permits to temporarily visit our life to test our faith, patience, loyalty, and love (e.g., Job). But we do.

Without "all might" from the Almighty, we repeatedly falter in our spiritual furnaces, wildernesses, and floods, dishonoring and disappointing Jesus and forfeiting His full approval for service (Col. 1:11). With it, we "stand fast," as Paul urged us (Phil. 4:1; Eph. 6:13), overcoming all challenges and challengers. Though injustices and indignities beset us we abide wondrously unaffected, in close fellowship with Jesus, steadfast worship, and faithful service. Our example powerfully draws unbelievers to the faith (cf. Acts 16:27–34; 28:6, 7–10). We also deeply satisfy the Lord by continuing to honor Him even while we suffer the dishonors, disappointments, and defeats He permits to test us.

Since this joyful endurance glorifies Christ, the divine strength that fuels it is called His "glorious power" (1:11)—the suffering strength that, when manifested in our lives, glorifies Him, or "the glory-strength God gives" (THE MESSAGE).[60] Paul was suffering strength incarnate (2 Cor. 11:23–33; 12:7–10) and his joyful endurance of many cruel tests—stonings (Acts 14:19–23), brutal beatings (16:16–25), riots (19:23–41; 21:27–40), death plots (23:12–33), lengthy incarcerations (24:27), shipwrecks (27:1–44), snakebites (28:1–6)—repeatedly brought Christ great glory.

This power is also "glorious" because as the Bible, Israel's history, and church history often demonstrate, God uses not sweet worldly success but suffering well endured to transform our characters into the image of Christ who, as a "man of sorrows," "despised and rejected of men," and "acquainted with grief" (Isa. 53:3), endured well many sorrows in His family, hometown, ministry, betrayals, and brutal redemptive sufferings. As we humbly trust and obey Him in our trials, deep and permanent changes occur. We begin thinking spiritually, not carnally, being concerned with others first, not ourselves. Christ, His Word, and His calling become more important and selfish pursuits less. Our besetting sins wither and fall away. Our spiritual discernment becomes quick, our vision clear, and recognition of God's voice sure. We begin

---

60. One definition of *glory* is the condition of highest achievement. While we think a Christian's condition of highest spiritual achievement lies in very fruitful or large-scale ministry works, in fact the highest manifestation of God's grace occurs when we suffer adversity well—continuing to seek God, love His Word, worship, work faithfully, pray always, trust God's promises, and walk in love without the slightest trace of discontent, resentment, self-pity, or envy of others. That's glorious overcoming, like the glorious One, Jesus. And it brings Him eternal glory!

loving and joyfully serving all Christians, even strangers. Our ministry gifts grow more effective and our prayers powerful. Thus, suffering well endured expedites our spiritual maturity, and we become more like our glorious Lord—and ready for His return.

That is why Scripture teaches us how to suffer well (Matt. 5:10–12; 7:25–26; 1 Pet. 1:6–7; 4:12–16). It's why Jesus commended the Philadelphian Christians—and assured them they would be translated!—for "keeping the word of my patience" (Rev. 3:10); or "My command to persevere" (NKJV); or "my command to endure patiently" (NIV). For this divine endurance they needed divine power. That's why Paul prayed as he did for the Colossians and Jesus ordered His original followers to wait until the Spirit came upon them in power. He knew only "power from on high" (Luke 24:49; Acts 1:8) would impart strength to suffer below.

Acts shows repeatedly the "glorious power [Greek, *dynamis*[61]]" (Col. 1:11) the Spirit released in the first believers was multifaceted: for overcoming sin, subduing self-will, working hard, working miracles, operating gifts of grace, fivefold ministry—and suffering persecution well! One day they were working stunning miracles at the Beautiful Gate and the next enduring shocking injustices from the ugly Sanhedrinists. But in all situations the "all might" (1:11) within enabled them to stay close to Jesus, love one another, forgive offenders, and press on in their predestined

---

61. No mere human energy, *dynamis* means nothing less than "miraculous [divine] strength, might, ability." See J. Strong, *A Concise Dictionary of the Words in the Greek Testament and The Hebrew Bible* (Bellingham, WA: Logos Bible Software, 2009), s.v. "*dynamis*."

course…with unquenchable joy and thanksgiving! Suffering strength has persisted throughout church history.

The confessors and martyrs of the early church had it. So did the reformers, such as John Wycliffe, John Huss, William Tyndale, Martin Luther, and countless others. Centuries later, Adoniram Judson, William Carey, John Wesley, Hudson Taylor, Harriet Tubman, Pandita Ramabai, Corrie ten Boom, and many more Christian missionaries, ministers, and movers exemplified the strength to suffer well. Presently Christians in China, Africa, India, the Middle East, and elsewhere are being strengthened daily with Christ's suffering power. Statistical historians tell us since the beginning of the twentieth century Christian suffering worldwide has increased significantly. With the last days fast approaching, suffering strength is going to become more, not less important. Like Paul and the Colossians, we'll soon be praying daily for our churches and fellow believers to be "strengthened with all might, according to his glorious power, unto all patience and long-suffering with joyfulness; giving thanks." And we'll see our sufferings for Christ's sake as divine gifts and means of grace.

Matthew Henry stated:

> We are strengthened to "all patience" when we not only bear our troubles patiently, but receive them as gifts from God, and are thankful for them…this is even unto long-suffering, not only to bear trouble awhile, but to bear it as long as God pleases to continue it. It is with joyfulness, to rejoice in tribulation, to rejoice that we are counted worthy to suffer for his name [Acts 5:41], to have joy as well as patience in the troubles of

life. This we could never do by any strength of our own, but as we are strengthened by the grace of God.[62]

Henry lived as he lectured. After once being robbed,[63] he noted in his diary:

> Let me be thankful first because I was never robbed before; second, although they took my purse, they did not take my life; third, because although they took my all, it was not much; and fourth, because it was I who was robbed, not I who robbed.[64]

Are we ready to adopt this spiritual view of suffering for Christ's sake? Ready to ask for strength not merely to succeed in our worldly labors or ministry works but also to thrive in our rejections, injustices, defeats, and also under the vexing burdens we bear day after day in dealing with stubborn, seemingly hopeless cases—incorrigible unbelievers and Christians that haven't shown improvement in years despite many prayers and much forbearance? May the Almighty re-anoint us with "all might" daily, specifically with "strength that endures the unendurable and spills over into joy, thanking the Father" (THE MESSAGE). When we consistently walk in this suffering strength, our Refuge and

---

62. Henry, *Commentary in One Volume*, 1870.

63. Lest we imagine this couldn't happen to a godly man, remember Paul's testimony of being robbed (2 Cor. 11:26) and Job's record of the same—on a much grander scale (Job 1:14–15)! Peter adds we should "think it not strange" when our sovereign God, for reasons fully known only to Him, tests us in unexpected ways (1 Pet. 4:12; cf. Prov. 3:5–6).

64. Billy Graham, *Hope for Each Day: Words of Wisdom and Faith* (Nashville, TN: Thomas Nelson Publishers, 2002), 263.

Strength will come for us because we'll be thoroughly like Him and ready to live with Him forever.

1:15 The invisible God made visible. This verse begins Paul's presentation of the glorious, preeminent deity of Christ, "Who is the image of the invisible God" (1:15). Jesus is nothing less than the invisible God made visible, a theme repeatedly asserted in the New Testament (John 1:1–4, 18; 14:8–11; 2 Cor. 4:4; Heb. 1:3). How does this relate to Paul's teaching in Romans 1, which tells us the creation is God's great witness to the world that He exists (Rom. 1:18–20)?

Warren Wiersbe makes this distinction:

> Nature reveals the existence, power, and wisdom of God; but nature cannot reveal the very essence of God to us. It is only in Jesus Christ that the invisible God is revealed perfectly.[65]

Anyone, therefore, who wants to see and know God can do so by simply examining Jesus' character, disposition, values, goals, and ways of living and working. He perfectly represents who, what, and all God is. All the essential divine attributes and characteristic acts are plainly visible in the life and works of Jesus of Nazareth, including God's holy wrath and righteous judgments (Matt. 23:13–33; Mark 3:5; 10:14, NLT, ISV; 11:12–14; 11:15–17). Thus, He has "declared" the Father (John 1:18), or "made him known" (ESV), "explained Him" (NAS), "revealed God to us" (NLT), "fully explained deity" (WUEST), "shown us what God is like" (NCV), and "made him plain as day" (THE MESSAGE).

---

65. Wiersbe, *The Bible Exposition Commentary*, Vol. 2, 116.

"Image" (Greek, *eikōn*, Col. 1:15) means "likeness, portrait, figure, effigy, or image."[66] We know God forbade the Israelites from making any images of Him to worship and that the pagans did just the opposite, sculpting or molding material images of their deities and making them the centerpieces of their worship in temples or shrines (and miniature icons for domestic worship; see Gen. 35:2–4; Acts 19:24). Jesus was God's answer or response to the proliferation of pagan idols and icons—He was God's Icon! God made one "Image," and only one. Why? In His love He wanted this sight-dependent world to have a singular, sufficiently visible and tangible expression of Himself to draw us to Him. The Advent materialized the immaterial God. Thus, mortals discerned the immortal, not in imperfect artistic renderings of stone, wood, or precious metal, but in one perfect God-man precisely and fully portraying the wondrous image of the Godhead (cf. Gen. 1:26). This Father's facsimile exactly represents the original seated on the throne in heaven (John 14:9; Rev. 4:2–3). Our viewfinders with which we view this unspeakably beautiful God-spectacle are the four Gospels. Matthew, Mark, Luke, and John describe the respective "side" of the Image they, or the apostles they spoke for, saw, heard, touched, and observed over the three years of Jesus' ministry.

As we behold the masterpiece their inspired words paint, or "the glory of the Lord," day by day, seeking Jesus, praying, soaking in His Word, and obeying Him in our tests, we're

---

66. H. Liddell, *A Lexicon: Abridged From Liddell and Scott's Greek–English Lexicon* (Oak Harbor, WA: Logos Research Systems, Inc., 1996), s.v. *"eikōn."* Also see Spicq and Ernest, *Theological Lexicon of the New Testament*, s.v. *"eikōn."*

steadily changed into "the same image" by the power of the Holy Spirit (2 Cor. 3:17–18). The Father's Image is increasingly replicated in our thought, speech, and actions for others to see and come to Him (Rom. 12:1–2; Phil. 2:12–16; Gal. 1:24; John 12:32). While many Old and New Testament characters exemplify divine attributes, none reveal the full image of God's character without being distorted by human flaws or sin. Even the best—Moses, David, Peter, Paul—had faults. Only Jesus was the "express image of His person" (Heb. 1:3). And the Father doesn't want anyone or anything to confuse, blur, or block the one great, unblemished self-portrait He gave us.

Therefore we must never excessively promote any human, whether Mary, saints, martyrs, or Popes, however virtuous they are or appear. Nor specially gifted, knowledgeable, or successful ministers. Nor extraordinarily beneficent political leaders. Nor grand military leaders. Nor the finest philosophers, inventors, artists, or musicians. Nor anyone else. Why? Lest we worship another image in the house of God's Image, Christ, and thus reenact the folly of ancient pagan worship (Matt. 22:21). Nor should we ministers excessively build or puff our public images (branding), lest people think too highly of us and we become in even the smallest measure an icon blocking out the glory-light of God's only Image (cf. Acts 10:25–26; 2 Cor. 12:6). All this is implied in Paul's declaration that Jesus alone is the "image of the invisible God." But Satan has ceaselessly challenged this.

He has inspired Roman emperors, and many other emperors, kings, potentates, and princes since, to make divine claims or demand excessive veneration or allegiance and prompted many to publicize their "divine image" in statues, reliefs, other artwork, or coins.[67] Antiochus IV referred to himself as an epiphany, or manifestation of God. Hitler made the German people take an oath of obedience not to Germany or even the Nazi party but to him personally. The Japanese people as recently as the 1940s turned away when Emperor Hirohito rode by to avoid looking directly at their god. The ruling family of North Korea has also made divine claims. And, though less well known, many deluded fanatics, gurus, and cultists have claimed to be Jesus or God. Thus, Satan has for centuries defied Paul's declaration. And he's not finished yet.

Antichrist will be Satan's final and most blasphemous response to God's Image. Satan will craft a likeness or paint a portrait of himself in a human being and release him on the world stage to imitate Jesus' divine wisdom, grace, and power (2 Thess. 2:3–12), even placing his physical, supernaturally animated image in the yet-future Jewish temple in an attempt to preempt Christ's soon-coming Millennial coronation (Rev. 13:14–15).

So remember who alone is the "image of the invisible God" and let no other visible person or thing woo, wow, cow, or bow you till God's true Image returns.

1:15–19 The preeminence of the Son. In these verses Paul asserted the singular supremacy of God's "dear Son," Jesus (1:13). Why place Jesus on this literary pedestal?

---

67. Haman likely made divine claims (or was considered an agent of King Xerxes' alleged divine wisdom or power; note Xerxes' edict, Esther 3:2), thus explaining why Mordecai refused to honor him. Other likely reasons were: (a) as an Amalekite, Haman was under God's judgment (Esther 3:1; Num. 24:7), and (b) he was excessively proud (Esther 5:11; 6:6), which sin God abominates the most (Ps. 40:1–4; Prov. 6:16–7).

It's a vital correction to this world's vicious lie. Secular history presents Jesus in the lowest terms—a first-century Jewish peasant carpenter turned uncredentialed rabbi whose exceptional powers and captivating oratory launched a regionally impressive three-year religious campaign acclaimed by thousands...of ignorant Galileans! His devotees then mythologized Him and successfully deceived the whole Western world for twenty centuries! As if anticipating this response from the intelligentsia, Paul preemptively sets the record straight by describing Jesus in the most soaring terms, as He really is. He portrays Jesus apart from and above all other purported deities, persons, and things, visible and invisible.

Generally, Paul describes Christ as before and above every existing thing, including:

- The universe (cosmos), consisting of the material (visible) and spiritual (invisible) worlds

- The church, which is the worldwide body of born-again believers in Christ

More specifically, Paul expresses Christ's preeminence in seven ways:

1. He is the Image of God (the Father) (1:15)

2. He is the Creator of everything, material and spiritual (1:16)

3. He is the Coherer, holding all things together (1:17)

4. He is the first Priority, holding first place, in all creation (1:17)

5. He is the Head of the church (1:18)

6. He is the Firstborn of the new creation (1:18)

7. He is the Fullness of God (1:19)

Let's examine further these marvelous Christ-truths Paul unveils.

CHRIST THE IMAGE. Jesus alone is the visible "image" of the invisible God (1:15), the tangible representation of the mystical deity, the glorious, distant author of space landed on our humble, temporal *terra firma*. As He said to Phillip, "He that hath seen me hath seen the Father" (John 14:9). For more, see my previous entry, "The invisible God made visible," Col. 1:15.

CHRIST THE CREATOR. Like other New Testament writers, Paul affirmed Jesus created the entire (material and spiritual) universe (1:16; cf. John 1:1–3; Heb. 1:1–2).[68] Naturally, then, Jesus is greater than all He created. This refuted the early gnostics, who taught the Colossians that, since in their view the creation was evil, a good God couldn't have created it. Therefore, it was instead created by the Demiurge, or evil creator (or artisan) god.[69]

---

68. This harmonizes perfectly with Genesis' account of creation. "In the beginning, God created the heaven and the earth" (Gen. 1:1) by the agency and in the person of His Son, through the energy and power of the Holy Spirit (1:2). Thus, God—the entire, united, indivisible, triune Godhead—created the entire material and spiritual cosmos.

69. To counter these false claims and establish both the greatness of Jesus and the goodness of the material creation (Gen. 1:4, 10, 12, 18, 21, 25, 31), Paul presented Jesus, the holy Image and Fullness of God, as the hands-on Creator of the material world the Father designed and the Spirit energized.

It was Christ's creatorship that gave Him calm mastery over wind, waters, earth, plants, fish, animals, and mortal bodies. This explains how He stopped the winds and waves on Galilee; made healing balm from clay and saliva (infused with His divine Spirit-breath); spoke death to a barren fig tree; drew a haul of fish into Peter's net; ordered a fish to retrieve a denarius; caused demonic pigs to rush off a cliff; and healed sick, injured, maimed, and even deceased human bodies![70] Though beyond the creature's abilities, these wonders were easy to their Creator.

Paul further asserted Jesus created all natural and supernatural seats of government and offices, specifically "thrones, kingdoms, rulers, and authorities [of lesser rank]" (1:16, NLT). This speaks of not only the natural realm of political authority but also the spiritual realm that surrounds and influences this Earth, with all its invisible dominions, thrones, spirit-principles (chief rulers), and lesser demonic authorities (Col. 1:16; Eph. 6:12; Dan. 10:13, 20–21).[71] This

---

70. For these physical miracles see Matt. 15:29–31; 17:24–27; Mark 4:39; 5:13; 8:22–25; 11:12–14, 20; Luke 5:1–11; 7:11–17.

71. The four terms, "thrones, dominions, principalities, powers" (1:16) are best translated "thrones, kingdoms, rulers, and authorities" (NLT). Being "visible, and invisible," these speak of human and spirit rulers and spheres. Christ has created every "throne" (worldly or heavenly seat of authority), every "dominion" (kingdom, nation, or realm), every chief ruler (human, angelic, or demonic principle), every "power" (human or angelic authority of lesser rank). Thus, Paul refers to three layers of government: (1) visible worldly governments of nations, provinces, and cities run by human principals and authorities; (2) invisible demonic governments influencing nations, provinces, and cities and run by demons of varying rank under the authority of the "prince of this world" (John 12:31); and (3) invisible angelic governments over every nation, province, city, and church, sovereignly *overruling* all human and demonic authorities, turning them to do God's will as He pleases or as He responds to believers' prayers (Ezra 6:22; Prov. 21:1; Dan.

explains why Jesus reminded earthly rulers (John 19:10–11) and His disciples (Matt. 26:53) that He and His Father, not political or religious authorities, were still sovereign, even during His humble, self-emptying, first advent (Phil. 2:5–8). It's also why He easily commanded demons and they always obeyed (because "they knew him," Mark 1:34), though occasionally with verbal protests upon seeing Him or complying with His demands (Matt. 8:16; Mark 9:20; Luke 4:35–36).

Paul went further, declaring everything was created not only by but also "for" Christ (1:16), or for His pleasure, service, and honor. This is why in Revelation the Father and Son are worshiped together in heaven by all created things, including saints, angels, and even (in that day) animals, birds, marine life, plants, perhaps even microbes (see worship of the Father, Rev. 4:11; of the Son, Rev. 5:8–13; cf. Isa. 55:12)!

CHRIST THE COHERER. Paul said, "By him all things consist [lit., hold together[72]]" (1:17). Or, "He holds all creation together" (NLT), "all things continue because of him" (NCV), or "in and through him the universe is a harmonious whole" (WEY). Peter says Jesus does this by the power of His Word (2 Pet. 3:4–7; cf. Matt. 24:35). Here's our unshakable security: Jesus holds the universe together—astrologically, physically, spiritually, socially, nationally, ecclesiastically, domestically— by His supreme authority, pervasive Spirit, and sure Word. That's why the world wasn't destroyed by thermonuclear war in October 1962 during the Cuban Missile Crises, why the Cold War (1947–1991) never overheated, and why today,

---

10:10–14, 20–21).

72. Swanson, *Dictionary of Biblical Languages with Semantic Domains: Greek (New Testament)*, s.v. "*synistēmi.*"

whatever wars or rumors of wars swirl or devastation occurs from weapons of mass destruction, the world will continue, proceeding steadily toward the end God's Word prophesies. Even in the most chaotic time, the Tribulation, Christ will still be fully in control, personally releasing from heaven the seals that initiate the final acts of God's righteous judgment on Earth (Rev. 6:1, 3, 5, 7, 9; 8:1). For more, see my following entry, "The Coherer," Col. 1:17.

CHRIST THE PRIORITY. Paul said Christ is the "firstborn of all creation" (1:15) and is "before all things" (1:17), meaning "He existed before anything was created and is supreme over all creation" (1:15, NLT). Because Jesus (who was uncreated) existed before creation,[73] created all things, and holds all things together, He stands first in time, rank, and authority. Since by becoming incarnate He, as a man, entered into this realm of created things (Phil. 2:6–8), He's creation's first Priority, occupying its "foremost place" (WEY), "before" and above every created thing in the cosmos. Being older than everything, He has seniority and authority over everything, just as a "firstborn" son (1:15) holds first priority among his siblings in inheritance and family matters.

CHRIST THE HEAD. Besides these distinctions, Jesus is "head of the body, the church" (1:18; 2:19; Eph. 1:22; 4:15; 5:23).[74] He is the sole, sovereign ruler of the *ekklesia*

---

73. Thus, Paul also confirms Christ existed during the Old Testament period, intervening in His pre-incarnate manifestation, the "angel [special messenger, representative] of the Lord" (Gen. 16:7; 18:2, 16–17, 20–32, 33; 22:11–12, 15–18; Exod. 3:2; Josh. 5:13–15; 6:2–5; Judg. 6:12; 13:3–21; Num. 22:22–32; Ps. 34:7; 35:5–6; Zech. 3:1, 5–6; 12:8).

74. Comparing Colossians to Ephesians, Warren Wiersbe observes, "We can discover many parallels between these two letters. However, the emphasis in Ephesians is on the church, the body of Christ; but the

and its every member. By His Spirit He is creating, sustaining, guiding, defending, growing, testing, and will ultimately translate the body of believers, His eternal bride, to be wedded to Him in heaven. That "marriage of the Lamb" will officially launch their eternal union of love and labor (Rev. 19:7–9). For more, see my following entry, "Holding the Head," Col. 2:18–19.

CHRIST THE FIRSTBORN. Paul taught Christ was "the beginning, the first-born from the dead" (1:18; cf. Rev. 1:8). That is, He was the first man to rise and enter the new, eternal world of the redeemed (cf. John 14:2; Rev. 21–22), "leading the resurrection parade" (Col. 1:18, THE MESSAGE). So being the "beginning" of the resurrection, and having risen before any of the redeemed (1:18; Rom. 8:29; Heb. 12:23), Jesus is the "first" man in the new creation.

CHRIST THE FULLNESS. Paul added that, by the Father's pleasure, "all fullness" of the divine presence, powers, attributes, and blessings were in Christ (1:19). "For it was in him that the divine Fulness [sic] willed to settle without limit" (MOFFATT). For emphasis Paul repeated Christ possessed the "divine fullness," adding it was a "bodily" manifestation of the complete "Godhead" (2:9). This again directly refuted the gnostic heresy denying the materiality of Jesus' body (1 John 4:3)—and thus the efficacy of His redeeming sacrifice on the cross! For more, see my following entry, "The divine fullness of Christ," Col. 2:9.

---

emphasis in Colossians is on Christ, the Head of the body." Wiersbe, *The Bible Exposition Commentary*, Vol. 2, Col. 1:6b, note.

❧

These shimmering facets of the jewel of Christ's preeminence were just as valuable to the primitive (early) church.

One of the first great heresies faced by the church was Arianism, which claimed Jesus was a created being and thus not divine, not one substance with the Father, and not eternally preexistent.[75] Today various religions and teachers (Islam, New Age, Jehovah's Witnesses) superficially promote Jesus' moral teaching and good works yet deny His unmistakable divine claims. As stated, the secular academic world sees Jesus as an extraordinary figure in ancient history, yet merely human and thus fully explainable. The gnostics Paul rebutted in this epistle also wanted to reduce Jesus to a mere man. But Paul's lofty assertions won't allow this.

He proclaimed Jesus is the Image of God, the Creator of all, the Coherer of all, the first Priority, the Firstborn of the new creation, Head of the church, the Fullness of God, the Repository of all wisdom and knowledge (2:3), and Master[76]

---

75. Some Arians may have felt confirmed by a misinterpretation of Col. 1:15, which calls Jesus the "first-born" of all creation. The Greek (*prōtotokos*) here means "first–in line, birth [and thus time]; or [first in] rank and value." In this context, first in rank and value is appropriate. This associates Jesus with creation only because His *humanity and physical body* were created by the Father through the Spirit's power working in Mary's womb to facilitate the Incarnation (Luke 1:35). Thus, while Jesus' Spirit and soul remained part of and united with the Godhead and eternally preexistent, His body and human personhood (Jesus of Nazareth) alone were created in time. Since Christ still indwells that same body, now glorified, at the Father's right hand, He is correctly called the *prōtotokos*, or "first-born" Son of first rank and value of "all creation" (1:15). For the definition of "firstborn" above, see Kittel, Friedrich, and Bromiley, *Theological Dictionary of the New Testament*, s.v. "*prōtotokos*."

76. "Master" (Col. 4:1) is translated from the Greek *kyrios* meaning, "Lord,

and Judge of all (3:24–4:1), concluding He is the utterly, immutably, eternally "preeminent" One (1:18, ESV). He holds "first place in everything" (1:18, NAS), without rival or equal but with full "supremacy" (NIV) over "all things," including the universe and the spirit world, social order, church, and new creation. Thus, Jesus alone rightfully holds the titles King of kings and Lord of lords (1 Tim. 6:15; Rev. 17:14; 19:16). Christ's preeminence is the greatest truth in this context, epistle, and the whole Bible![77] But has this revelation affected your walk with Christ?

Will you diligently study the record of the Image's life to better know and worship the Father? Acknowledging Christ's creatorship, will you also remember He can create things now—resources, solutions, deliverances, healings, wisdom, and other answers to prayer—to help you navigate the deadly storms of life? Will you by prayer and faith trust the Coherer to hold your soul, family, church, and ministry together when adversaries and adversities try to tear them to pieces? Will you seek the Priority as your first priority every morning and in every decision (Matt. 6:33)? Will you let the Head control your thoughts, attitudes, emotions, works, and church? Will you through your morning watch and Bible

---

owner, ruler." Swanson, *Dictionary of Biblical Languages with Semantic Domains: Greek (New Testament),* s.v. *"kyrios."*

77. This is not to deny or diminish the supremacy of God the Father or the great theme of justification by faith (Hab. 2:4). While Jesus ever defers honor to His Father and justification by grace through faith remains the Bible's core salvific doctrine, Jesus is its indisputable central theme. The distinctive "testimony of Jesus," or message concerning Him, presented in each of the Bible's sixty-six books links them all as one message glorifying Him (John 16:14). Thus, John concluded, "The testimony of Jesus is the spirit of prophecy" (Rev. 19:10).

studies let the Fullness fill you full of His Word, Spirit, and peace (Exod. 24:12)?

If so, Christ will gain one more title: the Preeminent One in your life!

1:17 The Coherer. Like a cohesive substance, or binding agent, a coherer is one who holds things together. Paul revealed not random force but Redeemer force—the awesome, unlimited power of Christ!—is holding everything together:

> By him all things consist.
>
> —Colossians 1:17

Or, the Greek says, by Christ all things "hold together in their proper place or arrangement."[78] Or:

> All coheres in him.
>
> —Colossians 1:17, Moffatt

So Jesus is personally sustaining the order and arrangement of everything He created, visible and invisible (1:16). Since He's absolutely, irresistibly sovereign (Matt. 28:18), nothing can escape His benevolent, redemptive control (Rom. 8:28, nas). How does He hold things together?

By His Father's authority, Spirit's power, servants' prayers, and angels' intervention, always according to God's Word and in response to human need. Hebrews says He is "upholding all things by the word of his power" (Heb. 1:3). Or, "He holds everything together by his powerful word" (ncv). The

---

78. Swanson, *Dictionary of Biblical Languages with Semantic Domains: Greek (New Testament)*, s.v. "synistēmi."

Coherer's Word-based saving interventions result directly from His intercessors' persistent pleadings in the Spirit and faith (Mark 11:24; Luke 11:5–10; 18:1–8; Eph. 6:18).

History shows that as Christians prayed He often held things together when they were on the brink of falling to pieces.

The New Testament showcases this. When Jesus' disciples panicked while crossing stormy Galilee, He regrouped them by rebuking the winds and reminding them to keep believing in His presence, promise, and power regardless of contradictory evidence (Mark 4:35–41). When they were scattered, baffled, and afraid after His crucifixion, He regrouped them by a series of special appearances and reassurances (Luke 24:13–43; John 20:19–29; 21:1–14). When the early church was being divided by its former prejudices, He led the apostles to correct the injustices that had arisen (Acts 6:1–7); later He revealed through Peter and Paul His plan to unite all believers, Jews and Gentiles, together in one body (Acts 10:1–35; 11:17–18; Eph. 2:14–18).

Throughout human history He has used wise and benevolent leaders to hold nations and the world together through wars, depressions, disasters, and crises that otherwise may have destroyed the existing order. When the church has been on the brink of utter sinfulness, error, and spiritual death, He's raised bold reformers and revivers to restore its life and fruitfulness. He used key leaders—the founding fathers, Abraham Lincoln, Theodore Roosevelt, and Franklin D. Roosevelt—to reunite our nation when it was fractured, failing, and fearful. When great world wars erupted, He turned key battles at crucial moments to keep His prophetic plan—including Israel's key end-time national restoration in Palestine—on schedule.[79]

On a more personal level, He holds our lives, families, and churches together. When long or severe tests threaten to break our faith and union with Him, He sends timely sermons and teachings, illuminating books, inspired dreams, wise counselors, fresh refillings of His Spirit, and quickened Bible verses or passages to correct our thinking, restore our faith, and hold us close to Him. Then, after the Coherer comforts us, He sends us to help reunite our dysfunctional families and divided churches.

Today He's still holding everything together, controlling, limiting, turning, and guiding nations, leaders, and conflicts, all to in some way facilitate His grand end-time plan. Remember this wondrous Colossian-fact the next time a sudden crisis, loss, defeat, or disillusionment visits your life, city, church, or nation, making you feel things are coming unglued. And if to supremely test and establish your faith and loyalty Christ lets them come unglued (John 11:14; Job 1:13–19; Acts 27:14–20), He'll be there, more manifest than ever, holding *you* together in the midst of it (Ps. 46:1–3; Isa. 41:10–13). Why? So you can be a calming, unifying,

---

79. History buffs will remember some of these turning points in World War II: the Battle of Britain, the Battle of the Bulge, the Battle of Stalingrad, the Battle of Midway, and the second Battle of El Alamein, to name a few. Concerning the latter, British prime minister Winston Churchill said, "Now this is not the end; it is not even the beginning of the end. But it is, perhaps, the end of the beginning," and once the war ended added, "Before Alamein we never had a victory. After Alamein, we never had a defeat." Love that Churchill! See http://www.brainyquote.com/search_results. html?q=now+is+not+the+end (accessed April 21, 2016); also see http://www. brainyquote.com/quotes/quotes/w/winstonchu111299.html (accessed April 21, 2016).

sustaining force until the chaos passes. But the great key is trust.

So wholly rely on the Coherer. When everything is falling apart, don't try to hold it together by your strength, wisdom, methods, or influence. You are not the Coherer! Instead go to Him in whom "all things consist" (Col. 1:17) and humbly ask Him to hold together what's falling apart (or put it back together) for His name and mercy's sake and others' blessing. Then trust Him to do it. Meanwhile be sure you fully obey His instructions, corrections, and guidance. And in His time and way He will make what's broken whole again. Isn't this really the story of redemption?

When Adam sinned, his race and world began falling apart. From that moment God signaled His intention to send Christ (Gen. 3:21) and, by His blood, grace, power, Spirit, Word, and servant-minded people, put everything back together again "in their proper place or arrangement." An oversimplification? Perhaps. But correct? Absolutely! Knowing and relying on our Coherer makes life livable, loveable, and laudable. All praise to the Coherer!

1:20–22 The fullness of reconciliation. Paul declared Jesus has by His shed blood reconciled "all things" to God.

"All things" emphasizes the fullness of reconciliation, that it includes everything in heaven, Earth, and humanity (represented by the Colossians he addressed, "And you," 1:21). "All things...whether they be things in earth, or things in heaven" (1:20) also harks back to Paul's earlier description of Christ creating "all things" that exist, visible and invisible (1:16). So as Christ originally created "all things," now He's permanently reconciled the same—including the physical and spiritual worlds and everything and everyone in them—making it possible for anyone who repents of his (or her) sins and believes in Him to have "peace" with God restored (1:20; cf. Rom. 5:1; Acts 10:36). But heretics were trying to undermine the Colossians' faith by claiming Jesus didn't really possess a mortal body but only appeared to and therefore didn't pay the price of redemption, the shed blood of physical death!

To rebut this Paul emphasized the raw physicality, mortality, and materiality of Jesus' substitutionary sacrifice. Jesus reconciled us "in the body of his flesh" (1:22), or, "in his human body" (WEY), or, "his body of flesh" (ESV), or, "physical body" (NLT). Jesus "blood" paid our redemption (1:20); so Jesus freely bled real, hot, flowing, human blood, something no mere spirit could do. Jesus redeemed us "through death" (1:22); thus He experienced physical expiration, again, as no disembodied spirit could. Finally, Christ's physical body died on a very real, rough, wooden Roman "cross" (1:20), and that great expiration occurred in the full public view of many witnesses! So "in the body of his flesh" (1:20), "through the blood of his cross" (1:20), and "through death" (1:22) He redeemed us. Let the heretics be silent! But there's more.

Jesus not only "made peace" (1:20) between God and mankind but also between God and the elaborate habitat God lovingly created for man and placed him in: the cosmos and every living thing in it! That's an awesomely full reconciliation.

We may wonder why Adam's sin affected all creation. The reason is simple: God had given Adam "dominion" and authority over the whole creation (Gen. 1:26, 28–30; cf. Ps. 8:4–8). So when he rebelled and fell, not just every unborn human resident in his genes but also every created thing under his authority fell with him (Gen. 3:17). But with the incarnation of the second Adam, Jesus, and His victory over sin, self, and Satan on the cross, God's chief creation (redeemed humanity "in Christ") has now recovered its authority over the entire creation. This was foreshadowed in Christ's mastery of heaven, earth, demons, winds, and waters and will be openly manifested through the redeemed in God's kingdom (Heb. 2:6–11). What does this "Adam principle" mean to us?

Simply that when we sin, we jeopardize every person (spouse, children, subordinates) and thing (possessions, work, ministry) under our sphere of authority, possibly exposing them unnecessarily to the enemy's malicious work.[80] Conversely, as we abide in Christ and His Word, remain faithful in our calling, and intercede daily, everything in our personal "Eden" is kept safe by Christ's full redemption. Everything and everyone we have is covered under the saving blood and protecting angels of Christ (except, of course, during those special seasons when God lets Satan pass through our "hedge" of protection to afflict us to test and perfect our faith, loyalty, and endurance; Job 1:10–12). Here is real motivation to stay very close to our Redeemer and walk before Him in uprightness and spiritual maturity (cf. Gen. 17:1). Back to the fullness.

Paul's emphasis on the breadth of redemption reminds us that not just believers but "the creation itself" is also awaiting the glorious day of the Lord (Rom. 8:18–23, NIV). Like Christians, the whole creation is painfully enduring these last

---

80. Jacob's procrastination in responding to God's call to return (all the way) to Bethel (Gen. 31:11–13; 33:17; 33:18–19) led to the shocking, injurious, and shameful events of Genesis 34.

days before it is fully, manifestly redeemed. Romans 8:22 says creation is "groaning"[81] as in travail, yearning to be free from all the detrimental fallout from sin. So every part of God's original creation—the countless galaxies; our solar system; sky; earth; mountains; oceans; and all plant, animal, bird, and marine species—is experiencing labor pains as it, with us, awaits the great rebirth of God's kingdom in this Earth and, later, in the new heavens and Earth. This enflames my imagination.

Considering the spectacular aesthetic beauties of our present fallen Earth and heavens, I can only imagine how amazing the restored universe will be. Stunning! Pristinely glorious! The visual splendors, astounding vegetation, azure skies, sparkling waters, brilliant stars, and sweetly animated creatures Adam and Eve, rapt and satiated, beheld and enjoyed daily before their rebellion will all be ours...forever! Why? Our Redeemer's shed blood, expired body, and shameful cross paid for not a partial but a full redemption (cf. 2 Cor. 5:18–21).

Since He redeemed "all things," let's give Him our all—our fullest obedience, trust, praise, worship, service, and endurance in testing!

---

81. "Groaning" (Rom. 8:22) is taken from the Greek *systenazō*, meaning, "to groan together, to sigh together," as the Hebrews jointly experienced deeply painful and unrelieved grief of mind and body during their lengthy Egyptian bondage (Exod. 2:23–24). Similarly, all sectors of creation are moaning together over the degrading effects of sin, as in a great chorus of grief, until God's kingdom and its spiritually mature sons and daughters appear. For definition of "groaning" see J. P. Louw and E. A. Nida, *Greek–English Lexicon of the New Testament: Based on Semantic Domains*, electronic ed. of the 2nd edition, (New York: United Bible Societies, 1996), s.v. "*systenazō*."

1:21 Estranged by sin. Paul said before receiving Jesus the Colossians were "alienated" from God because their sinful "mind[s]" and "wicked works" were hostile to Him and His authority. "Alienate" is taken from the Greek *apallotrioō*, meaning "to estrange, exclude, [as a] foreigner."[82] Several versions state the Colossians were "estranged" (MLB, WEY, AMP), one says "strangers" (PHILLIPS), and others "separated" from God (Col. 1:21, NLT, NCV, GW). The principle here is, sin estranges us from God, creating an uneasy, tense distance or cold wall of separation between two parties previously close, familiar, and loving. Why?

God's love is holy compassion, not permissive pity. He freely forgives sin when we confess and turn from it, but because He is holy, He won't abide continuing sin or evil of any kind. The apostle John wrote, "God is light, and in him is no darkness at all" (1 John 1:5). If we "walk in the light, as he is in the light, we have fellowship" with Him and others who live in the light of His righteousness and Word (1 John 1:7; cf. Ps. 119:105). Whenever sin occurs, God begins withdrawing His fellowship; whenever it's confessed, He immediately restores fellowship (1 John 1:9).[83] Practicing sin, however, lets darkness remain, and this separates or estranges us from God. Not only this, it divides us spiritually from other Christians who are walking in the light.

---

82. Swanson, *Dictionary of Biblical Languages with Semantic Domains: Greek (New Testament)*, s.v. "*apallotrioō*."

83. Concerning 1 John 1:7, one commentator notes: "To walk in the light is to live in fellowship with the Father and the Son. Sin interrupts fellowship but cannot change relationship. Confession restores fellowship and immediate confession keeps the fellowship unbroken." See C. I. Scofield, *The New Scofield Study Bible* (New York: Oxford University Press, 1967), 1 John 1:7, note, 1342.

This explains the uncomfortable, distressing distancing that occurs between formerly close Christians when one remains faithful and the other begins practicing sin or altogether rejects Christ. Amos observed, "Can two walk together, except they be agreed?" (Amos 3:3).

So if after becoming Christians we choose to return to sin or evil in our motives, desires, or behavior and stubbornly resist conviction or correction, we repel the Lord, or worse, revolt Him (cf. Isa. 1:10–15; Rev. 3:15–16). James declares that seeking "friendship" with (acceptance or approval by, or conformity to) this sinful "world"—our satanically influenced, proud, amoral, self-serving, independent, God-denying-and-defying secular humanist culture—puts us "at enmity [hostility] with God" (James 4:4). John adds loving the temporal idols of this fallen world spoils our love for the Father, or alienates our affection for Him (1 John 2:15–17). To seek union with Christ's enemies makes us His enemies; to love things our Father hates makes us hateful to Him and eventually hate Him (Matt. 6:24; Rev. 3:16–17; Gal. 1:10; 2 Chron. 19:2). If this continues without repentance, it grows until we're totally estranged from God, like a spouse whose impenitent unfaithfulness destroys his marital love and, after years have passed, renders him a complete stranger to his former spouse.

Summing up, sin estranges us from Christ and those who walk closely with Him and increasingly excludes both from our lives. Does Christ seem strange and foreign to you today? If so, in some way, your sins are responsible. You have disobeyed God's Word, will, guidance, or correction; become offended at Him over hardships; held unforgiveness; succumbed to discouragement or unbelief; or simply neglected seeking Him and His Word as Scripture so often urges (Ps. 105:4; Isa. 55:6; Hosea 10:12; Matt. 6:33; 11:28–30; Heb. 11:6). Ultimately something is going to be estranged.

Let's honestly and fully evaluate our relationship to God and estrange our sins before they estrange us.

1:22–23 The presentation: the Redeemer's focus. Jesus died not only to reconcile us to God but also to ultimately "present" us to Himself in heaven, perfect in His sight and ready for eternal union with Him (1:22–23; cf. Eph. 5:25–27).

Paul described believers being presented in a gloriously purified condition, positionally and practically "holy and unblamable and unreprovable in his sight" (1:22). Our positional condition is our legal standing before God; our practical condition is our real present state or actual day-to-day progress in grace.

Positionally, we are already "holy…unblamable…unreprovable" in His sight because the Father has "imputed" the merits of Christ's righteousness to our legal account by grace through faith alone, or solely because we believe in Christ and His work of sacrificial death for us on the cross (Rom. 3:24–26; 4:20–24; James 2:23). When the Father sees or thinks of us in Christ, "in his sight" He sees us robed not in the spotty unworthiness of our remaining faults, frailties, and follies but in Christ's holy perfections, precisely as He saw Israel long ago.

In Balaam's day, Israel was under God's judgment, consigned to wander in the wilderness until forty years expired because of their stubborn sins of unbelief and idolatry. When Balak, King of Moab, tried to induce Balaam to curse the Israelites, though they were actually living in a substandard condition God declared them faultless in His sight. Why? Their ongoing blood sacrifices expressed faith in the saving blood of a coming Sacrifice (John 1:29, 36). Thus, God acknowledged their positional righteousness, choosing to focus on what He would ultimately make them rather than on what they were at the moment: "He hath not beheld iniquity in Jacob, neither hath he seen perverseness in Israel: the Lord his God is with him and the shout of a king is among them...Behold, the people shall rise up as a great lion" (Num. 23:21–24). This is the nature of judicial righteousness, which sees the elect through the eyes and work of grace.

One commentator notes:

> Christians are "without blemish"...in Christ [Col. 1:22, NIV], and also are free from accusation (*anenklētous*). This latter Greek word...connotes one who is unaccused, free from all charges. Satan is "the accuser of the brethren" (Rev. 12:10, KJV), but Christ is their "advocate" (1 John 2:1, KJV) or "defense" (1 John 2:1, NIV) before the Father. Therefore by the merits of Christ believers are free from every charge (cf. Rom. 8:33).[84]

This judicial righteousness aside, God also wants a practical manifestation of Christ's righteousness, or actual right living in our daily thoughts, speech, and activities. Not a profession only but also an expression of righteousness. To this end He is progressively sanctifying or purifying us in our daily trials, until we become "wholly" sanctified, or entirely set apart for God and His use as Jesus was, thoroughly changed

---

84. J. F. Walvoord, R. B. Zuck, and Dallas Theological Seminary, *The Bible Knowledge Commentary: An Exposition of the Scriptures* (Wheaton, IL: Victor Books, 1985), Col. 1:22, note, 674.

to consistently think and behave as He did (1 Thess. 5:23; see 5:12–24; cf. John 17:17). Thus, righteous living is godly living—the lifestyle of the godly One, Christ (2 Tim. 3:12). A few verses later Paul declared bringing Christians to this standard of entire sanctification, and thus fully preparing us for heavenly presentation to Christ, was his primary purpose in all his ministry labors (1:28–29). (See my following entry, "The presentation: the ministry's focus," Col. 1:28–29.)

Real, consistent, sanctified (godly) living in the believer's life is the reason God has given us positional righteousness. He intends positional righteousness to lead to practical righteousness, not polished hypocrisy hiding behind a paper shield of self-serving theology. Godly living is also the climax of the work of the Spirit and every minister in this church age (Eph. 4:11–13); they will stand down and rest when Christ's bride rises up and shines, ready to be presented to the Bridegroom in heaven after the Rapture (1 Thess. 2:19–20; Rev. 19:7–9). Think our presentation is unimportant?

Think again—and prepare to rearrange your priorities. There are at least *seven* references to this, the most dramatic and climactic event in every believer's life and the church's history. They are:

1. Watch ye, therefore, and pray always, that ye may be accounted worthy to escape all these things that shall come to pass, and to *stand before the Son of man* [presented to Him].
   —Luke 21:36

2. He who raised up the Lord Jesus shall raise up us also by Jesus, and shall *present us* with you.
   —2 Corinthians 4:14

3. I have espoused you to one husband that I may *present you* as a chaste virgin to Christ.

—2 CORINTHIANS 11:2

4. Christ also loved the church, and gave himself for it…that he might *present it to himself* a glorious church, not having spot, or wrinkle, or any such thing; but that it should be holy and without blemish.

—EPHESIANS 5:25–27

5. He [hath] reconciled [you] in the body of his flesh, through death, to *present you* holy and unblamable and unreprovable in his sight.

—COLOSSIANS 1:21–22

6. We preach, warning every man, and teaching every man in all wisdom, that we may *present every man* perfect in Christ Jesus.

—COLOSSIANS 1:28

7. Now unto him that is able to keep you from falling, and to *present you* faultless before the presence of his glory with exceeding joy.

—JUDE 24

Being sevenfold, this witness is perfect, or meant to completely or perfectly convince us of this topic's importance. Meditate upon these scriptures, memorize them, and make them your mission. John surely foresaw the presentation as being part of the glorious and joyous "marriage of the Lamb" (Rev. 19:7–9), since to this day it is customary for brides to be escorted and presented to their husbands in wedding ceremonies. Christ requested this grand presentation of His bride church in His high-priestly prayer (John 17:24) and, because it's so dear to Him, remains focused on it. But is our Redeemer's focus ours?

In antiquity, once a Jewish girl was engaged, her upcoming presentation to her husband became the most important thing in her life. Never far from her thoughts, she was thinking of it and preparing for it day and night. All born-again Christians are "espoused" to Christ (2 Cor. 11:2). Are we focused on our upcoming presentation—conscientiously trusting and obeying our Bridegroom's Word, following His guidance, quickly confessing our sins to Him, faithfully discharging His call, ever yearning and preparing to look on His face? Or have we forgotten we are headed for presentation and, like our Bridegroom, we should be joyfully focused on it? It's time we refocus on our Redeemer's focus.

1:23 Continue continuing. With unmistakable clarity Paul declared we will not partake in the presentation automatically, or simply because we've been born again. We'll be presented only "if we continue," grounded in (a) "the faith," and (b) "the hope of the gospel" (1:23) and "be not moved away" from them (1:23).

This faith is the essential gospel message, that salvation comes by grace alone through faith alone in Christ alone (John 3:16; 14:6; Eph. 2:8–9). Paul was reminding the Colossians not to waiver in their core beliefs, as the Galatian Christians had (Gal. 1:6–9; 3:1–11). They must continue relying only on Christ's redeeming work on the cross, His sacrificial death and blood, not on any of the grace-plus-works salvation plans offered then and now by false Christianity or other religions.

The "hope of the gospel" refers to our dual joyful anticipation of resurrection and Christ's appearing (1 Thess. 4:13–18; 1 Cor. 15:49–54; Titus 2:13; 1 John 3:2–3). Multifaceted, our "hope" also speaks of all the joys and blessings we anticipate in Christ: eternal life (Titus 1:2), glorified bodies (1 John 3:2–3) and a heavenly inheritance (Col. 1:5); a new earth, heavens, and Jerusalem (2 Pet. 3:13–14; Rev. 21:1–2); and the honor of beholding Christ's glory (John 17:24), increasing it (by Christ-honoring living), and sharing it (Col. 1:27; Rev. 2:26–28; 3:21).[85]

Paul's exhortation to "continue" is reminiscent of Jesus' call to "continue in my Word," or persevere in studying, obeying, and sharing biblical truth (John 8:31; cf. Ezra 7:10). Jesus promised this will lead to full liberty of life and soul (8:32, 36), whereas Paul here added it will give us full assurance of participation in the presentation.

To "continue" in God's Word (John 8:31), surely the equivalent of "continuing" in our gospel faith and hope without being "moved" (Col. 1:23), implies four things:

1. Don't stop short

2. Don't turn aside

3. Don't go back

4. Keep going forward

Some believers are initially excited about following the Lord but never become rooted in God's Word and ways

---

85. God delights to honor in His time, place, and way those who, rather than seek their honor, delight to honor Him at all times, in every place, and in every way (1 Sam. 2:30; John 12:26; Matt. 23:12; Esther 6:6–7, 9, 11).

(daily spiritual life disciplines). Consequently, when challenges or hardships come they stop short, no longer seeking Him (Luke 8:13). Others make a good start but then turn aside to worldly distractions, interests, lusts, or sins (8:14). Still others become offended with Christ at the severity, humiliation, or duration of their tests; His persistent chastening (Heb. 12:5–17); or His apparent indifference to their sufferings (Luke 18:1–8) and defect, abandoning their faith, church, and calling, and returning to openly sinful living, some even embracing atheism (2 Tim. 4:10; Heb. 6:4–8; 10:26–31; 2 Pet. 2:20–22). These three types are "moved away" from steadfast faith and hope—and assurance of participation in the presentation.

But Christ's faithful remnant, His "disciples indeed" (John 8:31), "continue" diligently, moving on by seeking, worshiping, trusting, and obeying Christ each new day, whether tried or triumphal in circumstances (Phil. 3:13–15). What rewards await "continuers"? Chiefly, an ever closer, richer, sweeter spiritual walk with Jesus (cf. Gen. 5:22, 24; Gal. 5:16; Phil. 3:10)! Also Jesus promised them full spiritual liberty (John 8:36), and Paul assured them of participation in the presentation. Are you, am I, assured? It's time for honest self-assessment.

Are you continuing in "the faith"? In "the hope of the gospel"? Or have you been "moved away" by stopping short, turning aside, or going back? Only steadily pursuing our faith and hope brings assurance. So there's only one wise option: continue continuing!

1:23 Enlarged by our large-scale gospel. To again counter the influence of the heretics, who claimed to offer soul-saving knowledge that only specially enlightened ones could discern, Paul reminded the Colossians of the largeness of the gospel. While gnosticism was only for a few, the gospel was for everyone: "This is the gospel...that has been proclaimed to every creature under heaven" (1:23, NIV). Christ's reconciliation of "all things" (1:20), Paul assured the Colossians, was spreading among all peoples "all over the world" (1:23, NLT).[86]

Has the gospel's largeness struck us? It isn't provincial legend, nationalistic mythology, ethnic folklore, or merely some humanly authored and flawed metanarrative. Rather, the message of our Redeemer's love is so real and powerful and large it saves all kinds of people in all lands, conditions, and periods.[87] No nationality, ethnicity, tribe, race, or socioeconomic group is excluded. Wide as it is, such a gospel has no room for petty prejudices: "Then Peter opened his mouth, and said, Of a truth I perceive that God is no respecter of persons: But in every nation he that feareth him, and worketh righteousness, is accepted with him" (Acts 10:34). Are we accepting whoever He accepts? Let's be enlarged by our large-scale gospel.

---

86. Christ repeatedly called us to preach His gospel everywhere to everyone and prophesied it would be preached to all nations "for a witness" before He returned (Matt. 24:14; 28:18–20; Mark 16:15–18; Acts 1:8; 2:5, 8–11; Rom. 1:8). This ensures universal evangelism but not universal conversion before the *Parousia*.

87. In his day Paul asserted the simple, Spirit-empowered gospel message is the "power of God" able to save whoever believes, Jew or Gentile (Rom. 1:16). Its power is undiminished in our secular, postmodern world. Are we sharing it with confidence whenever God opens "door[s] of utterance" (Col. 4:3)?

1:24 Christ's continuing sufferings—and Paul's amazing attitude. Here Paul presented the Colossians with six facts:

1. Some of Christ's sufferings "remain" (KJV; or are "lacking," ESV; or "continue," NLT) for Christians to bear in this age.

2. These "uncompleted pains" (PHILLIPS), or "the leftover parts of Christ's sufferings,"[88] are "for his body's sake," or to spiritually benefit the church.

3. Paul was helping complete ("fill[ing] up," KJV; or "participating in," NLT) these post-Ascension sufferings.

4. Paul was experiencing these sufferings "in my flesh," or in his bodily life (mortal state).

5. Christ, who lived in Paul's body and the body of the church, was also experiencing them: "All that Christ has to suffer in my person on behalf of the church" (MOFFATT); or, "There are things that Christ must still suffer through His body, the church" (NCV).

6. Paul "rejoice[d]" to participate in these sufferings for Christ and His church.

This is puzzling, since Jesus declared His sufferings "finished" on the cross (John 19:30). If Jesus' sufferings are "finished," why did Paul claim some remain? The short answer is

---

88. A literal translation. See Wiersbe, *The Bible Exposition Commentary*, Vol. 2, Col. 1:24, note.

Christ's former sufferings redeemed us; His remaining ones revive us.

Jesus' bodily sufferings from Gethsemane to Calvary purchased redemption. They alone are uniquely salvific, complete, and inimitable. His sufferings that "remain," which we share because we identify with Christ in a Christ-rejecting world (Phil. 1:29), neither forgive sins nor save souls, but God uses them to give us more of His Spirit, who, through the redemption, creates new life and releases fresh growth and blessings. Thus, they are necessary to facilitate the enlargement or blessing of His kingdom, the church.

To ENLARGE. The "rulers of the darkness of this world" (Eph. 6:12) tenaciously resist and attack the church every time her evangelists or witnesses invade their dark dominions with the light of Christ's (the Light's) Word (Ps. 119:105, 130). Every soul the Light wins and enters is to them a soul lost. So these agents of darkness attack light-bearers (Word-bearers) who, as they see it, are invading their kingdom. These vicious counterattacks were glaringly evident in Paul's ministry. Every time he evangelized a new city, region, or nation, he suffered for the Light (Acts 9:20–23, 27–29; 13:7–8; 14:7–19; 16:14–24; 18:11–12; 19:9–12, 23–34; 28:20).[89] Why? He was enlarging Christ's kingdom by establishing new churches.

To BLESS. These sufferings are also necessary to bless the church. Whomever God uses to reform, revive, teach, correct, encourage, or guide believers and churches will experience Christ's "afflictions"—grief, loss, misunderstanding,

---

89. As the biblical references noted demonstrate, frequently, but not always, Paul's resistance came from occult or idolatrous sources.

slander, rejection, attacks, injury, hatred, loneliness, and other thorns and crosses—for ministering blessings to "his body...the church" (1:24). In a fallen world, pain is always the price of new life (Gen. 3:16), including not only spiritual rebirths but also fresh spiritual blessings and transformative growth (Rom. 8:29; Gal. 4:19). Every time Christ has sent a reforming or reviving visitation (work, move) of the Spirit, someone somewhere has paid the suffering-price for that divine work. The Waldensians, Wycliffe, Huss, Luther, and their disciples suffered to usher in the Reformation. Zinzendorf, Wesley, and Edwards (and the Moravians, Methodists, and Congregationalists) suffered to bring in the First Great Awakening. Camp meeting leaders, Asbury, Finney, and others paid the price for the Second Great Awakening. Parham, Seymour, and others suffered rejection, misunderstanding, and mockery to birth the Pentecostal revival. Roberts, Kuhlman, and others were rejected and lampooned for being used to reintroduce Christ's compassionate miracles on a large scale.[90] And many others less known have felt the nails and the thorns that we might taste reviving spiritual water, bread, and honey from heaven.[91]

---

90. Admittedly Kathryn Kuhlman had her faults and eccentricities, as we all do, but the healing ministry of Christ by His Spirit through her ministry was stunning and well documented. Though challenged and dismissed by ardent cessationists, Kuhlman's ministry left a long line of dynamically changed lives for Christ in its wake. For more, see Craig S. Keener, *Miracles: The Credibility of the New Testament Accounts*, Vol. I (Grand Rapids, MI: Baker Academic, 2011), 459–468.

91. In the Old Testament period the true prophets suffered rejection, slander, mockery, and abuse to deliver their vital corrective and prophetic messages, which, when received, brought periods of new life, joy, blessing, and growth to Judah and the remnant in Israel (2 Chron. 15:1–19).

Luke plainly taught that the church is continuing Jesus' teaching and ministry (Acts 1:1–2). Paul added we're also sharing His sufferings (Phil. 1:29; Col. 1:24).[92] Though not redemptive, our "sufferings of Christ that continue" (1:24, NLT) are nevertheless necessary, facilitating God's periodic refreshment of His people, especially in periods of spiritual declension.

What kinds of sufferings are these? Three are apparent:

1. PHYSICAL SUFFERINGS: physical afflictions such as hardships, injuries, wounds, deprivation, exposure, torture, and martyrdom (Matt. 10:17, 21; Acts 27:18–20; 2 Cor. 4:10–12; 11:23–33; Phil. 2:27–30)

2. NON-PHYSICAL SUFFERINGS: mental and emotional stresses believers experience in their troubles and persecutions for Christ's sake (Matt. 10:18–19; 2 Cor. 1:8; 2:13; 7:5; Phil. 2:26)

3. SPIRITUAL BURDENS: weights, pains, or other sensations or discomforts felt in our bodies without physical cause resulting from the special operation (work) of the Spirit called "the word of knowledge" (1 Cor. 12:8). An expression of Christ's compassion, and a biblically authorized spiritual gift, these "words" are insights concerning people's needs conveyed

---

92. Jesus' historic sufferings fell into two categories, personal and redemptive. Long before undertaking His redemptive sufferings (passion), He carried personal crosses of misunderstanding, misjudgment, rejection, and other indignities from his brothers, hometown, synagogue, and the religious leaders of His nation (Mark 3:22; 6:1–6; Luke 4:28–29; John 7:1–5).

intuitively by the Holy Spirit rather than
by normal means of discovery (observation,
inquiry, communications, reason). They are
given only for ministry, never curiosity, to
prompt intercession, counsel, correction, deliverance, or healing for those who are afflicted
with sin, distress, or sickness. They may be
verbal (thoughts impressed on our minds by
the Spirit) or non-verbal (spiritual burdens
felt in our bodies) but always address pressing
needs (Luke 2:26–29; Acts 5:2–3; 14:9; 2 Cor.
4:10; Gal. 6:2; Phil. 2:26). Though mystical
to us, words of knowledge, when genuine, are
very practical, greatly helping Christians in
distress.[93]

---

93. By words of knowledge the Spirit enables gifted believers to "know"
physical, emotional, or other distresses troubling people so they may identify their specific problem for ministry. Thus, God the Holy Spirit confirms
Christ is ever present and intent on helping us through our adversities. This
increases our faith in Him, fuels our devotion, and fosters Christ-honoring
worship, testimony, and enhanced discipleship. Though Jesus generally set
aside His divine powers and prerogatives in the Incarnation, He manifested
not only miracles but also words of knowledge in His ministry to teach and
encourage us—informing a previously unknown Samaritan woman of her
love life (John 4:17–19), revealing to Nathanael private facts about his devotional life (John 1:48–50), and calling Zacchaeus by name though the two
had never met (Luke 19:5). Peter and Paul also manifested this gift when
Peter exposed Ananias' secret sin (Acts 5:2–3), and Paul discerned a cripple's
faith for healing in Lystra (Acts 14:9). (Conversely, Paul came to know of a
death plot against him by natural means of discovery—a message from his
nephew—not by a word of knowledge, Acts 23:16.) Some evangelicals argue
because Scripture is all-sufficient (2 Tim. 3:16–17) this and other spiritual
gifts aren't necessary. Yet by naming, illustrating, and never retracting them,
Scripture explicitly authorizes and implicitly recommends these extraordinary works of the Spirit when needed (1 Cor. 12:1–11). Some have denied we
need spiritual gifts, or worse, branded them occult. Did our infinitely wise

Paul's attitude concerning his share of these sufferings was amazing. Instead of rebelling, grumbling, or pitying himself, he rejoiced! "[I,] Who now rejoice in my sufferings for you" (1:24). Some Christians will do anything to avoid suffering for Christ's sake (2 Tim. 4:10). Others learn to accept and dutifully endure it. Few embrace it so fully they actually "rejoice" (though Jesus taught this, Luke 6:22–23; Acts 5:41). Paul was one of these select Christians who suffered gladly (as did Peter, 1 Pet. 4:13–14, 16). How did he do it?

He had the full power of the Spirit, to be sure (Acts 1:8), but that wasn't all. He also had full spiritual insight. He understood not just that sufferings would come but why. They come:

- Because our ministry is blessing others. Paul's special revelations blessed Christians everywhere—including us (1:25–26; 2 Cor. 12:7–10; 2 Pet. 3:15–16)!

- Because our prayers are effective. Paul's private intercessions and public prayers brought spiritual growth, healings, miracles, and

---

God biblically authorize gifts we don't need? Occult works are demonic imitations of the Spirit's true works of compassion. Not only were they not authorized or used by Christian ministers in Scripture, they are condemned in Old and New Testament alike and are shown to be practiced by people who are not devoted to Christ or God's Word (e. g., Simon Magus, Acts 8:9–11).

deliverances to many (Acts 19:11–12; 28:8–9; Phil. 1:8–11).

• Because we are focused on Christ's will for the church. Through His teaching Paul aimed to prepare many mature, spiritually minded disciples for presentation to Christ in heaven, "perfect in Christ Jesus" (1:28; cf. 1:22; Eph. 5:25–27).

• So God can give us more revelation, life, or power for His people. Realizing God always gives new life through death experiences (John 12:24), Paul knew every time he "died" to self by willingly suffering for Jesus, God raised him to a higher spiritual plane and released new "life" (life-giving messages, mercies, wisdom, counsel, prophecies, miracles) through him for His people (2 Cor. 4:8–12).

• So other believers won't have to suffer. Paul realized that when he suffered "for his body," fewer members would have to. Aware many ministers were unwilling to suffer for Christ (Phil. 2:20–21; Acts 20:29–30), Paul apparently determined to bear the sufferings of as many members of Christ's body as he could. Moffatt thinks he intimated a desire to bear them all, if possible: "I would make up the full sum of all that Christ has to suffer in my person on behalf of the church" (Col. 1:24, Moffatt).

- So Jesus can draw nearer. Jesus feels our sufferings as acutely as we do (Acts 9:4–5). As the body's Head, when any member suffers, by His Spirit Jesus is present suffering with us (Matt. 25:40, 45; Acts 9:1, 4; 1 Cor. 12:26–27; Rev. 2:13).[94] To confirm this, He sometimes manifests to comfort sufferers in their lowest moments (John 14:21, 23) and did so repeatedly for Paul (Acts 23:11; 27:23–24). Thus, Paul realized he never suffered alone! Jesus, for whose kingdom, honor, and people he suffered, was suffering alongside him...in his very body (Gal. 2:20; Isa. 41:10; 43:2; Heb. 13:5). And every time he suffered Jesus drew nearer (Dan. 3:25)!

- To expedite Christ's coming kingdom. All Christian sufferings are helping prepare the way for Christ's kingdom: "We must go through many hardships to enter the kingdom of God" (Acts 14:22, niv). Every suffering we bear, then, brings us that much closer to

---

94. God designed our bodies so that every pain detected by nerve receptors in the peripheral nervous system is immediately transferred via our nerves to the brain (head) which instantaneously detects the cause of the affliction and orders the body's response. So Christ our Head feels every painful impulse we experience in His body and orders our response by His Spirit bringing to mind appropriate portions of Scripture. The Head's scriptural response-impulse comes more quickly and clearly if we abide close to Christ, obedient, and full of His living, breathing Word (John 14:26; Acts 11:16).

Messiah's glorious thousand-year kingdom on Earth! One commentator notes the Jewishness of this view:

> The expression *Christ's afflictions* [Col. 1:24] is to be understood against an OT and Jewish background with its notion of the afflictions of the end time. These were called the "birth-pangs of the Messiah," those pains and woes which would occur before the arrival of God's anointed ruler, the Messiah. In the NT they occur between the first and second comings of Jesus. The exalted Christ is in heaven and before his return he suffers in his members...
>
> These *afflictions* have been limited by God; the quota will be complete when the end comes. All Christians take part in these sufferings; it is through them that we enter the kingdom of God (Acts 14:22; 1 Thess. 3:3, 7). Suffering with Christ is essential if we are to be glorified with him (Rom. 8:17). Through the sufferings he endures in his own flesh, Paul contributes to the sum total, to *what is still lacking*...[95]

Realizing these truths, Paul determined to pay whatever cost was necessary to bless God's people—and "most gladly" (2 Cor. 12:9–10)!

---

95. D. A. Carson, R. T. France, J. A. Motyer, and G. J. Wenham, editors, *New Bible Commentary: 21st Century Edition*, 4th ed. (Leicester, England; Downers Grove, IL: InterVarsity Press, 1994), Col. 1:24, note, 1267.

This "understanding" kept Paul unoffended, strong, and fruitful even in his worst troubles (Prov. 2:5). So complete was his acquiescence that he seemed oblivious to afflictions, desiring only to bless and mature more Christians (Col. 1:28–29). One commentator notes:

> Paul devoted his life to the care of the church. Paul did not ask, as do some believers. "What will *I* get out of it?" Instead he asked, "How much will God let me put into it?" The fact that Paul was a prisoner did not stop him from ministering to the church.[96]

Moreover, Paul prayed that God would work in the Colossians until they too rejoiced in their sufferings "for his body's sake" (1:24; cf. 1:11). Is his prayer being answered in you?

Are you facing the facts Paul presented: Christ's sufferings remain, they are for His body, you should bear them, Christ shares them with you, and He wants you to rejoice in them. What's your attitude toward Christ's present sufferings in your life? Are you rebelling? Murmuring? Weakened and soured by self-pity? Abandoning your duty or ministry to avoid further trouble? Accepting but not yet celebrating your thorns and crosses? Today is the day to learn this lesson.

Fully embrace your share of Christ's afflictions—with Paul's amazing attitude.

1:25 Fully teaching God's Word. Paul declared his mission was primarily to "fulfill the word of God" (1:25), or fully present and teach—so believers could fully apply and

---

96. Wiersbe, *The Bible Exposition Commentary*, Vol. 2, Col.1:24, note.

live—all the truths in God's Word. This is the essence of his ministerial "stewardship" (1:25, NAS) or "divine commission" (PHILLIPS). Thus, he purposed not to deny, conceal, downplay, or limit any part of the biblical message but rather to fully open, expound, and apply all it offers us. This full exposition is Pauline teaching, and we need more of it.

Some deny various biblical truths, misinterpreting key verses or passages due to doctrinal biases. Others omit or limit teaching on subjects they simply don't like. Both do disservice to God and those to whom they minister. God doesn't want any part of His message muffled, since at some point in our walk in this hostile world we'll need every truth, story, biography, history, precept, principle, proverb, parable, and prophecy He's lovingly and wisely inscribed in Scripture. Therefore, we need ministers who'll tell us not part but "all the counsel of God" (Acts 20:27), omitting none of the "weightier matters" (Matt. 23:23) and veiling none of the passages that present disliked truths. Then the Word will dwell in us "richly, in all wisdom" (Col. 3:16).

Paul referred to five categories of replete Bible exposition:

1. REVELATION. Biblical revelation is eternal truth about God, man, the past, the present, and the future that God has disclosed by His Spirit to prophets and apostles, which we couldn't have discovered by human reason. Paul's primary revelation disclosed in this context is the "mystery" of Gentiles being saved on equal terms with Jews (1:25, 27).[97] Biblical revelations are

---

97. "Mystery" is translated from the Greek *mystērion*. Anciently it referred to "hidden things" or "religious secrets," such as the secret rites and rituals

God's inspired disclosures of His purposes
and plans, the times, and what we need to do
to fulfill His purposes in our time (1 Chron.
12:32; 2 Cor. 12:1, 7; Acts 10:9–20, 28, 34–35;
Gen. 41:25–36).

2. WARNING. Paul reported he was diligently
"warning every man" (1:28). With fatherly and
shepherdly love he alerted others of dangers:
God's wrath, judgment, sin's deception, heresy,
loss of rewards, and so forth (cf. Luke 3:7–8;
Acts 20:28–31; 24:24–25; 1 Cor. 6:9–10; Eph.
5:3–7; 1 Tim. 4:13; 2 Tim. 4:2; Heb. 3:13; 1
John 4:1). While selfish callousness remains
silent, love warns.

3. WISDOM. Paul said he preached and taught
"wisdom" (1:28), or biblical good judgment
springing from fear of God (Prov. 9:10). Most
specifically, wisdom is found in Proverbs, the
Bible's other wisdom books, and Jesus' wisdom
sayings (cf. Matt. 5:2–10). It's also "comprehensive insight into the ways and purposes of
God" (AMP), as Joseph and Daniel exemplify
so excellently (Gen. 41:39; Dan. 1:20; 2:19–23;
5:11–12, 14).

4. PROPHECY. A prophet, Paul spoke under direct
inspiration to tell forth God's will or foretell

---

practiced by members of mystery cults (Mithras, Isis), which they swore not
to divulge to the public. In the New Testament *mystērion* speaks of a part of
the divine plan previously undisclosed by God but now revealed in its time
to the redeemed.

future events to comfort, strengthen, and prepare God's people (1 Thess. 4:13–18; 2 Thess.
1:7–10). Here he foretold the heavenly presentation of the church to Christ (1:21–23, 28) and
our hope of living forever in "glory" (1:27)—
sharing the glorious presence, radiant beauty,
regal authority, and fabulous abode of God (cf.
Rev. 4–5, 21–22). Scripture is filled with hope-
inspiring disclosures of "things to come" (John
16:13), especially God's, the church's, and
Israel's ultimate triumph over the evil one. And
ours!

5. TEACHING. Paul occupied much of his time
"teaching" (1:28), or presenting with organization and the Spirit's anointing the entire
range of biblical subjects: the nature and ways
of God; Christ's life, works, and messages; the
history of Israel, the world, the church, and
biblical biographies; life lessons, parables, and
precepts; God's commands and exhortations to
righteous living; His instructions for salvation,
sanctification, worship, and so forth. Noting
Paul connected "warning…and teaching"
(1:28), Henry adds, "When we warn people
of what they do amiss, we must teach them
to do better: warning and teaching must go
together."[98]

---

98. Henry, *Commentary in One Volume*, 1871. For an example, see 2 Timothy 3:16–17; 4:2.

Some deny, omit, limit, or minimize their presentation of one or more of these biblical categories.

For instance, passages that discuss suffering, judgment, hell, the Rapture, the baptism or gifts of the Spirit, miracles, pride, self-examination, confession of sins, prejudice, holiness, homosexuality, the conception of life, the Book of Revelation, loss of salvation, loss of rewards, forgiveness, faith,[99] divorce and remarriage, women's roles at home or church, to name some. Our individual preferences, denominational guidelines, personal experiences, congregational preferences, or current cultural or national trends may incline us toward or away from certain Bible books, passages, or verses. Are we prepared to get comfortable with these uncomfortable passages? To preach the Word the Spirit wants fully presented even when it's unpopular or "out of season" (2 Tim. 4:1–2). Two questions seem appropriate.

First, am I willing to fully teach and obey all these potentially uncomfortable subjects? Do I have courage to do so? Second, are my congregants or students willing to hear and practice them? Do they have a hearing or an "itching" ear (Rev. 3:22; Isa. 50:4–5; 2 Tim. 4:3)?[100] Our answers will tell

---

99. The recent Word of Faith movement among Charismatics misused biblical promises and principles of faith for shallow worldly ends, chiefly personal gain. Many evangelicals have overreacted to this by neglecting, or even omitting, teaching and preaching on the biblically central and vital subject of faith. (I remember one radio host losing all interest in interviewing me when I dared to quote Mark 11:24, a text often identified with the Word of Faith movement's excesses, concerning a need under discussion. But isn't this text God's Word too? Didn't Jesus speak it?) This is tragically wrong and self-opposing. To live well by faith, we need teaching on the promises of God rightly applied to not only God's kingdom interests but also personal needs and problems—and a lot of it!

100. A hearing ear is willing to hear whatever truth God wants spoken and

whether as God's pastors and people we are fulfilling or limiting His Word.

If ministers don't study, teach, and live God's truth as fully as possible, we're failing our stewardship "to present the Word of God in its fullness" (1:25, NIV), we're not "proclaiming his entire message to you" (NLT).[101] Those we minister to won't be ready for everything they meet since God inspired not just part but "all scripture" for the purpose of making us "thoroughly furnished unto all good works" (2 Tim. 3:16–17). Thus, our deficient presentation of God's Word will produce deficient Christians—and leave us blameworthy at the judgment (Acts 20:26–27), facing Christ's rebukes and many questions from our partially taught constituents: "Pastor, why didn't you teach us about this, that, or the other subject? Your unfulfilled teaching left us unfulfilled—spiritually underdeveloped and unprepared for our trials." One caveat.

This increasingly secular, arrogantly heady, Bible-rejecting postmodern world dismisses out of hand anyone who believes, much less teaches, the Bible as God's very infallible Word. Pastor, teacher, counselor, don't let them intimidate you. While they preach high-sounding, popular but unproven secular philosophies, continue heeding Paul's simple, sound advice to Timothy: "Preach the word!" (2 Tim. 4:1–2). Theology is still the highest science and vocation. Charles E. Fuller wisely said:

---

prepared to do His will, whatever that may be. An itching-ear Christian desires ("itches") only to hear biblical truths that suit its own interests. The first attitude is truth-seeking, the second self-seeking; the first brings spiritual growth, the second stagnation.

101. Ezra didn't make this mistake but earnestly undertook to study, practice, and teach all God's Law (Ezra 7:10).

> To know the Word of God, to live the Word of God,
> to preach the Word of God, to teach the Word, is the
> sum of all wisdom, the heart of all Christian service.[102]

Summing up, as with Paul, our stewardship is to fully present and practice God's Word. So be Pauline: Commit to teach and receive all God's Word.[103] There's no higher calling, service, or need. Nor any more timely. Soon the incarnate Word will personally appear to receive a people in whom all His Word is "made flesh," living and growing daily.

1:26–27 The mystery: Jesus living and ministering in us...gloriously! In the Old Testament era the Jews realized they would be used to save Gentiles (Gen. 12:3) but never dreamed Gentiles would be accepted by God on the same terms and with equal standing. Nor did they imagine God would permit His glory to dwell among Gentiles as it had in Israel. But now, through Paul, the "mystery" (God's "secret plan" [PHILLIPS] or "sacred secret"[104]) was known: God was saving Gentiles on equal terms with Jews, not by circumcision and law-keeping but by grace alone through faith alone in Christ alone (Eph. 3:2–11; 2:8–9). Thus, the previous spiritual partition between these people groups was gone (Eph.

---

102. See George Marsden, "The Born-Again Mind," *Christian History Magazine*, Issue 91: A New Evangelical Awakening, (Worchester, PA: Christian History Institute, 2006), 27.

103. For more on presenting all God's Word, see Deut. 32:46; Josh. 8:34–35; 2 Kings 23:2; Jer. 26:2; Ezek. 3:10–11; Luke 24:25–27; John 15:15; Acts 5:20; 10:33; 20:20; Col. 3:16; 1 Tim. 4:13–16.

104. Wiersbe, *The Bible Exposition Commentary*, Vol. 2, Col. 1:25–27, note.

2:14),[105] they were now "one new man" (2:15), in "one body" (2:16), "fellow heirs" (3:6), with "no difference" (Rom. 10:12–13; Gal. 3:26–28). Furthermore, believing Gentiles would experience God's glory along with believing Jews! And that wasn't all.

God would live and work not just with but *inside* and *through* them: "And this is the secret: Christ lives in you" (1:27, NLT). Jesus' plan, therefore, is to live in us all and minister through us all, Jews and Gentiles. That's the core mystery Paul presented in Colossians. How wonderful! For Jesus to forgive and justify us by grace is one piece of wonderful news, but this—that He who created everything, is preeminent over everything, and in whom is the very fullness of God should live in us daily (1:15–19)!—is awesome beyond the power of words to express! That's the mystery...in theory.

In practice, whether Jesus' life and ministry are indeed manifested in us and our "Colossian" (primarily Gentile) churches is another matter. For that, we must abide in Christ, closely and constantly, like branches remain one with their vine (John 15:1–8), continue studying and obeying Christ's Word (John 8:31–32), and ever seek more of His Spirit (Eph. 5:18–21). These issues determine not theoretically but

---

105. The spiritual division between Jews and Gentiles was vividly represented in the courts of Herod's temple. A small wall (four and one-half feet high) stood between the Gentile and Jewish courts with signs posted in Greek and Latin warning that Gentiles who proceeded beyond this wall (balustrade; or in Hebrew, *soreg*) would be subject to, and held responsible for, execution. In Ephesians 2:14 Paul said the spiritual division symbolized by this wall no longer existed in God's sight. To not offend unenlightened Jews, however, Paul continued to respect the balustrade regulation, though he was brutally attacked, arrested, and held in custody for over four years for allegedly bringing a Gentile into the Jewish courts (Acts 21:28–29).

practically how much or little of "Christ in you" manifests. This is true individually and corporately.

The Amplified reads, "Christ within and among you" (1:27, AMP). This is an excellent rendering, since "you" (KJV) is singular and plural: "Christ lives in 'you' the Colossian Christian and 'you' the Colossian church" (author's paraphrase). Christ is in all born-again believers and our assemblies too, working in us personally and among us communally[106] in "the hope of glory"—in anticipation of transforming us to witness, reflect, and thus increase His "glory," or majestic divine honor, beauty, and authority (Rev. 5:8–12).

The early church let Jesus live in them and minister through them, and this led to periodic manifestations of His glory among them—wondrous conversions, healings, deliverances, and other enviable instances of divine guidance and intervention (Acts 8:26–40; 12:20–23). This wasn't accidental. Jesus specifically bequeathed His "glory" to His people (John 17:22). We have every right, then, to pray for His glory to dwell in and among us—and hope to be changed by it into His glorious image. It has happened before.

Moses was a man transformed by God's glory. For forty days on Mount Sinai he entered the glory (manifest presence),

---

106. As Jesus taught, the present aspect of God's kingdom, His spiritual and hidden kingdom, "his body...the church" (Col. 1:24), exists in and among all who believe on and obey the King (Luke 17:20–21, ISV, NCV; John 18:36). When He returns to Earth, this will radically change. His kingdom will then be a visible, political, worldwide kingdom, initially a thousand-year kingdom on this Earth and subsequently the same on the new Earth...forever (Dan. 2:35, 44; 7:26–27). But now, our "glory," or cause of delight, is that we may have "Christ's presence among you" (Col. 1:27, MOFFATT). Christ wants us to believe in His nearness by faith (Heb. 13:5) and also sense it (John 14:21–23). Is His presence discernible in your private and congregational life and worship?

soaked in the glory, and was infused and altered by the glory until he radiated the glory (Exod. 34:29–35). Thus, he was changed "from glory to glory" by the power of the Spirit (2 Cor. 3:18). Peter and John lived in the glory—Christ's presence—before and after Pentecost until His boldness shined through them (Acts 4:13). Stephen also lived in that glorious divine communion until Christ's forgiveness radiated through him (Acts 7:60). When angels, who stood perpetually in God's heavenly presence, announced Jesus' birth, they reflected the glory of God on their persons: "The radiance of the Lord's glory surrounded them" (Luke 2:9, NLT); or, "The glory of the Lord filled the area with light" (GW). This suggests the glory-light of heaven, radiating from God's very heavenly essence (Rev. 21:23–24; 22:5) or His manifested presence on Earth (as we commune deeply with Him) permeates its inhabitants and radiates from them. The physical glory (light) seen upon Moses and the angels was but a manifestation of the inner spiritual glory of God's truth, grace, righteousness, and power and the glorious works of compassion flowing from Him (Mal. 4:2; Matt. 4:16, 23–25).

"The hope of glory," therefore, suggests we too are predestined for this wondrous glory-transformation—to enter, be filled with, changed by, and radiate the indescribably awesome glory-light of Jesus (Acts 4:13; 1 Cor. 15:49–53). Time to check our light meters.

Are we shining or whining? Walking in light or darkness? Reflecting Jesus' glory in our attitudes, conversations, activities, labors, and reactions to life's myriad of adversities or blocking it by disbelief or disobedience? The lost souls of this sin-darkened world, whether they ignore or despise us, need desperately to see the light of Jesus in us. If they see it, many will come to Him (John 12:32). May we immerse ourselves in the "glory"—the Word, presence, worship, and closeness of Jesus—until our hope of glory reproduces the glory of our hope in us and through us.

1:26 The revelation goes on…according to His Word. Paul described the "mystery" as having been "hidden from [past] ages and from generations," then added, "but now [it] is made manifest to his saints" (1:26). This shows the unfolding of God's self-revelation and His eternal truth and plan is a progressive work (Eph. 3:4–5). Each age or dispensation has received more light than its predecessor until the full Light, Christ, appeared before us all, in whom is "hidden all the treasures of wisdom and knowledge" (Col. 2:3). And the revelation didn't end with His appearance.

Through Christ, the church's Head, and through the Holy Spirit He gave her, the New Testament scrolls were given. This revelation, given by Christ through chosen inspired writers, includes not only the "mystery" of the Gentile-Jewish church, which Paul presents in Colossians and Ephesians (1:26–29; Eph. 1:9–10; 3:2–9; 6:19), but also other biblical prophecies, such as the end-time apostasy (2 Tim. 3:1–4:4; 2 Thess. 2:1–3), the Rapture of the church (John 14:1–3; 1 Cor. 15:49–53; 1 Thess. 4:13–18), a plethora of key doctrines (e.g., justification by faith, Rom. 5:1; Israel's present condition and future conversion, Rom. 9–11; Christ's judgment seat, Rom. 14:10–12), and the summation of all prophecy and eschatology[107] in the Book of Revelation. Does Revelation terminate biblical revelation?

---

107. Eschatology (lit., "last things-study") is simply the study of history's final events—the end times, judgment, and the hereafter. In this chronically

Absolutely! The Book of Revelation, and biblical canon it closes, will never be enlarged, that we know (Rev. 22:18–19). But spontaneous prophetic revelation is not precluded by the New Testament. To the contrary, it validates the ecclesiastical gift of prophecy and office of prophet for this age (1 Cor. 12:10, 28–29; Eph. 4:11), nowhere removes them, and gives repeated examples of their sound and beneficial ministry in the early church (Acts 11:27–30; 13:1–2; 16:6–7; 27:10, 21–26, 34). Why? God has appointed prophetic ministry as a kind of supplement to biblical revelation, which, while wonderfully adequate, is not exhaustive in the information it proffers the redeemed (1 Cor. 13:9).

For instance, Scripture tells all of us generally how to behave wisely yet tells none of us specifically which decisions we should make at crucial junctures in our personal lives, ministries, or work (for example, marriage, career choices, purchases, job decisions, education). So while the Bible offers a broad divine message for all Christians, prophecy offers a more intimate divine message applicable only to the one receiving it (cf. Acts 21:10–11). Usually, but not always, these personal, spontaneous prophecies are given by the Spirit to help us through very difficult experiences or seasons by giving us words of individual correction, guidance, or encouragement not disclosed in scriptural texts yet so perfectly addressed to our exact circumstances, feelings, and problems that we're sure they've come from the Lord (1 Cor. 14:3, 24–25). Thus, while navigating the troubled waters

---

unsure world, it's indescribably comforting, inspiring, and motivating to understand the sure future God has revealed (Rev. 1:3). Are you building your life-house on the solid-as-a-rock prophecies of God's Word?

of life, prophecy helps us set our course, stay on course, avoid wrong courses, and reset our course when necessary.

Besides this personal aspect of prophecy, God also still forewarns His church, and even nations, of "things to come" (John 16:13). These inspired present-day predictions are always given on a need-to-know basis and never replace biblical prophecies. Instead they complement them, addressing key events, changes, blessings, or challenges that lay just ahead and aren't addressed by either Old or New Testament prophecies. Why are these "interim prophecies" given spontaneously? So, like the gifted "children of Issachar," who knew their times and what Israel ought to do (1 Chron. 12:32), Christians may have full insight into our times and what we should do to honor Christ, forward His plan, spread His gospel, pass our tests, minister effectively, and help us and others be ready for His appearing (cf. Acts 11:27–30). But vigilance is essential in connection with all spontaneous prophecy.

If genuine, prophetic revelation will always fully agree with and thus further confirm or clarify the body of biblical truth. It is intended only to accompany and compliment, never to equal or replace, Bible study and teaching. We live by every "word" of Scripture (Luke 4:4), not the latest spontaneous prophecy, however uplifting.[108] Scripture soberly

---

108. Some churches have lost this crucial balance. They unduly emphasize spontaneous prophecy and neglect vital biblical exposition. Spiritual health can't be sustained without regular, rich feedings in the green pastures of God's Word (1 Tim. 4:13, 16; 2 Tim. 3:14–17; 4:1–4). Conversely, by rejecting spontaneous prophecy outright leaders deny their people key spiritual aid Christ wants to give them in crucial hours of trial. And, ironically, while asserting Scripture's authority, such leaders reject its obvious validation of spontaneous prophecy (1 Cor. 12:10, 28–29; 1 Thess. 5:19–21)! Realizing the

warns there are many deceptive prophetic spirits abroad, and we must not to be gullible (1 John 4:1), urging us rather to carefully examine all alleged prophetic messages and trust only what we confirm to be of God (1 Cor. 14:29; 1 Thess. 5:19–21). If inspired, prophetic words will never contradict the written Word (2 Tim. 3:16–17). If they do, we are to immediately reject them and, if their messenger continues speaking invalid utterances, deny him (or her) further speaking opportunities, however spiritual they seem (Isa. 8:19–20; cf. Titus 3:10). That's a biblically balanced approach.

So while Scriptural revelation is irreversibly inscribed forever—what a rock to build on in these stormy times!—God's prophetic revelation goes on. But it must be carefully examined by biblically mature Christians and never allowed to rival biblical exposition. Then it will aid, not mislead; comfort, not confuse. Let's get biblically balanced!

1:27 The true riches—His Word! While referring to the glorious "riches" of God's "mystery," Paul described it as part of Scripture ("the word of God, even the mystery," 1:25–26). This link shows Paul considered not only the "mystery" but all God's Word to be spiritual riches, or true eternal wealth— the most valuable substance we may seek! No surprise here.

Scripture repeatedly states God's inspired Word (with its true truth claims correctly understood, humbly believed, and diligently obeyed) is more valuable than all the riches in this

---

gifts are complimentary, and manifest only as needed, we should neither try to initiate nor stifle prophetic messages. When truly gifted members receive them, their messages should be released with pastoral permission, in order, and with mature elders assessing their content (1 Cor. 14:26–33, esp. vv. 29–31).

world (Ps. 19:9–10; 119:72, 127, 162; Prov. 3:13–15; 8:1–11). Paul urged Timothy to "hold fast" to the scriptural teaching he had given him, describing it as a priceless truth-deposit (2 Tim. 1:13–14). Jesus also described the true, Bible-based knowledge of God and the faith springing from it as "true riches" (Luke 16:11) and urged the materialistically satiated Laodiceans to seek it instead of more worldly wealth (Rev. 3:18).[109] Are we listening? Learning? Changing?

Has it dawned on us that true riches are spiritual, not material? In the Word, not the world? Are we actively mining God's Word wealth—searching its precious golden truths and gems of wisdom daily—or disinterested, yet pursuing Mammon vigorously?

1:28–29 The presentation: the ministry's focus. Again Paul referred to the presentation of Christ's people to Him in heaven. (See my earlier entry, "The presentation: the Redeemer's focus," Col. 1:22–23.) As stated earlier, the condition of our being "perfect in Christ Jesus" before God (1:28) is both positional and practical, legal and actual. Clothed in Christ's righteousness, every born-again believer is already legally "perfect [complete, whole] in Christ Jesus" (1:28), having implanted within him (or her) by grace the divine nature of Christ with all its gracious and perfect virtues (2

---

109. From God's perspective, "true riches" are also souls—ultimately the elect who've been redeemed, sanctified, transformed into Christ's character image, and presented to Him in heaven (Col. 1:22, 28). These, and not gold, silver, or rubies, are Christ's valuables, His personal treasure, the fabulous inheritance-reward He looks forward to receiving and enjoying forever: "His holy people who are his rich and glorious inheritance" (Eph. 1:18, NLT). Are souls valuable to us?

Pet. 1:4). But God intends more, and Paul knows it. So he issued a ministry manifesto.

To all he declared his ceaseless, strenuous ministry labors were aimed at preparing the Colossians, and all others to whom he ministered, for the day they would be officially presented in heaven for marriage (eternal union) to Christ (1:29). Paul's passion was that long before that shining event, they would, while still in this world, become "perfect" in spiritual maturity, or consistently Christlike in all their ways: "We train everyone…in order to set everyone before God mature in Christ" (1:28, MOFFATT; cf. Gal. 4:19). This, he affirmed, was his goal as a minister of Christ:

> We warn everyone we meet, and we teach everyone we can, all that we know about him, so *that we may bring every man up to his full maturity in Christ*. This is what I am working and struggling at, with all the strength that God puts into me.
> —COLOSSIANS 1:28–29, PHILLIPS

In his previous reference Paul spoke of presenting the Colossians "holy and unblamable and unreprovable in his [Christ's] sight" (1:22–23), which is another way of describing them as "perfect in Christ Jesus," or spiritually mature (1:28). His repetition emphasizes his manifesto's importance. This also suggests that not only Paul but also all ministers should focus their ministerial efforts—studying, praying, preaching, teaching, writing, counseling—on this end: "that we may bring every man up to his full maturity in Christ." Or, in James' words, that those we minister to may become "men of mature character, men of integrity with no weak spots" (James 1:4, PHILLIPS).

Simultaneously, while writing the Ephesians,[110] Paul said this is the very purpose of the fivefold ministry. Christ "gave" us ministers for our "perfecting," or to faithfully teach and train us until we are "no more children" but like a "perfect [mature] man," comparable to the graciously wondrous "fullness of Christ" (Eph. 4:11–13). This spiritual maturity enables us to function in true unity and share and grow in the true faith and knowledge of God (Eph. 4:13). It also enables us to live and minister corporately (as a body of believers) like Jesus did corporeally (in His body of flesh). Like our spiritually mature Lord, our churches and ministries should become "a perfect man [body of believers], [growing even] unto the measure of the stature of the fullness of Christ" (Eph. 4:13). This is a very high goal, but Paul assured the Philippians he was "confident" God would assist and bless this vital work of maturity training: "Being confident of this very thing, that he who hath begun a good work in you will perform [complete, accomplish, perfect] it until the day of Jesus Christ" (Phil. 1:6). When the body of Christ lives and ministers in this world as maturely as Jesus did in Galilee, the fivefold ministry's work will be complete, this age will end, and the presentation will follow. Therefore Paul's personal ministry manifesto (Col. 1:28–29) and his revelation of the purpose of the ministry (Eph. 4:11–13) agree. Paul's manifesto *is* the core purpose of all ministry, and every minister should therefore adopt it.

Pastor, teacher, elder, counselor, mentor, is Paul's focus in ministry yours: to help present every Christian fully

---

110. Like Paul's epistles to the Colossians, Philippians, and to Philemon, Ephesians was written during the two-year period Paul was imprisoned in Rome (Acts 28:30–31).

mature—fully grown, completely developed, without persisting defects, "spiritually adult"[111]—in Christ? Ponder it until you're gripped, girded, and guided by this passion for the presentation: "that we may present every man spiritually mature in Christ Jesus" (1:28, WUEST); or, "to bring each one into God's presence as a mature person in Christ" (NCV).

1:28 Every individual counts. Three times in this verse Paul mentioned his ministry to "every man." Note my emphases:

> Whom we preach, warning *every* man, and teaching *every* man in all wisdom, that we may present *every* man perfect in Christ Jesus.
>
> —COLOSSIANS 1:28

This emphasis by repetition shows Paul believed every individual counts and therefore ministered to individuals as frequently and earnestly as to churches.[112] This valuing of individuals reflects God's viewpoint, and we need to be reminded of it often. Apparently, Paul remembered it daily as he valued, prayed for, and ministered to "every man." Why do we sometimes fail to realize the importance of one or two souls? Four reasons seem apparent.

First, pride. We may consider ourselves too gifted, knowledgeable, well-trained, or credentialed to help just a few and thus despise the "day of small things" (Zech. 4:10). Second, godly desire. In our divinely-inspired zeal to bear "much

---

111. I've borrowed this phrase from J. B. Phillips. See J. B. Phillips, *The New Testament in Modern English: Revised Edition*, Phil. 3:15, 415.

112. He was also hinting that Christianity's teachings, contrary to those of the heretics wooing the Colossians, were for "every" person (Col. 1:28), not just (supposedly) specially enlightened ones.

fruit" (John 15:4–5, 7–8) by ministering to as many as possible, we may overlook the few or the one we're presently ministering to on a regular basis. Third, prejudice. We may discount someone's potential value to God because we see them through our worldly prejudices: They're too poor or rich, uneducated or educated, of a particular race or nationality, religious or secular background, and so forth.[113] Fourth, ignorance of God's ways. We've never learned from Scripture that God often thinks and works quite differently from us (Isa. 55:8–9) and doesn't always choose, gift, or send those whom we think He should.

Edward Kimball, the man God used to convert Dwight Moody, said this of him:

> I can truly say, and in saying it I magnify the infinite grace of God as bestowed upon him, that I have seen few persons whose minds were spiritually darker than was his when he came into my Sunday School class; and I think that the committee of the Mount Vernon Church seldom met an applicant for membership more unlikely ever to become a Christian of clear and decided views of Gospel truth, still less to fill any extended sphere of public usefulness.[114]

Additionally, we tend to overvalue crowds, assuming ministry to crowds is always more important than ministry to small groups or individuals. Why? We forget that a great throng may during testing prove to be of little worth. Of

---

113. Such reasoning is faulty because it's not what we bring to God but what God puts into us through Christ that He trusts and uses in His service.

114. See http://gracequotes.org/author-quote/michael-simons/ (accessed June 17, 2016).

Gideon's 32,000-man army, 31,700 proved themselves useless as God's servants. Conversely, a little band, once proven
and purified through testing, may with God's help accomplish great things. Gideon's 300 warriors delivered Israel,
and Christ's handful of apostles turned the Roman world
upside down.

Consequently, the Bible repeatedly shows God sending
some of His best servants to attend to the spiritual needs of
mere individuals or small groups through whom He subsequently worked directly or indirectly to bear much fruit. That
is, He used some of these individuals significantly, while in
other cases He worked significantly through those they influenced. Thus, ultimately, God may bear much kingdom fruit
through us in one step or several gradual steps.

Here are some biblical examples of God working indirectly to produce much fruit:

- He sent Jesus to minister to one woman in
  Sychar; then, through her, He reached first
  "many," and then "many more" in her city
  (John 4:5–30, 39–43, esp. vv. 39, 41).

- He sent Philip to minister to one man in the
  desert; then, through him, He reached a new
  nation (Acts 8:26–39).

- He sent Ananias to minister to one new convert, Saul of Tarsus; then, through his subsequent ministry and writings, He reached the
  whole world (Acts 9:10–17).

- He sent Paul to meet and minister to one
  woman (Lydia) in Macedonia; then, through

her, an outstanding church was formed, a
Roman colony (Philippi) evangelized, and a
new continent (Europe) opened to the gospel
(Acts 16:9–15).

- He sent Paul to Malta to minister to one man,
  Publius' father; then, through him, He reached
  many others on the island with healing (and
  surely the gospel!) (Acts 28:7–10).

- He sent Joseph to counsel one man, the
  Pharaoh; then, through him, Joseph ministered to all Egypt, all nations, and his famished
  family, through whom the Savior later came
  (Gen. 41:14–41).

- He sent Boaz to meet one poor, starving, wid-
  owed immigrant gleaning in his field, Ruth;
  then, through their union, God gave Israel a
  King David—and the world King Jesus (Ruth
  2:1–5)!

More recently, He sent Kimball to evangelize and teach an
apparently very unpromising young Moody; then, through
him, He (and in a lesser sense, Kimball) touched the world.
And powerfully! Consider this string of divine appointments
that followed Moody's conversion:

If Sunday school teacher Edward Kimball had not
been faithful to share his faith with a Boston shoe
clerk, the world might not have heard about Dwight L.
Moody, Billy Sunday, or Billy Graham. But Kimball
was faithful, and in 1856 Dwight L. Moody came to
faith in Christ, and the world has never been the same.

God called Moody into evangelism, and in 1879 while he was preaching in England, an evangelistic fervor was awakened in the heart of Frederick B. Meyer, the pastor of a small church.

Years later while Meyer was preaching on an American college campus, a student named J. Wilbur Chapman professed faith in Christ. Chapman went on to hold evangelistic meetings across America. He later hired a new convert (and former major league baseball player), Billy Sunday, to work as an advance man in his ministry. In a few years Chapman went into the pastorate, and Sunday began to lead his own evangelistic crusades.

In 1924 Billy Sunday held a crusade in Charlotte, North Carolina. After the meetings about thirty men formed the Charlotte Men's Club, which met on a regular basis for prayer. Ten years later the club met for a day of prayer and fasting in a grove of trees at Frank Graham's dairy farm. The main focus of the day was to prepare for an upcoming crusade to be held in Charlotte. One of the men, Vernon Patterson, prayed that "out of Charlotte the Lord would raise up someone to preach the Gospel to the ends of the earth." Patterson had no idea that the answer to his prayer was a few hundred yards away, pitching hay into feeding troughs. During the crusade led by Mordecai Ham, Frank Graham's son Billy committed his life to Christ.

Because Edward Kimball was faithful, the world has been blessed by the ministries of Dwight L. Moody, J. Wilbur Chapman, Billy Sunday, Mordecai Ham, Billy Graham, and thousands of other men and women the world has never heard of, like Vernon Patterson.

Church history is in large part a record of the faithfulness of people like Edward Kimball and Vernon Patterson.[115]

Oswald Chambers agreed God often uses minuscule beginnings to produce maximum fruitfulness:

> Never look at yourself from the standpoint of—Who am I? In the history of God's work you will nearly always find that it has started from the obscure, the unknown, the ignored, but the steadfastly true to Jesus Christ.[116]

This principle is true not only in the church but also in the wider world.

In February 1875, God providentially sent Elizabeth Everest to be the nanny of a newly born English noble in whom both his parents later proved to have little interest. His name was Winston Leonard Spencer Churchill. While his parents neglected him, Miss Everest nurtured him, reading him the Bible, praying with him, listening to his frustrations and fears, comforting him in his failures, on one occasion liberating him from a sadistic schoolmaster, and modeling the life of faith for him daily. She faithfully continued this hidden ministry throughout young Winston's troubled childhood.[117]

---

115. J. P. Eckman, *Exploring Church History* (Wheaton, IL: Crossway, 2002), 92.

116. Oswald Chambers, *My Utmost for His Highest* (New York, NY: Dodd, Mead, & Company, 1935), 251.

117. On his part, Churchill later responded with filial loyalty, speaking highly of her, arranging her funeral, and keeping her picture by his bedside till his death. For more, see http://stephenmansfield.tv/the-hidden-calling-of-elizabeth-everest (accessed December 11, 2015).

Churchill, we know, became a world-changer, whose courageous and tenacious leadership helped hold England and the Western world intact during the terrifying Nazi onslaught!

What if Kimball or Everest had not valued individuals? What if they or God's other servants cited above felt their preaching, counsel, or time was too important to be wasted on the few, the ignorant, the ordinary, the poor, or the young? Thank God they believed every individual counts.

We must remember what they learned, that God determines who we will minister to. We must therefore determine to pour out everything He gives us to bless, help, lift, challenge, or inspire them—knowing we're not just touching them but everyone they will touch the rest of their lives. We should also remember God may, as with Kimball or Everest, let us help someone predestined for exceptional things find his way through the daunting maze of life. This is God-thinking, or spiritual-mindedness (Rom. 8:6), and marks those who have been taught of God and trained to think like Jesus: knowledgeably (knowing God's ways), humbly (without excessive self-importance), with patient desire for fruitfulness, and without prejudices. When Jesus brings people to them, these committed servants stop, listen, and love them with undivided attention—perhaps remembering how others did so for them.

They believe, therefore, these three principles:

1. Whatever God thinks is important is important, however unimportant it seems.

2. Whoever God sends us is important.[118]

---

118. Nehemiah's "great work" (Neh. 6:3) of rebuilding Jerusalem's walls was

3. God values individuals as much as crowds.

These beliefs nurture humility, as we realize we are not too valuable to minister to one or two gathered in Christ's name (since *He* is present and ministering, Matt. 18:20). They nurture teamwork or a body mentality. We just perform one work or step as God directs, confident others will take up where we've left off and together, not individually, we'll finish His work. They nurture brotherly love, as we begin seeing others as God's sees them—blood-bought, faith-gifted, and having the same spiritual potential we have (Rom. 12:3). They nurture healthy self-esteem, as we remember that whenever we minister to just a few or even one we're doing something very important—helping bless Jesus' beloved bride and kingdom...forever (John 21:15–17).[119] They enable us to respond with equal enthusiasm—doing "whatever ye do...heartily, as to the Lord" (Col. 3:23)—whether one or thousands call for our assistance or ministry. Finally, and chiefly, they make us like Jesus, who always ministered with the same spirit and zeal whether speaking to thousands by Galilee (Matt. chapters 5–7), small gatherings of His disciples (Mark 4:34b), two on the highway (Luke 24:13–32), or one by a well (John 4:6–26). In each case Jesus gave the same quality ministry to "every man." Can the same be said of us?

---

great because it helped facilitate Israel's restoration and prepare for Jesus' first advent. But it was also great because God, who is great, gave it to him. Similarly, any person God entrusts to us for ministry is a "great work," however insignificant they may seem, because the Great One sent them—and we'll account to Him for our care of them (Heb. 13:17).

119. This helps us retain a healthy sense of self-worth in Christ when we're ignored or mocked for having "few sheep" (1 Sam. 17:28).

Remembering every individual counts will transfigure every ministry opportunity, however small and unpromising, into, in Paul's words, "a great door, and effectual" (1 Cor. 16:9). We'll give our full, loving care to whoever is before us—and our ministry will never be the same. Now that you've pondered this principle, pray it!

Father, for Jesus' sake, and the church's, from this moment forward, please help me remember every individual counts. Thank You! Amen.

1:29 Striving with or against Christ? Paul consistently sought Christ's will and cooperated with it. And his cooperation was not casual but strenuous, "striving" to do Christ's will as athletes give maximum efforts to win races. He testified he was pouring himself out to help Christians become spiritually mature and prepared for the presentation (1:28): "to which end also I am constantly laboring to the point of exhaustion" (1:29, WUEST).

One commentator notes:

> To this end Paul expended all his God-given strength. Developing maturity in believers took great labor (*kopiō*), or wearisome toil (cf. 1 Cor. 15:10, 58); and even struggling (*agōnizomenos;* cf. Col. 2:1; 4:12), or agonizing like an athlete in an arena.[120]

Thus, once he discerned Christ's will Paul pursued it diligently, enduringly, exhaustingly. In this he reflected Christ's determination to "always" cooperate with His Father's

---

120. Walvoord and Zuck, *The Bible Knowledge Commentary: An Exposition of the Scriptures*, Vol. 2, Col. 1:28–29, note, 676.

will—to His last drop of sweat in Gethsemane and blood on Calvary (John 8:29; Luke 22:42)!

Selfishness and sin keep us from following Paul's and Christ's example. Some cooperate with God only when His will is easy, profitable, or comfortably aligned with their preferences. When it isn't, they work against, not with, Him; in contention, not concert. The Bible showcases non-cooperative servants of God. When God led Jonah to visit Nineveh, he fled from it. Jacob wrestled with God when he should have welcomed Him. Peter withdrew from Gentile Christians in Antioch when Christ wanted him to fellow-ship with them. Jehoshaphat partnered with Ahab when God wanted him to protest against him. King Saul tried to eliminate David when God wanted him to mentor him. Back to Paul.

When Paul cooperated, Christ empowered him, "working" in Paul "mightily,"[121] or "with all the superhuman energy which He so mightily enkindles and works within me" (1:29, AMP); or, "I work and struggle...depending on Christ's mighty power that works within me" (NLT). And as long and hard as Paul worked, "preach[ing]," "warning," and "teaching" believers to be spiritually mature (1:28), Christ worked equally long and hard, energizing him within (cf. 2 Cor. 12:9a; Phil. 4:13). Henry says when Paul "laid out himself to do much good...the power of God wrought in him the more effectually."[122] Thus, Christ gives supernatural strength to those who cooperate with Him and will-

---

121. This word is translated from the Greek *dynamis*, which is used repeatedly in the New Testament to describe, as stated earlier, divinely miraculous power, strength, or ability.

122. Henry, *Commentary in One Volume*, 1871.

ingly carry that work as far as they possibly can, despite weariness, discouraging results, and adverse circumstances (cf. Rev. 3:10).

Oswald Chambers said:

> God does not give us overcoming life; He gives us life as we overcome. The strain is the strength. If there is no strain, there is no strength. Are you asking God to give you life and liberty and joy? He cannot, unless you will accept the strain. Immediately you face the strain, you will get the strength...
>
> Spend yourself spiritually, and you get more strength... The saint is hilarious when he is crushed with difficulties because the thing is so ludicrously impossible to anyone but God.[123]

Because Paul made it a point to always "strive according to his working" (1:29), Christ made it a point to always strive alongside Paul in his service—making him famously fruitful.

Are you becoming famously fruitful or an infamous failure? Cooperating or contending with Christ's will for your life? Don't let selfishness or sin abort your life work...or weariness in well-doing (Gal. 6:9). Remember, as you contend with Christ's will, you forfeit His strength; as you cooperate, He strengthens you; as you agonize, He re-energizes you. So give yourself "wholly" (1 Tim. 4:15) to Christ's work—especially conducting or assisting ministry that helps Christians mature—and He'll give you all the strength you need to finish your course and win your race.

---

123. Chambers, *My Utmost for His Highest*, 215.

Chapter Two

GETTING DOWN
TO BUSINESS

*Since doctrinal correction was Paul's primary purpose in
writing this epistle, this second chapter finds him getting down
to the business at hand: attacking the Colossian heresies.*

*To refute the false truths troubling the Colossians, Paul
presented for their perusal more towering true truths
about Christ—the Repository of all wisdom, Fullness of
the Godhead, spiritual Circumciser, greatest Triumphator,
Substance of biblical shadows, and Head of the body
of the church to whom we should ardently hold.*

*So, with Paul, and with the Colossians,
let's get down to business.*

2:1–4:18 Spiritual maturity detailed. Given that spiritual maturity was Paul's overarching purpose in ministry (1:28), all his epistles, including this one, contributed to this ultimate goal. Whether by letters presenting doctrine (Romans), acknowledging gifts (Philippians), correcting conduct (1 Corinthians), defending his ministry (2 Corinthians), disclosing spiritual realities (Ephesians), presenting end-time truths (1, 2 Thessalonians), guiding ministers (1, 2 Timothy, Titus), urging reconciliation (Philemon), or refuting heresy (Galatians, Colossians), Paul always aimed to sanctify and mature believers. How did he do so in Colossians?

Paul's introductory prayer (1:9–14) obviously targets spiritual maturity. His description of Jesus' awesome creatorship and preeminence (1:15–19), revelation that Christ lives in us (1:27), and subtle prophecy that we'll be officially presented to Him one day (1:22–23, 28) inspire the caliber of faith, love, hope, and obedience that alone produces a spiritually mature heart and lifestyle. The remaining chapters (2–4) expound in greater detail spiritual maturity as Paul taught and lived it. Let's examine Paul's points of perfection.

Christians who are "perfect" (1:28, completely developed and consistently spiritually minded) are: knit together with other Christians in love (2:2); spiritually rich with full assurance springing from insight into God's Word, purposes, and character (2:2); confident all wisdom is hidden in Christ (not worldly philosophies or other religions) (2:3); not deceived by heretics' persuasive arguments (2:4); living and worshiping in divine order (God's priorities, values, ways) (2:5); steadfast in faith—"rooted and built up…and established" in God-confidence (2:5, 7); submissive to Christ's lordship, receiving and walking in His teachings (2:5–6); profusely thankful to

God and duly grateful to people (2:7); unspoiled by anti- or extra-biblical philosophies and traditions (2:8); confident God's very fullness is in Christ (He's no mere extraordinary man) (2:9); confident Jesus rules the entire spiritual realm (2:10, 15); circumcised from their "flesh's," or old nature's, control (2:11–13); free from Jewish (or other) legalism (14:16–17, 20–22); appreciative of but not worshiping angels (2:18); aware Christ alone (and no man) is Head of the church (2:19); self-disciplined but not ascetic (2:23); focused on and seeking heavenly, not worldly, goals (3:1–2); content to live humbly "hidden" in Christ (3:3); joyfully anticipating Jesus' appearing (3:4); mortifying their lusts and greed, knowing they anger God (3:5–6); sure God's wrath is as real and valid as His grace (3:6); consistently "put[ting] off" their old man's sinful attitudes and actions (3:8–9); consistently "put[ting] on" Christ by increasing their knowledge of and obedience to Him (3:10); abandoning all their prejudices, realizing "Christ is...in all" and "there is no respect of persons" (3:11, 25); humbly pursuing love and unity in light of their underserved election (3:12–14); letting God's peace judge their soul's condition (3:15); "rich" in (full of) God's Word (3:16); singing worshipfully "to the Lord" regularly (3:16); doing everything "heartily," as to Christ, "giving thanks" (3:17, 23); faithfully discharging their marital and family duties (3:18–21); obedient employees or fair employers (3:22; 4:1); expecting Jesus to reward or punish them fairly in life and eternity (3:24–25); persevering in prayer with vigilance and thanksgiving (4:2); praying for "doors of utterance" (divinely appointed speaking opportunities) for their ministers (and themselves) (4:3–4); interacting with unbelievers wisely (4:5); making the most of their time and opportunities (4:5); speaking always with grace (4:6);[1] practicing and encouraging comforting brotherly fellowship (4:7–9); taking fatherly oversight of younger believers (4:10); free from grudges against those who formerly failed them (4:10); complimentary of zealous intercessors and ministers (4:12–13); eager to share excellent teaching with others (4:16); exhorting others to fulfill their ministerial responsibilities (4:17); consistently praying for grace for others (4:18). Why did Paul enumerate these particulars?

He knew ideals aren't enough. We need a path of practical instructions that help us reach our ideals. Thus, he first informed us we are to be "present[ed]" one day "perfect [mature] in Christ Jesus" (1:28) and then described the specifics of the spiritually mature "walk" (2:6). But even this isn't enough unless we adopt his goal.

Is Paul's goal in ministry our goal in life? Are we willing to steadily seek, live, and share these ways of spiritual maturity so we may prepare ourselves and others for the presentation? Now that you've pondered the ideal, possess it. Practice spiritual maturity in detail.

2:1 Paul, an open book. Paul desired to disclose his true condition to the Colossians: "I would that ye knew what great conflict I have for you" (2:1); or, "I want you to know how much I have agonized for you" (2:1, NLT). Later he added, "Tychicus will tell you all the news about me" (4:7, NIV), or "give you a full report about how I am getting along" (NLT). This shows Paul wasn't a closed-off minister, cold, withdrawn, aloof. To the contrary, he was an open book, warm, personable, approachable, freely sharing his feelings

---

1. See Ps. 45:2; Luke 4:22; Acts 6:10; Eph. 4:15; 2 Tim. 2:24–26.

and experiences with fellow believers to help them conquer their own trying emotions and situations. This took exceptional faith and courage. Why?

Too often familiarity breeds contempt. Yet, knowing this innate human tendency to criticize and dismiss people around us (or more broadly to judge others first and then examine the facts, Matt. 7:1–5), Paul still opened up to his students. Surely he trusted God would preserve his favor with them and, if they misjudged him, would convict them. Thus, he concluded the benefits of candid testimonials outweighed their risks. Not only in Colossians but also throughout his letters Paul shared the full range of his feelings.

He told his readers when he was: blessed (Phil. 4:10, 14); troubled about their spiritual condition (1 Thess. 3:1–5); shocked with their inconsistent faith (Gal. 1:6); angry with heretics (Gal. 5:12); disappointed by abandonment (2 Tim. 1:15); thankful for loyal friends (2 Tim. 1:16–18); delighted with overcomers (2 Thess. 1:3–4); frustrated by persisting unspiritual attitudes (1 Cor. 3:1–4); outraged over lack of church discipline (1 Cor. 5:1–13); offended by irreverence at Communion (1 Cor. 11:17–22); inclined to exercise discipline if necessary (1 Cor. 4:21; 2 Cor. 13:2); regretful of having to discipline (2 Cor. 2:1–4); unsure of his future (Phil. 1:20–25; 2:23); desiring to go to his heavenly home (Phil. 1:23); brokenhearted by apostates (2 Tim. 4:10); hurt by believers' indifference yet glad to keep loving them (2 Cor. 12:15); pleased to honor fully committed ministers (Phil. 2:19–24; 2:25–30); grieved over selfish ministers (Phil. 2:21); grateful for friends' sacrificial loyalty (Rom. 16:3–4); weary from excessive labors or hardships (2 Cor. 11:27–30); wary of wolfish ministers intruding (Acts 20:28–30); elated at wonderful ministerial opportunities (1 Cor. 16:9); relieved he had discharged his sacred ministerial responsibilities (Acts 20:26–27); overwhelmed with sufferings (2 Cor. 1:8; 4:8–12); thankful for prayer support (2 Cor. 1:11; Phil. 1:19); expending agonizing effort (Col. 1:29–2:1); blessed to find zealous intercessors (Col. 4:12–13); urgently seeking relief from affliction (2 Cor. 12:8); humbled by a rejected petition yet revived by spiritual insight (2 Cor. 12:9–10); hopeful his students would forgive their offenders (2 Cor. 2:7–11; Philem. 12–21); hopeful contentious leaders would reconcile (Phil. 4:1–3); pleased with ministers who made the most of their second chances (2 Tim. 4:11); refocusing on finishing his calling (Phil. 3:12–14); vexed with his inconsistent obedience (Rom. 7:14–24); blessed by financial support (Phil. 4:10); and joyful over spiritual victories (1 Cor. 15:57). Thus, the man, with all his loves, hopes, and fears, was fully disclosed in his messages. What purposes did these self-disclosures serve?

Pondering Paul's many severe adversities for Christ's sake stirred his readers' mercy so they wouldn't so readily judge him over petty things. It also stirred their faith and courage; if Paul could overcome by grace, so could they![2] Conversely,

---

2. How many great characters in church or world history have been inspired to church-, nation-, or world-changing quests by hearing or reading one believer's extraordinary testimony? When the Spirit whispers, "If Christ helped him or her do this, He'll help you too," there's no limit to what we can accomplish in God's will. Thus, one overcomer reproduces another. George Mueller, seeing the example of A. H. Franke in Halle, Germany, builds by prayer and faith alone his own orphanage, schools, Bible publishing, and missionary support ministries in Bristol, England. William Carey, hearing of the Moravians' bold foreign missions, wonders why Baptists and others can't do the same and launches his own Indian mission—which inspires countless other Protestant missionaries. Got an inspiring testimony? Tell it, and watch what God does!

seeing his weaknesses humanized him and kept them from thinking too highly of him despite his amazing revelations, ministry gifts, and spiritual power (cf. 2 Cor. 12:6–7). But a warning is needed.

Discretion is always advised when considering negative self-disclosures. Confessing sins and failures can be taken too far. Before baring our souls, we should (1) be sure we're speaking to spiritually minded Christians and (2) prayerfully consider if doing so will edify and encourage them or leave them disillusioned and discouraged. Some things should remain between us and God.[3] The Holy Spirit will lead—showing us when to open or close the pages of our autobiography—if we'll wisely follow. What should we learn from this?

Pastor, teacher, elder, be candid, an open book before your congregation, unafraid to share your true feelings and experiences. See them as fellow soldiers facing the same fight against the same foes (Eph. 6:12) and remember your testimony may be as effective as your teaching, possibly more.[4] Congregant, don't fall into the trap of familiarity. Criticizing your ministers over petty things makes you devalue them— and the vital messages and corrections God sends through them. Instead appreciate them for the gifts they are, the One

---

3. Paul, for instance, lamented that sometimes he did things he knew he shouldn't do, yet didn't specify what these transgressions were (Rom. 7:16, 19, 21).

4. David Wilkerson shared with his readers many of his inner conflicts and tests, defeats and triumphs, and griefs and joys as a Christian and minister. This both comforted and challenged me. Truly, experiences can motivate as much as expositions. In them we see how to apply God's Word and ways to our life, how the Spirit works, speaks, leads, checks. They confirm that while we all may fail, we all may also conquer carnality, shed bad attitudes and habits, and reach new levels of consistently spiritual Christlike living.

who has sent them, the Spirit speaking through them, and the heavenly purpose they serve.

2:1 Paul, the agonizing athlete. Paul wanted the Colossians, Laodiceans, and other Christians who had never met him to know "what great conflict" (2:1) he had endured in his "labor" (1:29) to minister to them. In the Greek, "what great conflict" suggests an agonizing effort put forth by a contestant in athletic competition. Paraphrasing, Paul was saying, "I pray you could be a spectator to the agonizing struggle I've experienced in the race of my ministry labors for you."[5]

Paul's prayer was abundantly answered: Acts 13–28 showcases for the ages his agonizing struggle to minister to not only Colosse and Laodicea but the whole world. As we read Luke's inspired record, we sit in a great arena beholding, wondering, cheering for Paul, glorifying his amazingly faithful grace-Giver—and gaining ever more confidence that if Jesus helped Paul win his agonizing race, we can win ours too by His strength (cf. Phil. 4:13; 2 Cor. 12:9–10). Do we understand agony?

Agony involves both physical and psychological suffering. It therefore summons the uniting of our whole being and all its powers—while suffering bodily weakness or sickness, mental puzzlement or confusion, and unrelieved emotional turmoil and anguish—to achieve a great goal. Few things in life demand such a herculean effort, but finishing the race

---

5. "Conflict" (Col. 2:1) is translated from the Greek *agōn*, meaning "to engage in intense struggle involving physical or non-physical force against strong opposition." See Louw and Nida, *Greek–English Lexicon of the New Testament: Based on Semantic Domains*, electronic ed. of the 2nd edition, s.v. "*agōn*."

Christ set before Paul demanded just that (Acts 9:15–16). Thus, Paul revealed the great price he had paid, and was still paying, to fulfill his commission to bless God's people.

Paul's language suggests he sees himself as an athlete running a grueling race with both unscrupulous opponents trying to trip him up and those twin demons, exhaustion and discouragement, trying constantly to convince him to quit for his own comfort or safety. But having none of it, Paul struggled on, expending maximum effort to finish the course His Master put before him and gain the prize He offered (Heb. 12:1–2; Phil. 3:13–14).

Many since have experienced various forms and degrees of agony to finish the courses Christ set before them. They've agonized in hard, cold prisons or work camps, like John Bunyan, Corrie ten Boom, Dietrich Bonhoeffer, and Watchman Nee. They've suffered on long, exhausting journeys like the dangerous trans-Africa treks endured by David Livingstone or the ceaseless travels of Francis Asbury. They've endured lengthy banishments from their homeland, as did William Tyndale and Nicholas von Zinzendorf.[6] They've plodded through merciless missions that exposed them to grueling adversities, baffling lack of success, or devastating personal losses, as did Adoniram Judson, William Carey, and Eric Liddell. They've faced a steady stream of potential or actual violence while living or ministering in predominantly Muslim or Hindu cultures or Communist, Fascist, or despotically ruled countries. Others have suffered an agonizing home life, opposed and oppressed by abuse, aban-

---

6. Tyndale's banishment from England was self-imposed, while Zinzendorf's expulsion from Saxony was by royal edict.

donment, slander, or other cruelties with no relief in sight. When pressed to their physical, psychological, or emotional limits, these surely reexamined Paul's amazing endurance (Acts 13–28) and drew fresh encouragement to press on in their struggles, giving Christ their maximum effort. Their examples are calling us to follow them.

So let's keep running. Give the maximum, not the minimum, effort to win your demanding "race"—the course of God's will as it plays out in your family, work, ministry, or mission (Heb. 12:1–3). Selflessly determine by God's grace to finish your race, however agonizing, refusing to let self-pity, fear, or selfishness turn you inward and make you quit.

2:1 Laodicea, a privileged church. Besides Jesus' comments in Revelation 3:14–22 and indirect references in Acts 19, the only biblical mention of the Laodicean church is in Colossians (2:1; 4:13, 15–16). Let's note five ways Scripture shows Laodicea was a privileged assembly.

First, it was apostolically founded. Acts 19 tells of Paul's remarkably fruitful ministry in Asia, headquartered in Ephesus (19:9–26). For two years he taught in Tyrannus' lecture hall daily, making disciples who then (perhaps sometimes with him) went throughout Asia evangelizing, discipling, and founding the seven churches of Asia (including Colosse and Hierapolis). So whoever founded the Laodicean church preached Paul's gospel, taught his doctrine, shared his emphases, and practiced his methods.

Second, the Laodiceans were taught by Paul. Although it appears they never met him (2:1), Paul instructed them through letters. They received, read, and expounded his Colossian epistle (4:16), another apparently addressed to

Laodicea[7] (4:16), and his other epistles, which were hand-copied and circulated throughout the churches (and contemporaneously considered Scripture by Peter, 2 Pet. 3:16).

Third, they were covered by constant intercession. Having overseen the Asian churches for at least two years, Paul surely interceded for them all, including the Laodiceans, regularly. But he wasn't alone. Epaphras, an elder (perhaps pastor or teacher) who ministered to the Laodiceans, was "always laboring fervently" for them in prayer that they would "stand perfect and complete in all the will of God" (4:12–13).

Fourth, they enjoyed the sweet, supportive fellowship of the Colossian Christians—a solid church (1:3–5, 8; 2:5) with some excellent leaders (1:7; 4:12–13, 17; Philem. 1–2), though under heretical attack (2:4–23). Paul ordered the Colossians to "salute" (4:15, KJV) the Laodiceans. This hinted the Colossians extended warm, loving greetings to their Laodicean brothers and sisters regularly. "Salute" (Greek, *aspozomai*) means "welcome, embrace, to proffer the greeting" and clearly denotes personal contact between the two churches, which were only about twelve miles apart and connected by a major Roman highway, making travel convenient (a half-day's walk) and comparatively safe. "Embrace" one another may further imply the "holy kiss" so widely practiced by Christians—and

---

7. This reference to a Pauline epistle "from" (or "to," 4:16, NLT, WEY) Laodicea is sufficient to establish that, though not extant, it existed. The uncertainty whether it was written "from" or "to" Laodicea is inconsequential. If written to the Laodiceans, they would have read it; if written from, they also would have known its contents. Remember all apostolic letters were hand-copied and distributed for reading in all the churches. So Colossians 4:16 proves the Laodiceans had digested yet another inspired Pauline epistle.

recommended in five separate epistles (Rom. 16:16; 1 Cor. 16:20; 2 Cor. 13:12; 1 Thess. 5:26; 1 Pet. 5:14)!

Fifth, they had the direct, personal, ministerial care of the Son of God through the letter He dictated to them by the apostle John (AD 95), which contained His infallible examination and loving, precise corrections, which, if heeded, would have corrected all their spiritual ills (Rev. 3:14–22). This was the greatest privilege and advantage of all.

Of apostolic founding and ministry, multiple letters from Paul, oft prayed for by zealous intercessors, warm fellowship with other churches, Jesus' personal attention—can it get any better than this? Yet we see the Laodiceans' eventual response was...lukewarmness! They were so obsessed with and possessed by money and "goods," and so proud of it, they felt they needed "nothing" (Rev. 3:17)—even Jesus! Whether they ignored or enacted Jesus' vital corrections (3:18), the fact remained theirs was a privileged church.

So is yours and mine! Like Laodicea, our churches are founded through faith in four apostolic gospels.[8] Though we've never seen Paul, he's ministered in our churches countless times through his letters—all thirteen! Either presently or in the past all our churches have had zealous intercessors praying for them. We've all enjoyed sweet, supportive fellowship with other Christians and churches. And we've all had special attention from Jesus, who has often sent His personal encouragement, correction, instruction, and assistance

---

8. The four New Testament evangels from which our faith in Jesus springs are fully apostolic. Matthew and John were Christ's handpicked apostles, while Mark and Luke inscribed their records of Jesus' life, teachings, and works from the recollections of Peter and the other apostles (and other "eyewitnesses," Luke 1:2).

in our spiritual walk through our pastors, visiting teachers, the Spirit's convicting voice, the invisible but invaluable work of angels, and the entire New Testament!

Are we responding better than the Laodiceans? Abandoning our compromise (spiritual or moral lukewarmness), materialism, and religious pride (Rev. 3:15–17)? Responding when Jesus knocks at the door of our hearts (3:20)? Buying "gold tried in the fire" to prepare for His soon coming (3:18)?

2:1–2 Promoting unity. Paul promoted sweet, close unity between the Colossian and Laodicean churches, as well as other assemblies in Asia: "I want them…knit together by strong ties of love" (2:2, NLT). Why?

Christ's awesome church-building work in Asia through Paul (Acts 19) was under awful satanic assault through church-spoiling heretics (Col. 2:4, 8, 16, 18). Now more than ever the churches of Asia needed to come together and stand together for the true gospel ("the truth of the gospel," or, "the grace of God in truth," 1:5–6) and against the heresies encroaching on them. So do we!

Today our churches are constantly being assaulted by satanically inspired thought stuff and social phenomena in society and in our churches: secular philosophies, false religions, errant Christian doctrines, foolish religious fads, political divisiveness, sectarianism (denominational superiority), racial tensions, or other despiritualizing, demoralizing, or divisive influences. All churches need to be ready to come together and stand together so we can work together to preserve our common gospel, faith, commitment, and spiritual values and lifestyle in our increasingly atheistic, materialistic, and self-serving culture. Then together, in concert, as one, our churches can shine Jesus into the darkness, reaching out in joint evangelistic, educational, charitable, and missional works that bring souls to Jesus, strengthen His kingdom, change cultures, and prepare Christians for His return. Jesus prayed passionately for this unity (John 17:21–23).

Since He prayed, and Paul promoted, let's prayerfully pursue and promote true unity within and among churches!

> *Lord, help me, and help our church, walk in kind, patient love with one another and other churches until our hearts are "comforted...[and] knit together in love." Soli deo Gloria!*

2:2 Filled with the Comforter? Paul prayed that the Colossians, Laodiceans, and other churches would be "comforted" (2:2), or as numerous translations render, "encouraged" (esv, niv). The sense here is that they may be encouraged and thus comforted.[9] But how?

The sweet work of the Holy Spirit! Jesus said in His absence the Holy Spirit would comfort us, even assigning Him the title Comforter (John 14:16–18, 26; 15:26; 16:7). Logically, then, the more we're filled with the Comforter, the more we can comfort others. Paul stated his intent to comfort the Colossians not once but twice (2:1–2; 4:7–8). How characteristic.

Paul was always working to comfort Christians' souls:

9. "Comforted" (Col. 2:2) is translated from the Greek *paraklēthōsin*, which may be rendered "encouraged," "exhorted," or less commonly "comforted" (kjv), yet the latter seems to fit Paul's intent in this context. It describes one encouraging or exhorting so as to comfort. For the definition above see Kittel, Friedrich, and Bromiley, *Theological Dictionary of the New Testament*, s.v. "*paraklēthōsin*."

- Hastening to bring the Gentile Christians' monetary gifts to comfort the Jewish Christians in Jerusalem (when false teaching was trying to trouble and separate them)

- Sending Epaphroditus, whose fellowship and assistance he dearly needed, to the Philippians to relieve their fears about Epaphroditus' health (Phil. 2:25–28)

- Helping to build a fire to warm his fellow shipmates, though weary, wet, and cold himself, after their shipwreck on Malta's shoals (Acts 28:1–3)

- Quickly informing Philippi's jailer he and the other prisoners were still present to prevent him from committing suicide (Acts 16:27–28)

- Quickly informing the Philippian church he and Silas were free and safe to calm their anxiety over their condition (Acts 16:40)

Why? Paul was a consummately Spirit-filled, Spirit-obedient man.

Like him, Spirit-filled, Spirit-responsive Christians steadily exert a comforting influence. They seek to comfort others with God's truth (John 14:16–17, 26), which, when obeyed, creates peace, love, and unity.[10] Their counsels encourage troubled

---

10. By calling the Comforter the "Spirit of truth" Jesus implied *truth comforts* (John 14:16–17, 26). Knowing the truth comforts by clearing away the confusing, troubling contradictions of falsehood. Obeying truth further comforts us by giving us assurance Christ is with us, will answer our petitions (John 15:7–8; 1 John 3:19–22), and will never forsake us (Heb. 13:5–6),

hearts, warn unruly ones, and urge sinners to repent. They try to reconcile divided parties, whenever possible. They're eager to share good news to encourage the discouraged. They constantly edify others' faith with insights from the most comforting book, the Bible.[11] They point us to good things ahead, especially Jesus' return (1 Thess. 4:13–18). Their exhortations lift the oppressed and restore their joy and zeal.[12] All these exhortative or encouraging actions aim at imparting comfort of soul.

Just as certainly, carnally minded and sinning Christians, who lack the Spirit's fullness, too often trouble or agitate others by their bad attitudes, ungracious speech, selfish decisions, and offensive actions and reactions. Even if they received Christ's two primary works of grace, the net effect of their lives is to trouble, not comfort, those with whom they interact. The troubler, not the Comforter, works through them. And they're failing their calling.

We're called to represent "the God of all comfort" (2 Cor. 1:3), who faithfully and lovingly "comforteth those that are

---

thus releasing us from the nagging anxieties of a disobedient life. The Spirit of truth also comforts us by biblical insight, truth more deeply and accurately understood; biblical recall, truth remembered just when we need it; and biblical conviction of sin, the truthful acknowledgment we're not obeying the truth, which restores us in the light of truthfulness (1 John 1:7, 9). These are various phases of "the comfort of the Holy Spirit" (Acts 9:31).

11. Since it's inspired by the Comforter, the Word of God, when believed and received, imparts the strongest possible comfort to believers' hearts (Rom. 15:4; Luke 24:27, 32). This is especially true of the Book of Psalms (Ps. 119:50, 52, 76).

12. As in *The Pilgrim's Progress*, Hopeful's exhortations lifted Christian when they were crossing the river of death to reach the Celestial City. See John Bunyan, *The Pilgrim's Progress* (Old Tappan, NJ: Fleming H. Revell, 1979), 141–142.

cast down" (7:6), so comforting others is an integral part of our threefold Christian commission. Daily we preach, teach, or witness to comfort believers and non-believers by: fellowship, especially in perplexing times (Rom. 1:12; Acts 16:40); sharing God's Word, especially insights that have comforted us in our adversities (Rom. 15:4; 2 Cor. 1:4–5); teaching hope-giving Bible prophecy in these troubling last days (Rev. 1:3); loyally assisting suffering Christians, especially ministers (Col. 4:10–11); receiving penitent offenders seeking reconciliation with us (2 Cor. 2:7); exhorting discouraged members of our congregation, as Barnabas did (Acts 4:36); quickly sharing good news with suffering Christians (Prov. 25:25; 1 Thess. 3:6–7);[13] sharing prophetic messages, if so gifted (1 Cor. 14:3, 31; Gen. 40:5–13); reminding believers Jesus is coming for us *before* the Tribulation (1 Thess. 4:18; 5:9–11).

Comforting is a rewarding work. Every time we realize our efforts have comforted others' hearts, our hearts are comforted anew (2 Cor. 7:13). And there's more. God makes sure we reap what we sow by sending us comforters just when we need them (Gal. 6:7). Faithful comforters will never lack faithful comforters (Col. 4:10–11; Phil. 4:10, 14, 18). But not all Christians qualify.

There are different kinds of Christians: comforting, casual, callous, cruel. The regularity with which we yield ourselves to the Spirit or to sinful selfishness determines whether our hearts become softer or harder and our influence more comforting or troubling. Where are you? Are you:

---

13. Since Proverbs 25:25 states good news is like "cold waters" to thirsty souls, quickly sharing good news with stress-heated, trial-weary, hope-thirsty Christians is one way we give them a refreshing "drink of cold water" in Christ's name (Matt. 10:42).

- Comforting, promptly taking action to relieve others' stress and sorrows whenever possible?

- Casual, not very serious or urgent to render such relief?

- Callous, frankly unconcerned whether you comfort or vex other souls?

- Cruel, adding griefs and sorrows to those you could be comforting?

It's time we examine the net effect of our daily living on others.[14] And let's pray:

> Lord help me become like Paul, a Spirit-filled, Spirit-responsive Christian through whom rivers of the Comforter's consolation ceaselessly flow.

2:2 The riches and assurance of insight. Paul prayed the Colossians and Laodiceans would experience all the "riches" and the "full assurance" of "understanding" (2:2). That is, "the full riches of complete understanding" (NIV), "complete confidence that they understand God's mysterious plan" (NLT), or "the riches that come from a complete understanding of Christ" (GW). What does this tell us?

"Understanding" is translated from the Greek *sunesis*, meaning "insight,"[15] especially biblical insight, which is

14. See 1 Kings 18:17–18; Isa. 40:1–2; 61:1–2; 66:13; Matt. 9:22; Mark 10:49; Acts 9:31; 20:12 (10:38).

15. Literally, *sunesis* means "a running [or flowing] together," and when applied to our thoughts speaks of them coming together to a clear focus of comprehension, discernment, or insight. For definition, see R. L. Thomas, *New American Standard Hebrew–Aramaic and Greek Dictionaries*, updated

incredibly valuable and deeply stabilizing. The God-given ability to see beyond the superficial and obvious and discern the full, inner meaning of God's Word, its essence, latent messages, timely applications, historical parallels, and full range of instructions for our lives and churches, this is priceless and powerful. Biblical insight gives believers "full assurance" (Greek, *plērophoria*), or "complete certainty,"[16] in a very uncertain world. Therefore nothing is more valuable than knowing God's mind, grasping His grand, multifaceted redemptive plan, locating our part in that plan, understanding our times, and seeing clearly what we need to do, all as set forth in Scripture (cf. 1 Chron. 12:32). These rich insights are also powerful. They stabilize our souls in the stormy seas of life and keep us calm, strong, and steady in our walk and service, unmoved by opposition or sudden terrors. How do we get biblical insight?

By the illumination or enlightenment of the Holy Spirit. He authored the Word (2 Tim. 3:16–17), and He alone soundly interprets both its obvious (literal) and obscure (latent) messages. We gain this by studying the biblical interpretations of Spirit-gifted, Spirit-taught teachers. Also, by the inner witness of the Spirit as we prayerfully peruse God's Word while living a trusting, obedient life. The divine Teacher's witness, or inner illumination, is so assuring that we come to not hope but *know* biblical insights are rock-solid, thoroughly reliable in their truthfulness. This witness enabled prophets, saints, martyrs, reformers, and revivalists to stand firm in

---

edition (Anaheim: Foundation Publications, Inc., 1998), s.v. *"sunesis."*

16. Swanson, *Dictionary of Biblical Languages with Semantic Domains: Greek (New Testament)*, s.v. *"plērophoria."*

flooding Jordans of trouble and raging Euroclydons of opposition. Why? Firmly grasped by the Spirit who helped them grasp God's Word, they grew utterly certain of what they knew. The certainty of their insights cemented faith in their souls. And made them very valuable to God.

Joseph's greatest asset was his insight into: the meaning of his dreams and others'; the deep purpose of God in his years of suffering (Gen. 50:20); God's simple solution into Egypt's terrifying drought (41:34–36); and a way to test his brothers' truthfulness without harming them (42:18–20). Daniel's greatest gift was his insight into: dreams and visions; the handwriting on the wall; one of the causes of delayed responses to our prayers (Dan. 10:12–14); and how near God's time was for the end of Judah's captivity (9:1–2). Jesus had perfect insight into the sinful motive that spoiled all the Pharisees' impressive outward righteousness (Matt. 6:2, 5, 16; 23:5). Paul had insight into what typical Greeks and Jews of his day wanted (1 Cor. 1:22) and why God had caused spiritual blindness among the Jewish people (Acts 13:27–28; Rom. 11:20–25). Numerous pre- and post-Reform Christians insightfully discerned the gulf between the teaching of Scripture and the traditions of the Roman church. As time passed, God gave protestant leaders additional biblical insights that spurred further reforms and dynamic revivals (the Awakenings, Methodism, Evangelicalism, Pentecostalism, Charismaticism). All these insights in their own way gave God's people "assurance" concerning Him, their salvation, and their future hope in Christ.

So it's no wonder David prayed for "wisdom and understanding" for Solomon (1 Chron. 22:12), Solomon's writings praise their vitalness and value (Prov. 1:1–2, 5–6; 2:1–11), and

Paul prayed for Christians to possess the "full assurance of understanding." Perhaps the greater question is, Is David, Solomon, and Paul's desire ours?

Want the treasure of insight? Want its power to gird you till you're "completely certain" in these completely uncertain times? Then with worshipful prayer "get understanding" from teachers who have it and from the Spirit's witness in your personal Bible study (Prov. 4:5, 7). This insight—the "full riches of complete understanding"—will make you valuable and stable in God's service.

2:3 Christ, our Great Repository and Philosopher. Paul's statement should be interpreted in light of the verses that follow, in which he warns against being fooled by heretics (2:4) and spoiled by worldly philosophers (2:8).

The heretics troubling the Colossian church taught an early form of gnosticism that claimed the saving knowledge (Greek, *gnosis*) of God was accessible only to a select few, that those few were members of their sect, and that the Colossians should therefore join their sect—whose teachings denied the Incarnation, Christ's atoning death, and thus His redemption. The gnostics claimed that, upon joining, the Christians would be specially enlightened with the knowledge and wisdom of God. What was afoot?

Satan was tempting the Colossians as he had Eve. He was trying to get them to disbelieve and disobey Christ, who plainly claimed He was the *only* way to God and thus to His true knowledge (John 14:6), who called His Spirit the "Spirit of truth," and who taught His Spirit alone would "guide you into all truth" and "teach you all things" (John 16:13; 14:26). And why should they ignore Christ's claims? To have the "special" knowledge only revealed to and shared among the gnostics, thus elevating them to sit among the spiritual elites. This was a direct appeal to their intellectual pride. Through these gnostic advocates Satan was implying Christ's knowledge was inferior or inadequate and tempting the Colossians to seek knowledge outside of Christ that was "desired to make one wise" in their own eyes (Gen. 3:6).[17]

Paul countered here by reassuring the Colossians they already had full access to not some or most but "all" true knowledge and wisdom of God...in Christ! "Christ, *in whom* are hidden *all* the treasures of wisdom and knowledge" (2:2–3). Thus, they didn't need to seek purportedly divine knowledge or wisdom outside of Him. Certain influential early church scholars tried to reconcile Christ's comparatively new doctrine with preexisting, widely accepted Greek philosophy, but the church eventually learned the two do not have to agree. Christ's philosophy—His truth claims, consisting of His wisdom sayings, ethical code (Matt. 5–7), revelations, parables, and prophecies—stands absolutely alone without any need of corroboration from human philosophers (then Socrates, Plato, Aristotle; today Enlightenment, modern, or

---

17. Satan has done the same today by enticing secular philosophers and academics to believe through human reason and scientific method alone they may discover all truth (and thus be seen as "wise") apart from Christ and biblical revelation (Rom. 1:18–23, esp. v. 22). Also, Satan deceives cult leaders, false prophets, and even some Christian pastors with the notion that they have exclusive access to special revelation, who then call people to join their elite group, much as the gnostics did in Colosse. Shun all exclusivity, superiority, or any other form of spiritual pride. God is no respecter of persons, and while not all Christians enjoy the same knowledge of Christ, all can if they will—through the same Bible, by the same Spirit, in the same grace.

postmodern). They could, and should, unashamedly believe, rest, and rejoice in Christ, their great Philosopher.[18]

Not only are "all the treasures of wisdom and knowledge" found in Christ, but, according to Paul, they're "hidden" there (2:3). This implies they're beyond the grasp or apprehension of nonbelievers, however astute. "Hidden" also implies due to their immense value they're sealed, closely guarded, safely preserved, and thus unchanging through the ages. Truth in Paul's day is truth in our day; conversely, first-century error is still error in the twenty-first century, however cleverly repackaged and represented. So, ironically, the opposite of the gnostics' claim was true: wisdom and knowledge of God are found exclusively in Christ and available to even the humblest believers (Matt. 11:25–26)! Thus, ordinary Christians, not proud gnostics, were by grace the recipients of special knowledge.

Has this dawned on us? While we thank God for the fascinating, helpful, ever-increasing discoveries of true science daily, we should also realize spiritual and moral truths are as absolute and immutable as scientific or mathematical facts. And they're all found in Christ. He is the sole repository of divine wisdom and knowledge. We need not look to any other purported messiah, deity, prophet, oracle, mystic,

---

18. A philosopher (lit., "lover of wisdom") is one who seeks to discover truth (reality) or wisdom, primarily the great questions concerning our existence and the meaning of life and secondarily the particulars about every phase of our world and existence. Just as we rejoice in Christ our great Physician and Christ our great Psychologist, so Paul urged the Colossians and us to celebrate Christ our great Philosopher. That Paul taught Christ's teachings in the philosophical (or rhetorical) school (lecture hall) of Tyrannus in nearby Ephesus suggests he recommended Christ as the one true, superior, and all-sufficient Philosopher, at whose feet all people should sit, learn, and live (Acts 19:9).

pundit, philosopher, scientist, or religion, or any combination of them (New Age) to know the true God and true truth. The true God is fully revealed in Jesus, and true truth is encapsulated in His sayings specifically and the Bible generally. Thus, Jesus is our great Repository and Philosopher. How amazing and wonderful is this *gnosis!*

2:5 Colosse: a strong church under strong attack. Paul's statements concerning the Colossian church reveal that, though probably small in number, they were a spiritually potent assembly (1:3–5, 8; 2:5).

They had mature leaders (1:7; 4:12–13; Philem. 1–2), correct theology (specifically, their Christology, soteriology,[19] and an understanding of the "mystery" of the Gentile–Jewish church, 1:25–27), excellent order (2:5), steadfast faith (1:4; 2:5), lively heavenly hope (1:5), overflowing love (1:4, 8), habitual personal and intercessory prayer (4:2–3), sweet fellowship with other churches (4:15), the support of apostolic intercessors (1:3, 9–12), and apostolic teaching—by no less than the apostle to the Gentiles himself (1:1–2; cf. Rom. 11:13)! Yet despite this spiritual excellence[20] they were undergoing a very serious satanic attack from aggressive heretics desiring to sow ruinous errors in Colosse's field of truth (2:4–23). Strange?

---

19. Soteriology (lit., "salvation study") is the branch of theology examining the doctrine of salvation.

20. Weymouth quotes Ellicott: "After these words (Col. 2:5) we have no reason for doubting that the Church of Colossae, though tried by heretical teaching, was substantially sound in the faith." See Richard Francis Weymouth, *New Testament in Modern Speech* (Grand Rapids, MI: Kregel Publications, 1978), Col. 2:5, note #1, 541.

It shouldn't be. Satan attacks strong churches most severely and frequently. They are his targets of choice, not compromised or dead assemblies. (Note some thirty years later he left the churches of Laodicea and Sardis alone, but not the potent Philadelphia church, Rev. 3:1–22). Why this strategy? Satan doesn't want to disturb congregations in which he's already got a firm foothold through sin, heresy, schisms, worldliness, or lukewarmness. So he passes them by, opting instead to send his servants and demons to attack, overtly or covertly, devotionally hot, spiritually developing, truth-rich, increasingly fruitful assemblies. Is your church under satanic attack?

Is he troubling your congregation from within by heretics, rebels, Judases, self-serving leaders, earnest but ungifted prophets, troublemakers, sin-friendly attitudes, political strife, social or racial prejudices, distracting worldly interests, time-wasting programs or projects, or growing unfaithfulness? Or is he assaulting you from outside by persisting, unreasonable troubles or dogged persecution by hateful enemies? If so, don't take offense; take heart! Satan wouldn't attack your church unless there is something valuable to the Lord there, presently or potentially. Knowing this, the Lord has permitted the attack so that, as you respond correctly, He can turn it to serve His higher purpose: making your strong church even stronger (Rom. 8:28)! How should you respond?

Start by worshiping God in the middle of your mess! Praise and thank Him for, in His gracious love and wisdom, allowing Satan's assault. Better to be a strong church under attack than a conflict-free church that's weak and ineffective. Then deal with your problems as the Scriptures instruct you.

Refute error, assess prophecies, correct sin, abandon luke-warmness, eliminate worthless programs and projects, iden-tify and counsel troublemakers, forgive and pray for enemies, correct injustices, heal your divisions, and, most importantly, refocus on Christ and restoring your "Colossian excellence"— the things that have made your church strong. In these reforming and maturing fires your leaders will become stronger and more discerning, and new leaders and over-comers will be forged (cf. 1 Cor. 11:19, NIV). Every wise deci-sion they make will set a precedent that will help your church more easily settle future problems. When Christ brings your church to the other side of its troubled waters, it will be a purer, more devoted, and more fruitful vine in His world-wide vineyard (1 Pet. 5:10). Your people will be blessed and Christ honored—and Satan will regret he ever attacked you!

2:6–7 The road to established faith. Scripture declares no less than five times we are to live (or walk) by faith in God (Hab. 2:4; Rom. 1:17; 2 Cor. 5:7; Gal. 3:11; Heb. 10:38). But how?

Paul fully informed the Colossians. By inspiration he packed into a mere two brief verses a surprising amount of information on how we can live by faith and eventually become "established in the faith" (Col. 2:7). His words serve as an instruction manual for building a spiritual highway, which, if followed faithfully, will lead us into a life of estab-lished faith in Christ.

The Roman roads the Colossians knew so well and Paul traveled so frequently had in many instances five layers of construction materials. Similarly, Paul's "road" is comprised of eight layers of obedience. To construct by God's grace a life of established faith:

1. We "receive" Christ as Lord and Savior, thus being born again through the gospel message ("as ye have *received* Christ," 2:6). See John 1:12–13; 3:1–8.

2. We come under biblical teaching, thus becoming Christ's disciples, eager to learn God's Word and walk in His ways ("as ye have been *taught*," 2:7). See John 8:31–32; 2 Timothy 2:15.

3. We begin seriously doing or practicing God's Word, thus honoring Christ's lordship ("Jesus the [your] *Lord*...so *walk* ye in him [His Word]," 2:6). See Matthew 7:21; Luke 6:46; James 1:22–25.

4. We abide in Him and His Word closely and continue doing so faithfully as tests begin coming our way ("so walk ye *in him* [or abiding in Him and His Word]," 2:6). See John 15:1–8; Acts 11:23.

5. We form the habit of offering God thanks in every situation we meet ("abounding with *thanksgiving*," 2:7). See Ephesians 5:18; Colossians 3:17; 1 Thessalonians 5:18.

6. We grow spiritual roots by practicing these vital disciplines—receiving teaching, obeying God's Word, abiding closely, and offering

thanks ("*rooted*...in Him," 2:7). See Psalm
1:2–3; Jeremiah 17:7–8.[21]

7. Faith-filled, Christlike character is "built
up"—forged, formed, and firmed—in us as we
continue our spiritual disciplines in stronger,
sometimes fiery tests of faith ("*built up* in him,"
2:7). See Romans 8:29; 1 Peter 1:5–7; 2:5;
4:12–14.

8. Finally, our faith becomes "established," as we
persist in our disciplined faith-walk through
very long trials of endurance (Revelation 3:10).
Our Christ-confidence becomes so deeply
rooted and firmly built, it becomes a permanent fixture in our lives. Thereafter, however
severe or long our tests, we walk by faith—
"that leaning of the entire human personality
on Him in absolute trust and confidence in His
power, wisdom and goodness" (Colossians 2:5,
AMP)—and help others do so ("*established* in the
faith," 2:7). See 1 Peter 5:10.

Are you adding these layers of Paul's roadway of faith into
your life? Are you persevering in your construction or pro-
crastinating? When Satan tempts you to turn aside to fascinating or alluring but hindering detours—worldly fads, lusts,
pleasures, greed, unbelief, murmuring, self-pity, self-centered

---

21. Roots provide trees with water, nourishment (nutrients), storage (water
and nutrients), strength, and stability. Similarly, spiritual roots refresh us
with the Spirit, nourish our faith and devotion, store vital truths in our
hearts for later use in trials, strengthen us to witness for Christ and resist
temptation, and stabilize our walk in this unstable world.

living—take none of them. With God's grace assisting you, keep building your highway of faith according to Paul's instructions until you're fully "established in the faith." Then help others build their road: "Clear the way for the people; Build up, build up the highway" (Isa. 62:10, NAS).

2:4, 8 Spoiled? Paul warned the Colossians, "Lest any man should beguile you" (2:4) or "spoil" you (2:8), "beware!" Of what?

Beware the dangers of subtle intellectual temptations. They confront us wherever non-Christian or quasi-Christian philosophers, academics, or self-professed free thinkers offer flawed ideas—false truth claims and doctrines—for our acceptance. If we believe these false truths, Paul asserts they will "beguile" (2:4) and "spoil" us (2:8).[22] A return to spiritual health will not occur unless we again believe and obey the true truth claims of Scripture rightly divided (John 8:32; 2 Tim. 2:15). What's at risk?

Our steadfast, childlike faith in Jesus and all that springs from it—our close, daily walk with Him, divine guidance, worship in spirit and truth, winsome Christian witness, and fruitful kingdom ministries (2:5–7)—these are in danger of being "spoiled" or ruined by "empty philosophies and high-sounding nonsense" presented in "well-crafted arguments" (2:4, 8, NLT). Their crafty inspirer, Satan, is as intent on ruining our walk with Christ as Christ is on improving it

---

22. While the "spoilers" Paul referred to in this context are philosophical, theological, and ideological, there are others. Conspiracy theories, for instance, should be investigated on a case-by-case basis with careful distinctions made between facts and hypotheses, realities and rumors. While not theologically harmful, such issues are mentally entangling, waste our precious time and energies, and may cause us to misjudge others. The wise stay focused on the things that matter.

(cf. Gen. 5:22, 24; 6:9; Ps. 81:13; Zech. 3:7). Our spiritual walk is based on, fed, and sustained by our childlike trust in Christ's character and Word. So Satan aims to destroy that simple trust by troubling our minds with complex, confusing, unproven, and unbiblical anti-Christian ideas. Realizing this ever-present danger, Paul called the Corinthians, and us, to hold fast to "the simplicity[23] that is in Christ" (2 Cor. 11:3) so we wouldn't be tricked by clever, sophisticated philosophical or religious reasonings that spawn doubt or disbelief in God's Word, as Eve was (Gen. 3:1–6).

Paul's inspired warning proves, yes, though born again, Christians may be taken captive by false teachings (in Col. 2:4, 8, philosophical; in Col. 2:16–23 and Gal. 1:6–9, religious) if we don't watch:

> Be careful that nobody spoils your faith through intellectualism or high-sounding nonsense. Such stuff is at best founded on men's ideas of the nature of the world and disregards Christ.
>
> —COLOSSIANS 2:8, PHILLIPS

> Watch out lest (Satan through) clever secular intellectuals capture(s) your mind by causing you to believe empty, deceptive philosophies built upon the false truth principles and traditions (or rudiments) of worldly wisdom rather than on Christ's wisdom.
>
> —COLOSSIANS 2:8, AUTHOR'S PARAPHRASE

---

23. Or, "The simplicity [single-hearted loyalty] and purity [uprightness of life]" which had characterized their faith in Christ from the beginning. See K. S. Wuest, *The New Testament: An Expanded Translation* (Grand Rapids, MI: Eerdmans, 1961), 2 Cor. 11:3.

Key here is the term "spoil" (2:8). It is translated from the Greek *sylagōgeō*, meaning "to carry off booty; to carry off one as a captive (and slave)," henceforth controlling them.[24] This warns of Satan taking us as his captives, or prisoner-spoils of spiritual war, henceforth controlling us through the philosophical or ideological lies he has sown in our minds (2 Tim. 2:26). The last phrase in this verse is another key: " . . . and *not after Christ*" (2:8).

The ensnaring teachings Paul warned of are any *not* in agreement with those of our great Philosopher, Christ—the whole range of His teachings, including His truth claims, wisdom sayings, revelations, parables, and prophecies.[25] Paul's assertion that "all the treasures of wisdom and knowledge" are hidden in Christ (2:3) implies that as followers of Christ's teachings we are already enrolled in the fullest, truest, and most satisfying and honorable school of philosophy. Since our Teacher holds "all wisdom," we simply don't need secular philosophers, ancient, modern, or postmodern, to guide us into the basic eternal truths concerning the big questions of life: Where did we come from? What is the meaning of life?

---

24. J. Strong, *Enhanced Strong's Lexicon* (Bellingham, WA: Logos Bible Software, 2001), s.v. "*sylagōgeō*."

25. As Paul alluded ("and not after Christ," Col. 2:8), all heresy will clearly contradict at least one Bible verse. So the best defense against it is a broad and ever-growing knowledge of God's Word—the only infallible standard of eternal truth by which we assess the veracity of every teaching. To develop sharp discernment, we must also obey the biblical truths we hold (John 7:17), stay close to the Lord (and thus full of His "Spirit of truth," John 16:13), pray for the Spirit's help in detecting error (John 14:14), and learn to trust His unerring discernment when He alerts us to the presence of doctrinal imbalance or error (1 John 2:26–27). Paul, who also practiced these measures, excelled at discerning error (cf. Acts 15:1–2; Gal. 1:6–7; 1 Tim. 6:3–5).

What is truth? How do we discover truth? Who is God? How did the universe get here? How will life end? And so forth. We already have these questions adequately answered in Christ's teachings specifically and God's comprehensive revelation, the Bible, generally. But not everyone agreed with Paul.

One of the church's earliest disputes over how to interpret Scripture (hermeneutics) led to the establishment of two distinct schools, one advancing allegorical interpretations (Alexandria) and another literal interpretations (Antioch). The former originated from the teachings of Clement of Alexandria, who was influenced by the Hellenistic Jewish philosopher, Philo,[26] and whose teaching philosophy was continued by his extraordinarily prolific student, Origen. All three—Philo, Clement, and Origen—believed they could and should reconcile Greek philosophy with Hebrew, and later Christian, revelation.[27] Thus, they continually searched the Scriptures for allegorical interpretations they claimed did this. The Antioch school discerned correctly that Greek philosophy and divine revelation were not always compatible.

---

26. There were other Jewish Hellenistic philosophers in this period. "Diaspora Jewish writers praised 'philosophy,' and some, like Philo, combined it readily with ecstatic experiences (cf. 2:18). (Josephus, a Palestinian Jew writing for a non-Palestinian Gentile audience, even calls Judaism a 'philosophy'...and describes the different Jewish movements as philosophical sects...many Jewish apologists, including Philo and Josephus, accused the Greek philosophers of plagiarizing Moses.)" See Keener, *The IVP Bible Background Commentary: New Testament*, Col. 2:8, note.

27. Of Philo, one source states he was "the first to attempt to synthesize revealed faith and philosophic reason"; another that, "His work attempts to combine Plato and Moses into one philosophical system." See http://www.britannica.com/biography/Philo-Judaeus (accessed April 21, 2106); also see http://en.wikipedia.org/wiki/Philo (accessed April 21, 2016).

The early church father Tertullian later concluded, "What has Athens to do with Jerusalem?" Or, what does worldly philosophy have to do with Judeo-Christian theology? What agreement is there between the philosophers and the prophets, between intellectualism and inspiration? But the Colossians were not yet so fully convinced. Hence Paul's warning for them to steer clear of the gnostics and others who peddled the secular wisdom of Athens or the blended philosophies of Philo, and in later years, those of Clement and Origen.

However, Paul wasn't forbidding academic study of the world's various philosophical and religious belief systems to gain an accurate understanding of them. This is essential for Christian apologists and polemicists and helpful for pastors and missionaries as they minister the faith to people emerging from very different belief systems. Biblical evidence hints Paul himself may have studied philosophy at some point, since his hometown (Tarsus) hosted a major university specializing in Stoic philosophy[28] and he quoted pagan philosophers and poets in his brief sermon on Mars Hill (cf. Acts 17:28). Paul was warning the Colossians not to believe or practice any teachings, philosophical or religious, that contradicted biblical truth. Then, as now, the canon of Scripture is our guide in distinguishing false truth claims from true truth. Jesus said definitively, "Thy word is truth" (John 17:17; cf. Ps. 119:128; 2 Tim. 3:15–17).

Paul also warned of "the tradition of men" (2:8). A tradition is simply any belief or practice handed down as true

---

28. W. A. Elwell and P. W. Comfort, *Tyndale Bible Dictionary* (Wheaton, IL: Tyndale House Publishers, 2001), s.v. "Tarsus."

or beneficial from generation to generation. There is nothing inherently false or evil about traditions. To the contrary, many family, ethnic, and national traditions significantly enrich our lives. They are only objectionable when held or practiced contrary to the commands or standards of God's Word (cf. Mark 7:9). Christianity itself has many acceptable traditions. "There is a true Christian tradition,"[29] notes one source, speaking of the core beliefs and practices Christians have observed regularly from the beginning of the church age that spring from God's Word and which we observe to honor the Lord (cf. 2 Thess. 2:15; 3:6; 2 Tim. 2:2). Traditions were, and still are, universal. The Jews had their traditional rabbinic teachings (Matt. 15:1–9) and the Greeks their philosophical traditions (2:8). And later the Roman church developed its traditions, as did virtually every Orthodox and Protestant denomination that has followed, including Pentecostals and Charismatics.

Paul warned specifically against believing mere man-made traditions are authoritative and binding upon us, that we must embrace them to be saved, or, being saved, to become more spiritual and Christlike. This is why he pointed out that the "rudiments" (2:8, basic elements, principles, spirits[30])

---

29. Wiersbe, *The Bible Exposition Commentary*, Vol. 2, Col. 2:8–10, note, 125.

30. "Rudiments" (2:8) is translated from the Greek *stoicheion*, meaning, "any first thing (or first in a row, as the alphabet)." First things are basic things or fundamentals. Here *stoicheion* refers to the basics, or basic elements, principles, or spirits. That is, the basic elements of the natural world, basic principles of worldly philosophies or religions, and the basic or ranking demonic spirits ruling the realms of worldly philosophy and religion (and invisibly inspiring all heresies—though Christ, whenever He pleases, overrules them [2:10], as He did by prompting Paul to author this, his corrective epistle to the Colossians, 2:10). For definition, see Strong, *Enhanced Strong's Lexicon*,

of the traditions threatening to spoil the Colossians were of purely human, not divine, origin. They were traditions "of men" (2:8), not of God, like those the Pharisees imposed—and Christ so repeatedly rejected. Thus, Paul concluded those traditions were "not after Christ" (2:8), or not born of or in agreement with His teaching and therefore neither authoritative nor binding. He concluded they were "vain" (2:8), or futile (lit. "empty"), and so powerless to help those who practiced them (cf. Heb. 13:9). Among the vain traditions being promoted among the Colossians were not only Greek philosophical traditions but also those of Jewish legalism, angel worship, and asceticism (2:14–23).

The danger with these and all unbiblical philosophies and traditions is twofold. First, we may abandon Christ's teaching to embrace them. Second, we may try to blend the two, attempting to put new philosophical patches on our old garments of Christian theology, something Jesus warned would fail (cf. Luke 5:36). Paul warns both options will "beguile" us and "spoil" our faith, rendering us Satan's captives and derailing our spiritual walk and destiny.

So, Christian, give thanks you already know and follow the only unerring philosopher, Christ. Never be ashamed of His wisdom and knowledge. To the contrary, search, revel in, live by, demonstrate, and recommend it daily. And concerning worldly, anti-Christian philosophies, however sophisticated and widely accepted, heed Paul's instruction: "Beware!"

---

s.v. *"stoicheion."*

2:9 The divine fullness of Christ. Paul declared "all the fullness of the Godhead" was in Christ while on Earth...and not mystically but "bodily" (2:9).[31] So Christ was the unique human repository of the divine fullness. God was not merely in Christ but was in Him repletely, with no part of His mystical, divine being left out.

Various translations help us grasp this more firmly. One adds Jesus was "giving complete expression of the divine nature" (2:9, AMP). Another, "It is in him that God gives a full and complete expression of himself" (PHILLIPS). One paraphrase states, "Everything of God gets expressed in him, so you can see and hear him clearly" (THE MESSAGE). What does this mean to us? Simply, if we want to fully understand who and what and all God is, we should study Jesus fully. We do so by receiving Him and His Spirit, prayerfully and persistently perusing all four Gospels, and exploring the balance of New Testament revelation, all while living a life of submissive trust in and obedience to Christ. Then, daily, we'll see more and more of the awesome divine fullness that resided in the Nazarene bodily.

Indeed, the full wonder of God was evident in Him. Over the course of His life and ministry, the Gospels describe Jesus acting or speaking so as to reveal the entire Trinity in His person:

---

31. As stated earlier, Paul's affirmation of the Incarnation refuted the gnostics' claims that Christ did not indwell a real body but only seemed to, since their view was that everything material, including human bodies, was the creation of the evil god of their dualistic belief, the Demiurge.

- The authority of the Father (Matt. 8:7–9, 13; Mark 4:39, 41; 11:14, 15–17)

- The submissive obedience of the Son (Luke 22:42; John 5:30; 7:16; 8:29)

- The awesome power and gentle, meek grace of the Spirit (Luke 4:14–15, 18, 22, 31–32), and that "without limit" (John 3:34, NIV)

- The Father's honoring of the Son (Mark 1:11; 9:7)

- The Son's honoring of the Father (John 2:15–16; 8:28–29, 49; 10:29; 14:28; 17:1)

- The Spirit's voluntary deference to the Father and Son (John 16:13–14)[32]

- The Father and Son's reciprocal honoring of the Spirit (Mark 3:28–29; Luke 12:10)

These incidents or statements help us understand that while the three persons of the Trinity are perfectly equal in their deity, authority, and essence (spiritual substance, Greek, *homoousios*), the Father, Son, and Spirit relate to themselves within the Godhead in very distinct ways, and there exists a clear chain of command or habitual manner of address and response.

---

32. This voluntary, love-driven deference of the Spirit for the Father and Son is confirmed in the Revelation, where John shows that in heaven, while the Spirit is fully and centrally present as deity (Rev. 4:5), the Father and Son are the prime objects of worship offered by the redeemed and angels forever (4:9–11; 5:8–9, 11–12, 13; 21:22–23; 22:3). We must remember the indivisible, enduring unity of the Godhead teaches us that to worship the Father and Son is to also worship the Spirit. When one Person is honored, all three are honored.

Want to know God? Fully? Receive, abide in, and study Jesus—fully! And in your thinking, praying, and living, relate with equal faith and awe to all three Persons of the Trinity that indwelt Him. Praise and worship the Father, Son, and Holy Spirit. Obey the Father's will, the Son's words, and the Spirit's guidance until by grace your life is an increasing reflection of Christ's, filled with "all the fullness of God" (Eph. 3:19). That's a lot of fullness, so start or continue filling today!

2:9–10 Our completeness in Christ. Paul reasoned with the Colossians in the clearest, simplest terms. "All the fullness of the Godhead" was in Christ (2:9; 1:19), Christ was in them (1:27), so they were therefore "complete in Him" (2:10). Consequently, they needed no other deity, way of salvation, supernatural power, overshadowing helper, or way of worship other than what they had already discovered and lived in "in him." Why?

In His amazing fullness, Christ filled every vital role in the drama of their lives. As their great Savior (John 14:6; Acts 4:12; Col. 1:13–14), Shepherd (John 10:11–16), Physician (Matt. 8:16–17; Luke 4:23), Psychologist (John 4:16–19, 29; 5:6), Provider (Phil. 4:19), Defender (Luke 18:1–8), Companion (Heb. 13:5), and Philosopher/Teacher (John 3:2; Col. 2:3, 8), He covered all their human needs, spiritual and physical. Thus, they required nothing and no one to complete their lives. But something else bears on this subject.

Our completeness Himself, Jesus, urged with imperative language that we receive the fullness of the Holy Spirit (John 16:7–15; Acts 1:4–5, 8). Humbly following His instructions, the early church diligently urged their converts to receive not only Christ but also the fullness of the Spirit, thus practicing two primary works of grace (Acts 8:12–13, 14–15; 9:5–9, 17). So why the apparent contradiction? Why did Paul say Jesus is enough, yet Jesus said we also need the Spirit?

The answer is, as a man, Jesus received the fullness of the Holy Spirit when He was baptized by John (Luke 3:21–22). Then He possessed not only the Father's nature but also the Spirit's power in His human body (4:1). All this together—the divine nature and Spirit—comprised "the fullness" indwelling Jesus. So when Paul declared us complete "in Him" (Col. 2:10), he meant, "Ye are complete in Him [and the Spirit who indwelt Him]." Or, "You are complete when all the fullness that indwelt Christ as a man also indwells you." Paul's ministry confirms this was his intent. When in Ephesus Paul met twelve students he assumed were Christians. He asked, "Did you receive the Holy Spirit when you believed" (Acts 19:2, NKJV). Or, paraphrasing, "When you first believed in Christ, did you also receive the Holy Spirit?" When they replied they hadn't, and didn't even know there was a Holy Spirit (19:2), Paul's response was unhesitating and undeniable. First, he first shared the gospel (19:4). Second, when they had received the gospel (and Christ), he baptized them in water (19:5). Third, he prayed for them to receive the fullness of the Spirit, which they did (19:6). If the fullness of the Spirit was not a necessary part of the fullness of Christ, Paul's actions were incorrect and misleading, as were his other writings that addressed this issue (2 Cor. 1:21–22; Eph. 1:12–13). Thus, his personal ministry and writings reveal we need the fullness of the Spirit to be "complete in him [Christ]."

We may assume whoever founded the Colossian church (Epaphras or other disciples Paul trained and sent throughout Asia from his headquarters in Ephesus, Acts 19:9–10, 26), would have followed Paul's methods. So the Colossians would have interpreted Paul's declaration, "Ye are complete in him," as referring to their having received Jesus and the Spirit. Thus, they could tell their gnostic suitors, "Gentlemen, we don't need what you're promoting. We're complete in our Savior and all He's given us."

We can say the same. The wondrous, divine fullness of Christ, His Spirit, and a life lived close to Him daily completes us. Not arrogantly but humbly we can affirm we don't need any other purported deity, religion, or spiritual support system to see us through life and eternity. When appealed to by followers of Allah, Buddha, the Hindu gods, the Maitreya,[33] Mammon, the coming Beast, or any other messianic pretender, we may respond, "No thanks!" and quietly and confidently walk on, "complete in him."

2:10 Head of all authorities. For the second time in this epistle, Paul, who already declared Christ's headship over Christians (1:18), asserted Christ's supreme universal authority. Jesus is "the head of all principality and power" (2:10; cf. 1:17–18), or "head over every ruler and authority" (NLT). Or, paraphrasing, "His power extends over everything" (THE MESSAGE).

So all authorities—human, angelic, demonic—are now and forever subject to Christ as a body is to its head. Thus, Scripture assigns Him the loftiest title, "KING OF KINGS

---

33. The purported great coming teacher of the New Age movement.

AND LORD OF LORDS" (Rev. 19:16; cf. 17:14; 1 Tim. 6:14–15). Jesus proclaimed His supreme authority at His ascension: "All authority has been given to me in heaven and on earth" (Matt. 28:18, NAS). Have we pondered the implications?

If we believe His authority is supreme, we'll be supremely confident on His missions. Whatever work He puts before us, whatever ministry He assigns us, whatever difficult circumstances He leads us into, no matter what opposition we face, we'll rest knowing the consummate Authority is with us, not those who ceaselessly and senselessly reproach or resist us. Despite their worst, He will see us through, giving us all the favor, support, provision, protection, and success we need to finish His kingdom work. No longer easily intimidated, we'll grow increasingly assured, secure, poised.

Even ungodly authorities won't intimidate us. We'll respect but never fear them, honor but never cow before them. Why? We'll know Christ is their "head" (2:10). Whether they know it or not, they're subject to His will. If they wrong us, it's only because He's permitted it for His higher purposes in our lives (Rom. 8:28).[34] His grace will support us while we suffer injustice or mistreatment, and His faithfulness will ultimately turn our troubles into triumphs—for His glory, our joy, and others' instruction and encouragement in the faith

---

34. Jesus demonstrated this supreme confidence in His Father's overarching control when he informed Pilate His Father's authority trumped the governor's (John 19:10–11). Peter, John, and Paul exemplified the same when facing hostile councils and courts (Acts 4:10–13; 25:10–11). Are we ready to praisefully share this confidence that, "In the center of the circle of the will of God I stand; there can come no second causes, all must come from His dear hand." Quote is public domain content from Mrs. Charles E. Cowman, *Streams in the Desert* (Grand Rapids, MI: Zondervan Publishing House, 1965), 238.

(Phil. 1:12–14). Strengthened by this confidence, we'll go forth to spread the gospel, make disciples, and serve Christ's kingdom interests fearlessly: "Go ye, therefore, and teach all nations" (Matt. 28:19). But not foolishly.

There is a fine line between holy boldness and unholy brashness, and we must prayerfully seek to find that line and never exceed it. Christ defends us while we humbly and zealously serve His will. But if we proudly or stubbornly pursue our own initiatives independently of Him, needlessly expose ourselves to our enemies' attacks, attack them in the same unscrupulous way they do us,[35] or defy or disrespect authorities in an un-Christlike, rebellious spirit, we'll earn not His praise but His corrective punishment—often through those very authorities! Better to be humble than humbled and comforted than chastened.

And how comforting it is to know that, while submissively following Jesus' call, "all authority" is with us! His angels will assist us (Acts 12:7–11) and leaders will cooperate with us. And eventually every demon will flee (Phil. 2:9–11), critic fall silent, adversary surrender, and mountain of opposition move (Mark 11:23).[36] Why? As long as we are with Him, "the head of all principality and power" is with us.

---

35. One of the most difficult tasks Christ assigns us is to not resist enemies who resist us but rather to consistently choose to respond to their lies, plots, hypocrisy, and injustices according to His high standards, not their low behavior. Jesus' "love your enemies" teaching is the last word on this subject (Matt. 5:38–48), and our consistent, humble obedience to it marks the completion of our spiritual maturation process. Thus, Jesus appropriately closes the passage with the words, "Be ye, therefore, perfect [spiritually mature], even as your Father…is perfect" (Matt. 5:38–48; cf. Rom. 12:17–21).

36. Though they occur rarely, there are situations in which we must not only pray believingly to our Father for help (Phil. 4:6–7) but also bind, loose, and command in His authoritative name (Matt. 18:18–20; Mark 11:23) in order

2:11–13 Christian circumcision. Besides being under attack by gnostics, the Gentile Christians in Colosse were apparently being pressured to submit to circumcision by Jewish Christians or heretics influenced by the "Judaizer" doctrine.[37] Paul combated this error by explaining Christian circumcision.[38]

He described it as a divine, not a human, procedure: "The circumcision made without hands" (2:11).[39] It occurs in two stages, degrees, or depths:

1. Immediately at salvation, as Paul describes in this context (Col. 2:11–13)

2. Progressively, as we're being entirely sanctified, or fully set apart for God and His use by

---

to move the unseen forces that, like imposing mountains, defiantly block us from moving forward in Christ's kingdom will or work (Eph. 6:12). Paul not only called on God but also commanded in God (Acts 13:6–12; 16:16–18). As we walk closely with Christ His Spirit will help us discern such times (Eccl. 3:1).

37. The Judaizers were Pharisaic Christians (former Pharisees converted to Christ) who, apparently to avoid or diminish Jewish persecution, insisted that Gentiles become Jewish proselytes, and thus be circumcised, before they could become Christians. Though their doctrine was officially rejected some ten years earlier by the first church counsel (c. AD 50; Acts 15:1–29), they persisted in promoting it to the detriment and division of the church.

38. The best and only lasting remedy for falsehood is truth. Truth endures. Said the Truth incarnate, "Ye shall know the truth, and the truth shall make you free" (John 8:32). When you can do nothing else to reason with those in the grip of false doctrine, simply state, and whenever possible restate, the enduring truth in humble love and without the slightest bit of strife or contempt (Eph. 4:15). Whether they accept or reject it, they'll eventually meet it again. Paul here employed this simple method.

39. In Scripture what is done "without hands" means *without human hands* and is therefore an act of God (Dan. 2:34, 45; 8:25). Christian circumcision is further discussed in Rom. 2:25–29; Phil. 3:3.

consistently spiritual thinking and living (1
Thess. 5:23)

The very term *circumcision* immediately brings Jewish circumcision to mind. Circumcision was the prime sign of
authentic Jewishness, faith in Abraham's God, and participation in His covenant (Gen. 17:9–14). Aside from its minimal
health benefits, Jewish (physical) circumcision is ultimately
powerless to save us (1 Cor. 7:18–19) and by itself imparts
no spiritual benefit. But Christian circumcision differs from
Jewish circumcision.

Jewish circumcision is natural; Christian circumcision is
supernatural. Jewish circumcision is physical; Christian circumcision, spiritual. Jewish circumcision concerns the body;
Christian circumcision, the heart. Jewish circumcision is
performed by humans;[40] Christian circumcision, by Christ.
Jewish circumcision is irreversible; Christian circumcision
can be reversed.

Initial Christian circumcision occurs at conversion when
we experience salvation by grace alone through faith alone
in Christ alone and receive His nature and Spirit (Rom.
3:30; 4:8–11; Gal. 5:6). Thus, it has the utmost spiritual value
(Rom. 2:25–27). Receiving Christ's nature and Spirit frees
us from not the presence but the control of our old fleshly

---

40. Today some Jews allow their children to be circumcised in hospitals
by pediatricians on the second day, as is typically done in American hospitals when circumcision is requested. More Orthodox Jews often employ
the services of a (Hebrew) *mohel*, a Jew trained in *brit milah*—the surgical
and religious procedures involved in Orthodox Jewish circumcision rites.
See https://en.wikipedia.org/wiki/Mohel (accessed April 21, 2016); also see
http://www.myjewishlearning.com/article/the-mohel/ (accessed April 21,
2016).

nature and its sinful acts in our bodies, all the various "works of the flesh" (Gal. 5:19–21). The presence of Christ's imparted life and righteousness supernaturally liberates us, enabling us *not* to sin so we may now lead a life of holiness as we seek to please our wonderful, new Savior. In brief, God's grace gives us the power to control the old nature that formerly controlled us: "You were made free from the power of your sinful self" (Col. 2:11, NCV). Thus, its dominion is "circumcised," or cut away. This always produces a noticeable turning from sin in the new convert's life (1 Pet. 4:3–4). This is symbolized by our water baptism, which Paul refers to here (2:13) and which in Christianity's earliest years was usually executed immediately after conversion (Acts 2:41; 8:12–13, 36–38; 9:18; 10:47–48; 19:5).

Christian circumcision furthermore marks us as being true Jews (Rom. 8:29)—and now utterly reliant upon the faithfulness of God, not mere human goodness, wisdom, and ability (Phil. 3:3). The spiritual nature of Christian circumcision also marks Christ-rejecting ethnic Jews as being false Jews, since they reject God's only appointed spiritual Circumciser (Rom. 2:28). Foreseeing this, in the Old Testament period God called the Jewish people to circumcise their hearts (Deut. 10:16; 30:6; Jer. 4:4; 6:10; Ezek. 44:7). Today He is calling us to do so.

Since Christians still possess a sin nature and free will, and can therefore choose to sin as long as we live in our mortal bodies, God calls us to a deeper, fuller, second circumcision as Christians. Our fleshly (old, fallen) nature is not "eradicated" (eliminated or removed), as some teach. To claim this is self-deceptive (1 John 1:8) and, though rarely done, if taken to an extreme it can lead to an extraordinary state of denial that justifies obviously sinful behavior.[41] Instead, God's plan for our fleshly nature is that we "mortify" it (Rom. 8:13; Col. 3:5)—render it powerless, dormant, and *as dead*, by steadily choosing to obey Him rather than it. If the circumcision we receive at salvation eradicated our sin nature, Paul would not have charged us to circumcise or cut away ("mortify," "put off," or "put away") the sinful behavior springing from it and "put on" Christ's thoughts and ways. Yet Paul clearly and repeatedly did just this in his epistles (Rom. 8:6–13; 13:12–14; Gal. 5:16–26; Eph. 4:17–25; Col. 3:5–9). What is the "flesh" that must go?

Broadly, "flesh" is all fallen humanity, or unredeemed human stuff (Isa. 40:5–6; 49:26; Joel 2:28; Luke 3:6). Personally, our flesh is our innate Adamic or fallen nature, or "old man" (Col. 3:9), sometimes referred to simply as "sin"[42] (Rom. 7:17). Practically speaking, our flesh is *the person we were before receiving Christ* and *the person we are presently when not abiding close to Him* (John 15:5b). Our "old man" always expresses itself through the "carnal mind"—unspiritual thought patterns, or ways of thinking unrenewed by God's Spirit-inspired Word (Rom. 8:7).

---

41. A shocking and rare example of this delusion is the original Oneida Community sect that settled in Oneida, New York, in the nineteenth century, led by John H. Noyes. For more information, see https://en.wikipedia.org/wiki/John_Humphrey_Noyes (accessed April 21, 2016); also see http://www.britannica.com/biography/John-Humphrey-Noyes (accessed April 21, 2016).

42. Sin is the fallen nature with which we are all born that is inclined to disbelieve God, reject His authority, and rebel against His will. Sins are the whole range of wrong motives, thoughts, words, actions, and reactions that spring from this nature, producing behavior that displeases and dishonors God.

Our flesh nature, with all its wrong attitudes, desires, and behavior, is comprised of both higher, more refined elements and lower, cruder elements. While we all share the same fleshly nature, it expresses itself differently in each of us. Some are troubled greatly by one or more forms of flesh thought or behavior and comparatively little by others. Here are seven general manifestations of our common fleshly nature:

1. PROUD FLESH is the satanic assumption of or desire for superiority that infects us all. It seeks to be first, above, or better than others in every activity and quest and causes us to vainly imagine we are superior even when we're not. It constantly competes and refuses to complement or cooperate. Constantly comparing, it ceaselessly seeks recognition, spurns anonymity, mocks humble ones, despises contentment, and envies anyone who seems better off. Vain, it's only interested in appearance, not substance, in others opinions of itself, not God's (Prov. 6:16–17).

2. RELIGIOUS FLESH is inclined to be and act religious but worships the wrong god or the true God wrongly—that is, in its own way, as Cain did, not in God's requested way (Gen. 4:1–5, 7; Acts 17:22–23; Rom. 10:1–3; Heb. 11:4). Inspiring and sustaining all false religions, and false Christianity, religious flesh worships purported deities with devotion, zeal, good works, rituals, rigors (asceticism), and sacrifices but

does not recognize the deity and sole saviorship of Jesus Christ (Phil. 3:4–6). Or, it professes to worship Him but does so in ways contrary to New Testament teaching (Gal. 3:1–5; 4:9–11; Col. 2:16–17, 18, 20–23).

3. IDEALISTIC FLESH, springing from the remnants of Adam's original goodness, inspires uplifting but nonbiblical human optimism. In songs, poems, or essays it naively envisions an elusive human utopia and inspires praise of political or social leaders who we hope will lead us there. But it always ignores the problem of sin, the solution of the Cross, and the lordship of Christ (Acts 17:28). It inspires high ideals but cannot save.

4. INTELLECTUAL FLESH inspires secular humanistic philosophies and intellectualism. It believes unaided human reason and scientific methods can discover all truth apart from biblical revelation. Consequently, it rejects or mocks biblical statements when they don't seem plausible to reason, putting human intellect above heavenly inspiration, man's word above God's. It also inspires dead Christian intellectualism— born-again Christians focusing excessively on theology, doctrinal debate, creeds, and academic Bible study and forgetting the greater importance of personal devotion to Jesus, worship, obedience, and loving fellowship with all

genuine believers, including those with different opinions.

5. INDEPENDENT FLESH inspires individualism and creates a perceived world of self within the larger real world. This self-centered spirit inspires people to live to serve, preserve, and prosper themselves without regard for others' welfare. It is stubbornly, sometimes fiercely independent, idolizing self-sufficiency, refusing assistance, idealizing isolation, downplaying fellowship, and ignoring the fact that without others we're incomplete.

6. WORLDLY FLESH produces blind, thoughtless, slavish conformity to whatever is popular or glamorous in our society. It's the bandwagon mentality, doing whatever we see others do merely because they're doing or promoting it—in politics, social movements, fads, fashion, or other new things on the worldly scene (1 Sam. 8:5b). The committed Christian will not blindly conform to the latest rage or fad (Rom. 12:2; 1 John 2:15), nor blindly reject it without pausing to see, as sometimes occurs, if it does have real value or meaning.

7. LUSTFUL FLESH encourages the immediate and unrestrained gratification of all bodily desires—for sex, food, addictions, comforts, or other carnal cravings—with no regard for the consequences. This is unrefined, fallen humanity in its most degraded condition. It is

self-indulgence and sensuality deified and the ruin of many a person, marriage, family, and society (cf. Rom. 1:24–27; Gal. 5:19).

We often overlook the first six forms of flesh while condemning the seventh, but full spiritual circumcision occurs when we turn from them all. God will never accept any "flesh" as "good" (Rom. 7:18).[43]

Therefore His Word bids us cut off all flesh (Col. 3:5–9). This deeper, more permanent circumcision of the heart—entire sanctification—occurs gradually as we radically adjust our thinking by steadfastly reading, studying, and most importantly obeying God's Word (Rom. 12:2). This joyful voluntary immersion in pondering and practicing biblical truth changes our perspective. Increasingly we make decisions through the lens of God's Word and so come into fuller agreement with His mind on all issues. The further this progresses, the more Christ our Circumciser, by His Spirit, operates on our soul to remove our fleshly thinking. As a result, we become increasingly "spiritually minded" (Rom. 8:6)—and a fully circumcised Christian with "the circumcision made without hands" (Col. 2:11). The issue then is, Will we continue?

Sadly but undeniably, due to offenses, temptations, or other disillusionments some Christians turn back to unspiritual living. Thus, their flesh life reasserts itself, and their spiritual interests, thinking, and conduct wanes. In some cases, this continues to their tragic end (2 Pet. 2:19–22). However, like the

---

43. Christ had no sin nature and thus was the only truly intrinsically, entirely "good" man since Adam's original condition before the Fall (Matt. 19:16–17; John 2:24–25; Heb. 4:15).

Israelites at Gilgal, they may be recircumcised if they repudiate and abandon the fleshly thinking and habits they have allowed to slowly creep back into their lives.[44] Why is this important?

As at Gilgal, it removes the "reproach of Egypt" from us (Josh. 5:9). This reproach is threefold. First, God's grief and reproach over our carnality ends (cf. Rev. 2:4; 3:1; 3:15–16). Second, unbelievers can no longer justly reproach us because we're walking in the Spirit, like Christ, and neither misbehaving nor reacting to them with unspiritual attitudes. Third, we're freed from the self-reproach that so persistently harasses our consciences when we "walk...after the flesh" rather than in the Spirit (Rom. 8:1). And as our reproach rolls away, God's rewards roll in.

There are tremendous benefits to spiritual circumcision and recircumcision. It pleases God, liberates Christ in us, sanctifies us and our churches, and fully releases the Spirit and His power among us. And, most importantly, it enables us to experience full spiritual victory and enter our promised land: spiritual maturity! Just before Israel's Canaan conquest, God ordered Joshua to circumcise the people (Josh. 5:2). Then He gave them one victory after another as they possessed the land to His honor and their joy! The same thing had occurred forty years earlier. After Moses ordered his second son circumcised at the inn by the way (Exod. 4:24–26), God

---

44. Literally, of course, individuals cannot be physically recircumcised. But Scripture explains that Israel's national recircumcision was necessary for the younger generation born in the wilderness who had not been circumcised, as their fathers' generation had been (Josh. 5:2–9). Once these young men were circumcised, God considered the entire nation recircumcised, or restored to a purified, flesh-free condition. For Christians, however, after our spiritual circumcision we may slip back into unspiritual thinking and living and thus need recircumcision (Gal. 3:1; 5:1).

released him to lead Israel's great triumph over Pharaoh: the Exodus!

Need a victory, a lift, a rallying, an exodus, or deliverance from the oppression of defeat, fruitlessness, or hopelessness? Perhaps this very note is timely for you. Is the Spirit calling you to your Gilgal or inn by the way? Ready to roll away your reproach and be released for your next triumph? What spiritual victories will follow for your joy and God's honor if you abandon all your flesh and start consistently thinking and living after the Spirit (Gal. 5:16)?

2:14–15 Jesus our Triumphator—and His triumph! Paul said Jesus didn't stop at circumcising our flesh and forgiving our sins (2:13). He completely deactivated the Mosaic Law and all its regulations, which we struggled with and habitually broke, "blotting out the handwriting of ordinances that was against us" (2:14). Let's review how He did this.

At His baptism Jesus officially identified with sinful humanity (Matt. 3:13–15). He confirmed that oneness in Gethsemane and carried it to Calvary. So when the Romans nailed Him to the cross, they nailed all of us with Him— and all our sins, heavenly indictments, and sin-debts! Jesus died there in our stead to pay ("blot out," or cancel, 2:14) all our debts to God and indictments for violating His Law (the "ordinances"), for which violations we had been justly charged by heaven's court and maliciously condemned by hell's devils.

The "handwriting of ordinances" (Col. 2:14) which Jesus cancelled has a threefold application: (1) to all the Mosaic commands as given originally by God, but especially the burdensome Pharisaic expansion of them to 613 regulations (according to the Talmud); (2) to the indictment against us individually or the listing of rules we have personally broken, with their legal penalty (death); and (3) a listing of the massive sin-debt we owe God for breaking His regulations (cf. Matt. 18:23–27).

This key phrase is therefore variously translated:

> The handwriting of requirements that was against us…
> —COLOSSIANS 2:14, NKJV

> The written code with its regulations…
> —COLOSSIANS 2:14, NIV

> The record of the charges against us…
> —COLOSSIANS 2:14, NLT

> The debt which listed all the rules we failed to follow…
> —COLOSSIANS 2:14, NCV

> The record of debt that stood against us with its legal demands…
> —COLOSSIANS 2:14, ESV

Regarding our debt one commentator notes:

> The Jewish people believed that their sins were forgiven when they repented; records of sins would be blotted out on the annual Day of Atonement. Paul says the atonement occurred when the debt was nailed to the cross in Christ and thus paid.[45]

---

45. Keener, *The IVP Bible Background Commentary: New Testament*, Col 2:13–14, note.

Thus, Jesus' substitutionary death terminated and removed the Jewish ceremonial law's authority over us, or "took it out of the way, nailing it to his cross" (2:14). Has the gravity of this settled upon us? Nailed to Jesus' cross, the Mosaic ordinances are no longer in effect, their righteousness fulfilled and penalties paid in full forever by Him. So was the Law futile?

In other epistles Paul explained that, far from being a waste, the Law has served its purpose well. Like a school master, it has taught us vital truths and principles about God's nature, His will, righteousness, sin, judgment, worship, (and by its many types, shadows, and prophecies) Jesus, His kingdom, the Christian life, heaven, and numerous other New Testament realities. Thus, our "schoolmaster," having completed its divine mission, was at Calvary retired. There it also brought us to our new, eternal Master, Christ (Gal. 3:23–25; Rom. 7:4–6). Christians now may be justified, sanctified, know God intimately, and grow spiritually mature by faith, with the assistance of God's Spirit and Word and without perpetuating the legalistic elements of Jewish ceremonial law.

Also, by "blotting out the handwriting of ordinances," Christ has forever changed our condition and Satan's. Let's review this.

Previously Satan and his demonic "principalities and powers" (2:15) controlled us through our fleshly nature and sins and oppressed us by condemning us for breaking God's Law. But now, with our sins cancelled and Christ's righteousness imputed to us and manifested in us as we walk in obedience to His Spirit (Rom. 8:2–4), their control over us is "spoiled" (Col. 2:15, literally, "stripped, disarmed"[46]). Our former spiritual oppressors are left with no spiritual weapons or means of deceiving, oppressing, or harming us—*if* we abide in Christ (John 15:1–8)! As long as we "walk in the Spirit" (Gal. 5:16) they can neither control nor condemn us (Rom. 8:1). But that's not all.

While formerly lording over us, Satan was in a triumphant position, we were in bondage, and Christ was insufficiently honored. But now the situation is reversed. Thanks to the Cross and Resurrection, Satan is defeated, we are liberated, and Christ our Victor is properly exalted. Paul joyfully declared, "He [Jesus] made a show [humiliating spectacle] of them [Satan's principalities and powers] openly, triumphing over them" (2:15). His carefully chosen words "openly triumphing over them"[47] introduce Christ our Triumphator.[48] Let's go further.

Before Jesus' death there was no way opened into God's holy presence for sinful humanity. All had sinned (Rom. 3:23), and so none could enter. The righteous (Jewish) dead, though justified by faith in the Law's promise of a coming Lamb and reserved in the paradisiacal "bosom" of Abraham in Sheol, were still denied entrance to heaven and thus subject to Satan's limitations (Heb. 2:14b). (In Jewish thinking,

46. Swanson, *Dictionary of Biblical Languages with Semantic Domains: Greek (New Testament)*, s.v. "*apekdyomai*."

47. Remember there was no punctuation in the original Greek manuscripts of the New Testament. Thus, I've used none in this quote to better make the point.

48. A triumphator was a Roman general who, after achieving a great victory for Rome, was given its highest honor: an elaborate victory parade in Rome.

Sheol was the "place to which people descended at death,"[49] or the abode of deceased souls, made up of two radically different areas: "Abraham's bosom" for the redeemed [Luke 16:22] and "hell" for the lost [Luke 16:23–24].) Since Satan was still fallen humanity's master due to the submission of its federal head, Adam (Rom. 5:2; 6:16), he wouldn't release (nor would God's holiness permit) the Old Testament believers to enter the Father's full presence. This continued until Christ *triumphed* over "him that had the power of death ['authority over death' (WEY) or the dead], that is, the devil" (Heb. 2:14b) by dying for us on the cross, atoning for our sins, rising for our justification, and offering His blood on heaven's altar (Heb. 9:24–26).

After His death, Jesus descended to Sheol and freed the righteous dead from their temporary confinement to Satan in Abraham's bosom. Then, after His resurrection, He led them in a great victory parade into heaven and God's holy presence (Eph. 4:8–10; Ps. 68:18). While we know few details about this spectacular, unprecedented celestial event, it appears Jesus' victory parade was in some respects similar to a Roman triumph.

When Roman generals won a great victory in foreign lands, they were awarded an elaborate, prestigious victory parade—or triumph—in Rome. The victorious general, beautifully crowned and clad and riding a four-horse chariot, led his unarmed army clad in white robes through Rome's main streets before cheering throngs.[50] His entou-

---

49. Thomas, *New American Standard Hebrew–Aramaic and Greek Dictionaries*, updated edition, s.v. "*sheol.*"

50. By some accounts, a slave rode with the triumphator, periodically reminding him he was still a mortal and not a god so as to minimize his

rage was followed by a humiliated sampling of his chained, vanquished foes and carts full of exotic spoils and animals from the subjugated land. This grand parade continued all the way to Jupiter's temple on Capitoline Hill, where he honored the chief deity with sacrifices for (supposedly) giving him victory. Banquets, games, and other entertainments accompanied this joyful national celebration. Thereafter the general received the most distinguished title "triumphator" (originally *vir triumphalis*, or "man of triumph").[51]

When Christ our Triumphator led the liberated souls of the righteous into heaven, the demons didn't follow His procession, but they surely stood by, watching helplessly as He led a vast multitude of their former captives on a rapturous exodus from Sheol to heaven.[52] God hinted at this

---

pride and prevent any attempt at seizing imperial power. In the day of our victories, may Christ send His sober-minded love-slaves to keep us mindful of our true status, devoted to His praise, and pursuing the course He's assigned us...till He comes (Rom. 12:3; Gal. 6:3; 1 Pet. 5:5–6).

51. The tradition of the Roman triumph continues in the Western world to this day. In America, it has taken the form of ticker-tape parades in New York City, which have become our traditional way of honoring great generals—from Pershing to Eisenhower to MacArthur—after significant foreign triumphs.

52. Christ's triumph is not to be confused with His preaching *by the Spirit* through Noah (as He did through the prophets and does through Christian ministers today, 1 Pet. 1:10–11; 2 Pet. 1:21) to the wicked generation living before the Flood. Those souls are in hell *now* for rejecting Noah's (and by the Spirit, Christ's) preaching of "righteousness" *then* (1 Pet. 3:19–20; 2 Pet. 2:5). Jesus did not, as some claim, convert anyone through His "preaching" in Sheol, which wasn't an offer of salvation to the wicked dead but was rather a joyful announcement of the liberation His Cross had won for the righteous dead. Scripture nowhere promises one's spiritual status may change after death but rather asserts only divine assessment or "judgment" (Heb. 9:27)—not another chance at conversion—follows physical expiration. This underscores the importance of Christians interceding for the lost and

mighty release of the righteous dead when, immediately after Jesus' resurrection, "many" of "the saints that slept" (righteous Jews) were resurrected and permitted to visit many of their living family and friends in Jerusalem (Matt. 27:50–53). Christ also alluded to His glorious triumph when later declaring "all authority...in heaven and in earth" was fully and forever His (Matt. 28:18).[53] Glad Christ is your personal Triumphator? So am I.

But there's more good news. You can participate in His next Triumph! After He and His armies defeat Antichrist at Armageddon, overcomers will "walk with [Him] in white" (Rev. 3:4) as He rides victoriously down Jerusalem's main street to His yet-to-be-constructed temple, is coronated King of kings, and begins His thousand-year reign. How can you qualify for participation? Abide closely to Him, walk in the Spirit, and let this vision of Jesus' past and future triumphs inspire you, His faithful soldier, to conquer every test of faith, endurance, and loyalty He puts before you. Rise and overcome. Your Triumphator awaits.

---

being faithful witnesses of Christ and His gospel now in this time.

53. In a very different allusion to a Roman triumph, Paul said the many public indignities and abuse he and other apostles suffered from satanically inspired enemies (cf. Acts 14:19; 16:19–24, 37; 19:26; 21:27–31) made it seem that, albeit temporarily, the prince of this world had won a great triumph over them! Satan had seemingly forced them to march as a humiliating "spectacle" at the end of his triumph parade as if they were his vanquished enemies and spoils of spiritual war (1 Cor. 4:9–13). But Paul, strengthened by God's grace, willingly suffered these painful humiliations to continue blessing Christ's people and finish his course. Why? He knew Christ, the General of heaven's armies, would one day turn the tables and in His kingdom grant Paul the inestimable honor of "walk[ing] with me in white" (Rev. 3:4) in Christ's ultimate Triumph following His final, grandest conquest at Armageddon (Rev. 17:14; 19:14; cf. Matt. 25:31, 34).

2:16 Not one bit! Paul's injunction, "Let no man, therefore, judge you" (2:16), is a little confusing. We can't stop over-zealous religious people from passing judgment on us for ignoring their petty, self-appointed rules. But we cannot, and must not, let their rejections affect us. Paul was saying, "Don't adopt their criticisms. Don't yield to their demands any more than Jesus did the Pharisees' self-initiated legislations."[54] Or, simply, "Don't let them change your walk. Not one bit!"

This is another apostolic charge to "Stand fast, therefore, in the liberty wherewith Christ hath made us free, and be not entangled again with the yoke of bondage" (Gal. 5:1). Specifically, Paul had in view the bonds of legalism (2:16–17, 20–21), asceticism (2:23), and idolatry, which he warned, if continued, would result in loss of rewards (2:18). There's another bondage he didn't address here.

We Christians often misjudge and reject each other because our ways of worship differ. Remarkably, Christ required only that we worship "in spirit and in truth" (John 4:24) and left no specific, authoritative instructions on how to do so. We gain general instruction from Acts, Paul's epistles (1 Cor. 14; 16:1–2; 2 Tim. 4:1–4), and the history of the church (especially the early church; also called "primitive" or "ante-Nicene") and teachings of its fathers, but these at best offer suggestive examples. We correctly imitate their patterns as biblical traditions but err if we insist they are biblical imperatives (only John 4:24 uses the term "must" regarding

---

54. Hoping to awaken them, Jesus deliberately targeted the Pharisees' fastidious traditions (Luke 6:6–10). Centuries later, the Reformers refused to observe Catholicism's sacrosanct traditions (praying to saints, using icons), rituals (mass), idolatry (venerating Mary, the Pope), and sacraments because they were not grounded in Scripture.

our worship). Though all biblical examples of worship have authority and are instructive, justifying whoever imitates them, none dictate a single fixed order of worship to which we must all adhere. So the New Testament is largely silent on this topic—and many feel compelled to fill in the gap with their own sanctified wisdom.

God, however, seems content to leave worship methodology largely up to us. We do well to remember, "More important than how we worship is that we worship Christ."[55] We must be generous in allowing churches to worship "in spirit and in truth" according to their consciences and neither condemn their way nor try to force ours upon them. Therefore we may extend Paul's injunction to say, "Don't be intimidated when other Christians' criticize your way of worship. Worship as you feel the Bible teaches and Spirit witnesses—and let them do the same." But this won't stop your critics.

Zealous legalists, heretics, and amateur worship critics are, if anything, incurably nosey. In a heat of religious pride, they insist on imposing their scruples on others. When they openly or subtly press you, don't yield to their pressures but instead determinedly maintain your spiritual freedom, walking, serving, and worshiping by your understanding of God's Word, not men's rules (Matt. 15:9; Mark 7:1–13, esp. 7–9; Titus 1:14). This is easier said than done.

Even Peter yielded on one occasion to relentless, judgmental heretics, for which error Paul quickly corrected him (Gal. 2:11–14). Don't imitate Peter's capitulation. Hold Paul's line: Don't let the frowns of legalists or heretics change your

---

55. *Life Application Study Bible,* Col. 2:16–17, note, 2032.

free, joyful Christian beliefs, walk, work, or worship. Not one bit!

2:16–17 Shadows and substance. Paul said the regulations and ordinances of the Mosaic Law were a "shadow [foreshadowing] of things to come."[56] The "substance" (NAS), or "reality" (NIV), or "what is true and real" (NCV), is ours now in Christ as we live daily in His Word, Spirit, church, and ways of life and worship.

Paul's argument is irrefutable: If you have the real article, you don't need shadows or images of it anymore. The writer to the Hebrews agreed, teaching us the Law, including its foreshadowings, could not make us "perfect"—render us spiritually mature, or fully developed and complete in our worship, work, and walk with God (Heb. 10:1).

Here is a list of the "shadows" Paul cites in this context and a brief description of the New Testament realities of which they speak:

- "FOOD" (2:16, NKJV): This speaks of the Law's dietary restrictions, which established clean and unclean foods (Lev. 11:1–47; Col. 2:21). The New Testament reality is (a) food cannot save, damn, or spiritually defile or improve a believer's soul (Matt. 15:10–20; Rom. 14:17); (b) for believers all foods are sanctified by prayer, thanksgiving, and God's Word (1 Tim. 4:4–5); and (c) we are to avoid eating only unbled

---

56. The writer to the Hebrews agreed that the ordinances of the Mosaic Law are "the example and shadow of heavenly things" (Heb. 8:5; 10:1).

meats or any foods we know have been offered to idols (Acts 15:29; 1 Cor. 10:25–29).

- "Drink" (2:16): The Law forbade drinking of blood (Lev. 3:17; 7:26–27) and (implicitly) wine or other libations offered to idols (a form of idol worship, Exod. 32:6). The New Testament repeats these prohibitions and, while not ordering abstinence, warns us excessive drinking (drunkenness) renders us spiritually unfit for Christ's return (Luke 21:34–36).

- "Feast day[s]" (2:16): Israel's seven annual festivals (Lev. 23:1–43)[57] ordained in the Torah speak of key New Testament realities:

    1. Passover (Lev. 23:4–5): This celebration of salvation calls for the offering of the paschal lamb and saving application of its blood (Exod. 12:1–28). It speaks of Christ the "Lamb of God" (John 1:29, 36), or "Christ, our passover" who was "sacrificed for us" at Passover (1 Cor. 5:7), and whose blood alone saves us from eternal death when we repent and believe on Him.

    2. Unleavened Bread (Lev. 23:6–8): During this celebration of holiness only unleavened bread was eaten. This speaks of

---

57. Two other feasts currently celebrated by Jews worldwide, Purim and Hanukkah, originated after the writing of the Torah (Pentateuch) to honor God for delivering the Jews from Haman's genocide and helping them retake and rededicate their temple during the Maccabean period.

our need and willingness, after salvation by the Lamb's blood, to be sanctified by putting the leaven of sin out of our hearts, lives, families, and churches (2 Cor. 7:1; 1 Pet. 1:15–16). Jesus is our unleavened (sinless) "bread of life" (John 6:35).

3. FIRST FRUITS (Lev. 23:9–14): This celebration of the beginning of the (God's[58]) barley harvest, occurring on the third day after Passover, speaks of the beginning of the kingdom harvest. The sheaf of barley waived to the Lord by the high priest symbolizes "Christ the firstfruits" of the resurrection and the kingdom, who rose the third day (1 Cor. 15:33; Col. 1:18).

4. WEEKS (PENTECOST) (Lev. 23:15–22): This celebration of the wheat harvest, occurring fifty days (seven weeks and a day) after First Fruits, speaks of the advent of the Holy Spirit in power upon Christ's followers in the Upper Room fifty days after Christ's resurrection (Acts 2:1–4), which marked the birth of the body of Christ and church age. The two loaves offered to God during this festival symbolized the

---

58. The land was God's, the people were God's, thus their harvest was God's (Ps. 24:1). The people acknowledged this by "waiving" a sheaf of barley before the Lord (Lev. 23:11), thus symbolically consecrating it and the rest of the harvest to Him. Do we remember to "waive" our blessings before the Lord to acknowledge they are His and He alone has graciously given them to us?

two people groups, Jews and Gentiles, that would comprise the church. The unifying work of the Holy Spirit is seen in that the harvest was no longer "separate growths loosely bound together" but was now, as loaves of baked bread, "a real union of particles making one homogeneous body" in Christ.[59]

5. TRUMPETS (Lev. 23:23–25): This festival of regathering (Rosh Hashanah) is marked by the blowing of trumpets throughout the land to signal a great "convocation" (Lev. 23:24) after a long period of separation (since Pentecost). This symbolizes the Rapture, when Christ will blow His trumpet to regather Christians scattered throughout the world and in heaven unto Himself, thus terminating the church age (1 Cor. 15:51–52; 1 Thess. 4:13–18; cf. Rev. 4:1–2). The long interval between Pentecost and Trumpets symbolizes the lengthy period of the church age from Pentecost to the Rapture.[60] This beginning of the new year in Israel symbolizes our beginning of a new life at the Rapture—

---

59. Scofield, *The New Scofield Study Bible*, Lev. 23:16, note, 157.

60. According to one source, the Jewish priest would blow a trumpet to signal the people to leave their work in the fields and come to the temple for worship. What a beautiful picture of Jesus signaling to Christians worldwide to leave our fields of service to gather together to worship Him in heaven (cf. Rev. 4–5).

in Christ's presence "forever" (1 Thess. 4:17b, NIV).

6. DAY OF ATONEMENT (Lev. 23:26–32): This (Yom Kippur) is a convocation of conviction. The people gathered to grieve over their sinfulness and present to God an offering "made by fire" (23:27). This festival speaks symbolically of our place and day of atonement, the Cross. There, as Jesus' disciples grieved over betraying and forsaking Him, He offered Himself in fiery passion as an atoning sacrifice for sin (1 John 2:2). It also looks forward. Shortly after the Rapture, a repentant remnant of ethnic Jews in Israel (and worldwide) will grieve when they realize, stunned by the church's sudden, publicly predicted translation, Jesus is their Messiah after all (Rev. 7:1–8). This will spark a great revival as many Jews receive the Atonement (Christ and His saving blood) and many Gentiles, seeing this, also come to Him (Zech. 8:20–23; Rev. 7:9–17). Thus, as Daniel foresaw, God will "put an end to their [Israel's] sin" and "atone for their guilt" (Dan. 9:24, NLT).[61] Then, finally, Israel will be ready for the kingdom.

---

61. The Antichrist-worshiping world that fully and finally rejects the good news of God's proffered atonement through the revived Jewish remnant (Rev. 7:1–8) will experience the full and final wrath of His judgment in the trumpet and bowl judgments of the Great Tribulation (Rev. 8–9, 16; 2

7. TABERNACLES (INGATHERING) (Lev. 23:33–44): This celebration is memorial and prophetic. For eight days the Jews gathered in Jerusalem, built small huts (booths, tabernacles) with branches, and lived in them to commemorate God's faithful provision, protection, and presence among them in the wilderness. This also foreshadows the time they will live (tabernacle) with Him in the millennial kingdom (the Day of the Lord, Zech. 14:16–17) and later, the eternal kingdom (New Jerusalem, Rev. 21–22). Christians will also share these glorious periods of blissful cohabitation with God.[62] This festival came to be known as Ingathering since it coincided with the fruit harvest.

- "NEW MOON" (2:16): Israel's calendar was lunar-based. Every new moon the Jews observed festivities marking and celebrating the beginning of a new month (Isa. 1:13). Since, unlike the seven festivals, these were not ordered in Scripture, it's difficult to assign any meaningful symbolism to the new moon rituals.

- "SABBATH DAYS" (2:16): Every seventh day was a divinely establish Sabbath, or day of total rest

---

Thess. 2:10–12) and, ultimately, Armageddon (Rev. 19:11–21).

62. I've used some information about Jewish feasts from the very informative Web site *Hebrew for Christians*. See http://hebrew4christians.com/Holidays/Introduction/introduction.html (accessed February 19, 2016).

ordered by the Law (Exod. 20:9–11). Mercifully,
by requiring the Jews "not do any work,"
the Sabbath was designed to maximize their
quality of life by providing a day for much-
needed physical recuperation (Exod. 20:10).
It also honored God by memorializing His
resting from His labors on the seventh creative
day (Exod. 20:11). Symbolically, the Sabbath
represents our soul-rest in Christ. This occurs
when we cease trying to earn salvation by good
or religious works and accept Christ's finished
work in our behalf on the cross, thus resting
or reposing in faith in Him. Our Sabbath is
not any day of the week, seventh or first,[63] but
rather the entire church age, during which we
rest in Christ every day (Heb. 4:3–11).

Paul cited these legalistic particulars because they were
among those heretics were trying to persuade the Colossians
to adopt and, as stated, he insisted none were binding on
Christians. But there are other Old Testament passages not
part of the Mosaic Law that, while not binding, nevertheless greatly enrich us when by prayerful study we glean vital
truths from them for our lives. Let's consider some.

The mission of Abraham's servant to find, test, and retrieve
a suitable bride for his son (Gen. 24:1–67) symbolizes the
Holy Spirit's mission in this age—to find a bride church

---

63. Our first-day worship services are based on Christian tradition honoring the "Lord's day," or the day Christ rose from the dead (Luke 24:1–6;
Acts 20:7; 1 Cor. 16:2; Rev. 1:10). We are free to worship Christ this day or
any other so long as we neither believe this saves us or renders us spiritually
superior, nor condemn Christians who worship on other days.

for God's Son and bring her to Him in heaven. Moses and Aaron's epic confrontation with the oppressor Pharaoh foreshadow the final standoff between Antichrist and God's "two witnesses" (Rev. 11:3–6). The Psalms foreshadow Christians' innermost thoughts, emotions, and trust as we struggle with enemies, tests, defeats, delays, sorrows, and besetting sins. They also foreshadow Christ: Psalm 22 foretells His redemptive sufferings; Psalm 23, His present ministry as our Good Shepherd; Psalm 24, His return in glorious power to establish His kingdom.

Many of the Israelites' wilderness experiences foreshadow our experiences in the wilderness of this world (1 Cor. 10:11). The tabernacle design and use foreshadow truths about the church, our worship, and heaven. Israel's manna-bread in the wilderness speaks of Jesus, our "bread of life" in this world (John 6:35, 48), and all God's Word (Matt. 4:4). Israel's water from the rock speaks of our life-sustaining baptism and refillings with the Holy Spirit, and the biblical insights He gives, all of which come from our smitten Rock, Christ (John 4:13–15; 7:37–39; Acts 2:32–33). The Canaan conquest foreshadows our challenges in passing from elementary to mature Christianity and the nature of the spiritual warfare we face as intercessors (Eph. 6:10–18) and disciples committed to fully doing God's will.

King Saul's envy-inspired persecution of David explains many power struggles that trouble and divide ministers and churches. David foreshadows the "son of David," Christ (Matt. 21:9). The first part of Solomon's reign foreshadows Christ's glorious kingdom. David's men who faithfully shared his wilderness testing and later become respected leaders or warriors ("mighty men") in his realm represent overcomers who, for remaining faithful to Christ in testing, will be made honored leaders in His kingdom (Luke 22:28–30; Rev. 2:26–27; 3:21).

Israel's Babylonian captivity, which was caused by idolatry, speaks of the spiritual captivity that follows when any nation or church idolizes power and wealth more than God's truth and righteousness.[64] The post-exile rebuilding of the temple and walls of Jerusalem prefigure the rebuilding and reviving of the church from the Reformation forward. Nehemiah and Ezra represent uncompromising ministers and scholars dedicated to that great work. The Garden of Eden foreshadows the garden (paradise) of God in New Jerusalem. The fall of Lucifer due to pride foreshadows the inevitable demise of proud Christians, ministers, and political leaders (Luke 10:17–20). Israel's false and true prophets reveal key truths about false and true Christians, chiefly their readiness, or refusal, to suffer for speaking God's truth (Luke 6:20–23; James 5:10–11). Ahab and Jezebel foreshadow respectively weak leaders manipulated by unscrupulous, strong-willed wives. The sons of Issachar foreshadow Christian leaders gifted with exceptional insight into their times and wisdom to know how we should address them. The Song of Solomon foreshadows the sweet love of believers for Christ and His passion for them. Instead of breeding legalism, all these "shadows" bring inspiration. They are priceless biblical truths Paul would have us treasure, not trash.

While none dictate behavior mandatory for salvation, by studying them we better understand the substance or reality of Christian life. Like the different levels of precious findings

---

64. This is particularly evident in the decline of the Roman church from the time of Constantine to the Reformation.

buried in an archaeological tell, these inspired histories contain layers of insights that help us understand the characters, incidents, and trends we meet and give us hope of many wonderful "things to come" (John 16:13). This affirms, "All scripture is given by inspiration of God" and is highly "profitable" for our instruction (2 Tim. 3:16–17). The lesson here?

Don't live in or for Israel's legalistic shadows any more. We don't need them since we're living their reality every day in Christ! But ever search and ponder the Old Testament's truth-laden foreshadowings and be inspired by their rich insights.

2:18 On loss of rewards. Paul warned the Colossians if they worshiped angels (idolatry), they would lose rewards (2:18).[65] Whether all or part of their rewards would be lost he didn't say, but loss was certain.

"Let no man beguile you" (2:18). "Beguile" is translated from the Greek verb *katabrabeuō*, which describes a judge or umpire disqualifying a contestant in an athletic competition for some infraction of the rules, thus judging them unworthy and therefore depriving them of a reward.[66] It is rendered "disqualify" in some versions (ESV, NIV, NCV). Paul taught Timothy the same, namely, that we must keep God's biblical rules if we hope to be rewarded at the end of our earthly race: "If a man also strive for masteries, yet is he not crowned, except he strive lawfully" (2 Tim. 2:5); or, "Athletes cannot win the prize unless they follow the rules" (NLT).

---

65. As stated in the Introduction, the gnostics taught there was a bridge of angelic and other intermediaries between God and humanity and for this mediatorial work they should be worshiped (ct. 1 Tim. 2:5).

66. See Louw and Nida, *Greek-English Lexicon of the New Testament: Based on Semantic Domains*, electronic ed. of the 2nd edition, s.v. "*katabrabeuō.*"

While Paul addressed idolatry here, specifically angel worship,[67] the larger point is *sin disqualifies*. Christians who impenitently hold or practice any form of sin (sinful attitudes, motives, desires, behavior, [false] doctrine) will lose not their grace-given salvation but part or all of their works-based rewards in Christ (1 Cor. 3:12–15). John also warns we may lose part of our rewards, in his context, for believing and obeying false teachings (2 John 8).

Though an unpleasant subject, it's one we need to know not later but now, while we can still do something about it. Awareness that our Christian rewards, once earned by good works, can be lost by bad works should be a tonic. It should stir us to fear God, seek His Word-truth, respect His holiness, take obedience very seriously, embrace tests, and begin hoping for and working toward eternal rewards now in this life rather than merely craving more temporal rewards in this world (2 Cor. 5:9). This will round out our faith.

We already believe for every righteous seed-word or seed-act we sow God will one day reward us with a harvest (Ps. 126:5–6; Isa. 55:10–11; Gal. 6:7). We believe God is "a rewarder of them that diligently seek him" (Heb. 11:6). We believe God is "not unrighteous to forget your work and labor of love" we have shown in ministering to His people (Heb. 6:10). We believe our "labor is not in vain [without merit or reward] in the Lord" (1 Cor. 15:58). We believe obeying God's Word brings "great

---

67. We may not worry about angel worship tempting us. But if even the apostle John, who had repeatedly seen and worshiped Christ in his eternal divine glory (Rev. 1:10–17; 5:5–14), could be moved to prostrate himself before an angel (Rev. 19:10; 22:8), it behooves us to remember to in every way appreciate yet in no way venerate the supernatural beings God has assigned to help us in our arduous trek through this treacherous world (Heb. 1:14).

reward" (Ps. 19:11). We believe Christ will assess and reward us for our works in heaven (Rom. 14:10; 2 Cor. 5:10). And we believe this will occur soon after Jesus appears: "Behold, I come quickly, and my reward is with me" (Rev. 22:12). But we need one more conviction to complete the circle of our beliefs.

We also need to believe we can lose part or all of our rewards if we walk in disobedience to God. We can't precisely predict what or how great those losses may be, but we can be sure we'll lose rewards: some, most, all? And for eternity! May this sobering conviction—obedience matters! rewards are not automatic!—jar us out of our naïve acquiescence in disobedience and stir us to be alert and diligent in our personal obedience and God-given work or ministry. Let's joyfully keep God's rules and finish our race without disqualification!

2:18–19 Holding the Head. For the third time in this letter Paul asserted Christ's headship over "all the body" (2:19; cf. 1:18; 2:10). He concluded the angel-worshiping heretics mentioned earlier had never learned, or had forgotten, the headship of Christ. They were "not holding fast to the Head" (2:19, ESV); or had "lost connection with the Head" (NIV); or were not "keeping in touch with that Head" (MOFFATT). This was the primary reason they had been deceived by, and were now deceiving others with, wrong doctrines.

No minor point, Christ's headship over every church and Christian is proclaimed seven times in the New Testament (1 Cor. 11:3; Eph. 1:22–23; 4:15–16; 5:23–24; Col. 1:18; 2:10, 19). Have we gotten the message?

Are we allowing Jesus to have full sway over every aspect of our lives? Is He by His Word's authority and Spirit's guidance exerting His benevolent control over us daily? For this we must (1) be free from the ensnaring, controlling fear of man (Prov. 29:25); and (2) never submit to any minister, however widespread his authority or traditional his office, claiming to be head of the church. Like every human body, Christ's spiritual body has only one Head. So, Paul argued, we mustn't submissively venerate angels—or apostles, bishops, popes,[68] or other puffed-up leaders—posing as our head (or supposed "covering"). Christ alone is our Head, Lord, and Covering (Phil. 2:11)[69] and we must hold Him close!

---

68. Catholics regard the Bishop of Rome (Pope) as the "visible head" of the worldwide church who, as the purported Vicar of Christ, represents its invisible Head, Jesus. Yet nowhere does Scripture assign even the remotest form of headship to any mere human—apostle, bishop, father, or minister—but only and repeatedly to the divine Son, Jesus. The Bishop of Rome is unquestionably the head of the Roman Catholic organization, but Christ alone is Head of the worldwide body of Christ.

69. Though a charismatic evangelical, I don't see covering theology authorized in Scripture. Christ, and no man, is our "covering," to whom we must account hourly, and we will be assessed by ultimately, and who alone protects us from demonic assaults as we submit to His Word, guidance, call, and delegated authorities (Ps. 17:8–9; 27:5; 31:20; 32:7; 46:1; 91:1–4, 11–12; 1 Pet. 5:6–7). Yet Christ's Word requires us to humbly submit to the direction of our church, denominational, or ministry leaders, unless they (a) advise us contrary to Scripture, (b) practice sin, or (c) exceed their authority by trying to micromanage our lives in areas not addressed by God's Word. Christ often leads younger ministers to elder ministers for assistance and training, but never blind or total control. Such Timothys may wish to bless their Pauls financially, but tithes or offerings shouldn't be required to retain such counsel: "Taking the oversight...not for filthy lucre" (1 Pet. 5:2); or "Watch over them because you want to...because you are happy to serve, not because you want money" (NCV). If truly Pauline, our overseers will always respect and never try to usurp Christ's headship over us. They'll think and speak of themselves as Christ's servants, not our coverings, trusted by Him and accountable to Him to guide us ever further under the divine Covering—where daily we cultivate our sweet, direct, constant reliance upon our one, true Head. If we consider any minister, however godly, kind, or knowledgeable, to be our spiritual covering (authority and protector) we're

Here's how we do so. We cling to Christ in daily fellow-ship, taking time to "be with him" (Mark 3:14), meditating in His Word, praying, and offering Him thanksgiving and worship.[70] We submissively obey His Word in our daily situations (James 1:22–25). We confess any failure to do so, quickly and humbly, to our Head, thus remaining "in the light, as he is in the light" (1 John 1:7, 9). We seek and follow His confirmed guidance, whether plain or puzzling to our reason (Rom. 8:14). When He corrects our attitudes or behavior, whether by the Spirit's conviction, the Word's enlightenment, or a minister's counsel, we change (Rev. 3:19). We faithfully pursue whatever vocation or ministry He assigns, exercising the natural or spiritual gifts He's given us. By doing these things we "hold the Head"—and receive His benefits.

Paul specifically promised the benefits of spiritual nour-ishment, unity, and growth: "the Head, from whom all the body, nourished and knit together by joints and ligaments, grows with the increase that is from God" (2:19, NKJV). Or, "It is from him that all the parts of the body are cared for and held together. So it grows in the way God wants it to grow" (NCV; cf. Eph. 4:15–16). As long as we hold the Head, His blessing flows into and through us ... and we experience:

"not holding the Head" as we should (Col. 2:18–19). And finally, we should not automatically dismiss as unruly mavericks ministers who, while submis-sive to their ministerial, church, or denominational authorities, are not also submitted to the intimate scrutiny and spiritual control of a particular min-ister or apostle.

70. Barnabas wisely exhorted the new converts at Antioch to "cleave" to the Lord, or closely and earnestly follow, trust, and obey Him (Acts 11:23).

- Personal spiritual nourishment: "All the body, nourished" (2:19, NKJV). The Head nourishes our souls daily by blessing our Bible study, instruction, and contemplation and by refreshing us spontaneously day or night whenever we turn our thoughts to Him and His Word and worship Him with songs or the "sacrifice of praise...our lips giving thanks to his name" (Heb. 13:15).[71]

- Brotherly fellowship: We are "knit together" (Col. 2:19) in Christian friendship, providing us with more spiritual support and nourishment as we share the things of Christ (Prov. 27:17).

- Unity in ministry: We're also "knit together" in our churches and ministries for the Head. These productive ministerial fellowships that help build God's kingdom often result from the work of "joints and bands ['ligaments,' NAS]" (2:19), Barnabas-like ministers specially gifted and used as peacemakers and unifiers in

---

71. The union of a head with its body is like that of a vine with its branches; both are vital, not incidental, bonds. Only when we, the branches, are in constant union with Christ, our Vine, do we: enjoy "life more abundant" through regular infusions of spiritual life (John 10:10); receive purifying, fruit-producing corrections (15:2b); pray effectively (15:7); produce "much fruit" of the Spirit, converts, and disciples that "remain" (15:5, 16); prove ourselves true disciples (15:8; cf. 8:31); glorify the Father (15:8); experience full joy (15:11); become Christ's close friends (15:14–15); and receive a fuller insight into His will (15:15).

Christ's body and among His ministers (Acts 9:26–28).[72]

- CHURCH GROWTH, SPIRITUAL AND NUMER-ICAL: "Grows with the increase that is from God" (2:19, NKJV). By sustaining our union with the Head, we sustain our spiritual nourishment, unity, and growth. Daily the Spirit teaches, corrects, and transforms us increasingly into Christ's character image (Rom. 8:29) and the unity He desires (John 17:17–23). Ultimately this leads to church growth: more converts made disciples and disciples remade in the image of the Head for His honor!

Are we holding the Head or controlled by other heads? Is Christ "heading"—nourishing, correcting, guiding, controlling—all our attitudes, actions, ministries? Are we enjoying the nourishment, unity, and growth of His headship?

2:16–23 Dead to dead religion. Paul's "therefore" in Colossians 2:16 is very significant: "Let no man, *therefore*, judge you in..." Let's consider what precedes and follows it.

His line of thought in this context is as follows. By dying to deactivate the Law and cancel our indictments and debts of sin (2:14), Christ won for us a great triumph over Satan's

---

72. Thus, Colossians 2:19 may be paraphrased, "(These erring members of Christ's body are) no longer holding fast to the Head—from whom the whole body, being knit together by joints and bands (church ligaments, or joining ministers), and being nourished (by the fivefold ministry's teaching given by the Head), continues growing according to God's plan."

"principalities and powers," who previously condemned and bound us (2:15; cf. Rev. 12:10b). By our spiritual rebirth through His death and resurrection He furthermore circumcised our hearts from the control of our fleshly nature (2:11–13). Amazingly, "all the fullness" of God is in Christ (2:9), and, even more amazingly, with Christ in us we are "complete in him" (2:10), lacking nothing essential to full-orbed life with God. So as believers we have the greatest life, Christ's life, "life eternal" (John 17:3), the enviable "life more abundant" Jesus promised (John 10:10). Wow! What a life!

"Therefore," Paul concludes (2:16), since we have the fullest, richest, liveliest religion—living Christianity—we don't need dead religion. If we're already enjoying the utmost internal spiritual bliss, free-flowing life from Christ reviving us daily, why should we have any interest in dead religious externals we've already found to be dry, uninspiring, and void of power to change us? His reasoning is reminiscent of the angels' wisdom at Christ's tomb: Why should the living seek life among the dead (Luke 24:5)? After Paul's pivotal "therefore," he goes on to describe dead religion in Colossians 2:16–23 as various forms of "the rudiments of the world" (2:20).

These "rudiments" are the basic elements or principles of this world's religious teachings, or *the rules, rites, and rituals of false religion.*[73] Though blindly followed and respected, they are of not divine but human origin, "the commandments and doctrines of [mere] men" (2:22). Thus, they hold no binding authority over our lives. Essentially, legalism is any humanly

---

73. The more we enjoy the reality of God, the less we need rituals; the less we experience His reality, the more we cling to rituals. It's time we ask, Are we worshiping God in rites and rituals or "in spirit and in truth" (John 4:24)?

designed religious teaching that requires more of us than God requires.[74] What "rudiments" did Paul have in mind?

As stated previously, first-century Jewish Law, though now deactivated and rendered obsolete by Christ's Cross (2:14), continued to impose a plethora of requirements concerning diet, feast days, new moons, Sabbaths, separation from Gentiles (for ritual purity), and other things (2:16–17, 20–21). Mysticism (ancient mystery religions) advocated the worship of angels for their purported mediation between God and humanity (2:18–19). Asceticism ordered and glorified extreme fasting, what Paul called "neglecting of the body" (2:23).[75] Heretics were trying hard to sell all these "rudiments" to the unsuspecting Colossians. But, Paul asserted, they were dead to them now in Christ: "Wherefore, if ye be dead with Christ from the rudiments of the world…" (2:20). And he didn't stop there.

---

74. Matthew Henry paraphrased Paul's teaching, "Let no man impose those things upon you, for God has not imposed them." Conversely, license occurs when religious authorities permit or authorize more than God permits (e.g., immorality, covetousness, idolatry). For quote, see Henry, *Commentary in One Volume*, Col. 2:16, note, 1872.

75. While biblical warnings against gluttony are still valid guidelines for us (Deut. 21:20; Prov. 23:20–21), Paul taught, generally speaking, our status in God's kingdom (and relationship to our King) has nothing to do with our diet: "In the kingdom of God, eating and drinking are not important. The important things are living right with God, peace, and joy in the Holy Spirit" (Rom. 14:17, NCV; cf. Matt. 15:1–20; 1 Tim. 4:4–5). However, it's advisable, but never required, that we practice good nutrition whenever possible. While neither saving us, bringing us closer to Jesus, nor rendering us spiritually mature, healthy eating habits will help us feel better physically and serve the Lord better in the body till He comes (Acts 27:34; 1 Tim. 5:23). Thus, like bodily exercise, it profits us "a little" (1 Tim. 4:8, NKJV), or it is "of some value" (ESV, NIV).

He also explained why Christians shouldn't return to these dead elements of religion:

1. They are vain, unable to save our souls or circumcise the power of our fleshly nature (2:11–13, 23).

2. By serving them we imply Christ's sacrifice and the spiritual circumcision He's made available to us are insufficient to save us and make us spiritually mature (2:11–13).

An honest debater, Paul conceded that living by high-sounding religious rules, impressive rituals, and sacrificial rites make us appear wise, humble, devoted to God, and self-disciplined,[76] and may prompt others to laud us as holy men and women (2:23). But he tenaciously reasserted the key reality: these basic elements of religion do not make us better Christians. They can't, because they are dead—and we are alive!

Furthermore, he added, by pretending holiness through careful man-made rule-keeping, we do not really honor God ("not in any honor," 2:23). To the contrary, He is as dishonored by and displeased with our self-led religiousness as He was Cain's in the beginning (Gen. 4:3–5). And

---

76. The gnostics appeared wise by claiming special revelation not given to others and by suggesting various ways the Colossians should humble themselves, perhaps including by worshiping angels—whom they believed were due worship because they mediated between the human race in this unholy material world and a distant holy God. But Paul asserted it was all just an empty show, Pharisaic religious theatre (Matt. 23:5). True wisdom is found in Christ alone (2:3) and true humility in joyful obedience to His Word and will (3:23–24; Phil. 2:5–8, 12–16).

we only satisfy ourselves! By living in these "rudiments," we "satisfy [indulge] the flesh" (2:23), specifically, our religious flesh (religious pride)[77] and its desire to be "seen of men," as was so amply displayed by the Pharisees (2:23; Matt. 6:5; 23:5).[78] Thus, Paul correctly analyzed the situation. The heretics advocating these errors were motivated by religious pride—"vainly puffed up by his fleshly mind" (Col. 2:18)— and trying to stir the same in the Colossians.

Also, rather than help the Colossians' self-control, legalistic rules and disciplines had the opposite effect. They failed to help their adherents control their flesh: "They provide no help in conquering a person's evil desires" (Col. 2:23, NLT). So compliance left the Colossians not more holy but more hypocritical: white-washed sepulchers, clean outside but still harboring corruption inside; looking superior but still being inferior; talking spiritual things while remaining "yet carnal" (1 Cor. 3:1–3).

Additionally, the heretics' preference for "rudiments" over reality proved that, contrary to their boastful claims of wisdom and knowledge (*gnosis*), they were foolish and without the knowledge of God. They totally misunderstand not only the way God saves but also the way He frees us from our flesh or old nature—by the supernatural power of His Spirit and Word, not by mere human willpower executing self-imposed

---

77. On our religious flesh, see my earlier entry, "Christian circumcision" (Col. 2:11–13).

78. Again Henry notes, "Though there was a show of humility in the practice, there was a real pride in the principle. Pride is at the bottom of a great many errors." See Henry, *Commentary in One Volume*, Col. 2:18, note, 1872. Warren Wiersbe adds, "Somehow, adhering to the religious routine inflates the ego and makes a person content in his self-righteousness." See Wiersbe, *The Bible Exposition Commentary*, Vol. 2, Col. 2:16–17, note.

rules, however religious and well-intended (Rom. 2:29; 7:6; 8:1–4, 11–14).

Paul recognized this dead religion was for the spiritually dead, not for the spiritually reborn. Spirit-filled, fully alive, vitally-connected-to-the-Head Christians had no need of it! "Wherefore," he concluded, "if ye be dead with Christ from the rudiments of the world['s religions]" (2:20), why submit to them any longer (2:21–22)?[79] Sadly, little has changed since Paul's day.

A master of reinvention, Satan keeps repackaging the same old dead religion and reselling it to living Christians. He persistently tries to convince us to forsake the freedom and power of a satisfying Spirit-filled life to return to his dungeon of dead religion filled with its devices of torturous frustration.[80] We must learn from Paul's warning. When teachers or fellow believers begin stubbornly requiring compliance in debatable things—diet; holy days; the keeping of Sabbaths;[81]

---

79. He made the same appeal to the Galatians when they became ensnared in similar elements of dead religion (Gal. 4:9–12).

80. Martin Luther eventually became physically spent and disillusioned as an overzealous Augustinian monk immersed in ascetic rigors and empty rituals. He later concluded, "If I had kept on any longer, I should have killed myself with vigils, prayers, readings, and other work." See Ken Curtis, "Martin Luther: Monumental Reformer," *Christianity.com*, accessed February 5, 2016, http://www.christianity.com/church/church-history/timeline/1501-1600/martin-luther-monumental-reformer-11629922.html.

81. Even today some Christians insist we must keep a seventh-day Sabbath, Mosaic dietary laws, or Jewish festivals, such as Passover. Some churches slavishly hold their Catholic or Protestant liturgy as if it had special value. Others earnestly refuse to allow their people to observe the most basic, harmless Christian holidays, such as Christmas or Easter, or even birthdays, due to their former association with pagan beliefs. (Pagans also believe in and practice eating, sleeping, buying, and selling, but we still observe these daily life rituals without spiritual loss!) Others insist their people observe

the observance of Jewish festivals, terminology, or customs; non-observance of holidays, birthdays, etc.; total withdrawal from society; infatuation with or veneration of angels; undue exaltation of ministers[82]—Paul warns, beware! They are being drawn by the same subtle devil that inspired the well-crafted and alluring Colossian heresies. Sadly, neither Paul's "therefore" (2:16) nor "wherefore" (2:20) has registered with them. Be sure these key words register with you.

Never exchange live Christianity for dead religion.[83]

---

strict dress codes. Why do we stubbornly impose or slavishly obey such man-made religious rules and condemn those whose rules differ from ours? Didn't Jesus die to free us to worship Him according to His Word and our consciences? "Where the Spirit of the Lord is, there is liberty" in such non-mandatory debatable issues (2 Cor. 3:17).

82. If even godly Cornelius was moved to prostrate himself before a renowned minister (Acts 10:25), we should take heed lest we think or speak too highly of or bow too low before the Lord's anointed! And if Peter was quick to discern and halt such excessive honor, we should be too! "Peter took him up, saying, Stand up; I myself also am a man [just like you]" (10:26).

83. This includes avoiding dead churches (Rev. 3:1). It's been wisely said, "Don't put live chicks under a dead hen!" Applied to Christians, this means we shouldn't encourage growing Christians to attend spiritually life-less churches. Why do Bible-hungry disciples continue to attend churches with cold congregations, errant fundamental theology, little Bible teaching, unbiblical moral standards, or overtly worldly messages or methods? Immersion in apathy will eventually cool the hottest zeal (Rev. 3:15–17).

Chapter Three

REFOCUSING ON THINGS ABOVE— AND READDRESSING THINGS BELOW

After exploring Christ's preeminence and attacking heresies, Paul refocused the Colossians' attention. His tone was urgent: They must now look up!

Since their real life was in Christ, they should "seek" and "set" their hearts on "things above," not the popular, noisy distractions of this passing world. Why? Jesus will one day "appear," and they must be ready to live forever with Him. Once refocused on this powerful, prime hope of "things above," they should then readdress things below: mortifying their flesh, putting off old ways, putting on the new man, letting God's peace "rule," staying in God's Word "richly," doing everything "heartily, as to the Lord," and obeying God's instructions in every relationship.

3:1 A change of focus. Since the gnostics believed secret knowledge alone saved their souls, some of them felt no compulsion to live righteously. Paul would have none of it. After refuting their bad teaching, he exposed their bad living by teaching the Colossians how to live well.

Using different terms he instructed the Colossians, as he had the Philippians, to "work out your own salvation" (Phil. 2:12) and specified how they were to do so. Understanding human motivation, he began by focusing on what they love, think on, and seek, insisting these drivers must now be spiritual, not worldly (Col. 3:1–4). Building on these holy hopes, he constructed a very full description of mature Christian living (3:5–4:6).[1]

3:1–4 Live in your new life! In these verses Paul summoned the Colossians to higher things. Every Christian needs this exhortation periodically, since the constant pull of life in our worldly cultures tends to allure us to and entangle us in worthless, worldly things.

Paraphrasing, Paul says:

> Since you've risen with Christ, set your affections and thoughts on heavenly, not worldly, ends. Seek them diligently in your daily devotions and duties, because you've died to your old life and received a new life. So live in your new life. It springs from your hidden, private fellowship with Christ, who will one day appear and take you to live with Him forever in heaven.
>
> —COLOSSIANS 3:1–4, AUTHOR'S PARAPHRASE

---

1. For more, see my previous entry, "Spiritual maturity detailed" (Col. 2:1–4:18).

This "seek, set, for [because]" (3:1, 2, 3) gives a clear, accurate purpose and direction to our lives.[2] If we forget this primary exhortation, we'll stray. If we remember it, we'll live well, close to Christ and faithful in our worldly responsibilities because we're motivated by a higher, overriding goal of faithfulness to Him, our heavenly King, and His kingdom. If we temporarily lose this heavenly "set" (determination), we'll reset it. If our "seeking" lapses, we'll renew it. But always, with this "set, seek, for" deeply rooted in our soul, we'll move steadily forward spiritually. Now to Paul's words.

In these brief verses (3:1–4) he broached five key subjects: the life above, the life below, the hidden life, the secure life, and the end of life.

THE LIFE ABOVE. Based upon the Colossians' spiritual rebirth symbolized by their baptism (2:12–13), Paul exhorted them to live in and for their new life, that is, their personal relationship to Christ and destiny in His will and kingdom. He reiterated that, by Christ's substitutionary death, they are now "dead" (3:3) to all the old life—sin, selfishness, their previous worldview, life goals, habits, work methods, values, and the "rudiments" of religion (2:20, see vv. 14–23).[3] In their former life they had religion; now they had a personal Redeemer! They formerly lived in a circle of worldly inter-

---

2. I recently heard someone summarize Colossians 3 in three words: "Seek, set, sanctify!" Seek heavenly things (3:1), set your heart on them (3:2–4), and with this focus sanctify yourself (3:5–4:1).

3. Warren Wiersbe relates, "Years ago I heard a story about two sisters who enjoyed attending dances and wild parties. Then they were converted and found new life in Christ. They received an invitation to a party and sent their RSVP in these words: 'We regret that we cannot attend because we recently died.'" See Wiersbe, *The Bible Exposition Commentary*, Vol. 2, Col. 3:4a, note.

ests; now they thrived in a new realm of spiritual thinking and living (3:1) where one dominant relationship comes before and guides all others (3:2; Matt. 6:33; Col. 3:18–4:1). Therefore, Paul charged them to stay focused and live in their new life and ruling relationship.[4]

Specifically, they should "set" (fix) their hearts and minds on "things above" (Col. 3:2). Or, "give your minds to the things...above" (WEY). Or, "think about the things of heaven" (NLT) or the "realities of heaven" (NIV).[5] He asserted Christ was enthroned "at the right hand of God [the Father]" (3:1; Ps. 110:1; Acts 2:32–35; Rev. 3:21), thus reminding them they served One already possessing irresistible universal power over heaven and Earth (Matt. 28:18–20).[6] This heavenly soul-

---

4. This was most timely for the Colossians who, as stated earlier, would soon have their city (and "things on the earth," 3:2) rocked and devastated by an earthquake that would leave the city a mere shadow of its former self. It's just as timely for us in these last days, since Jesus' appearing to take us away, which draws closer by the day, will trigger the Tribulation period that will utterly dismantle the "things on the earth" as we know them (Rev. 16:17–20)!

5. For more on the "realities of heaven," read Revelation chapters 4–5 and 21–22. Are we presently studying and living in the essential truths, righteousness, priorities, attitudes, unity, and worship that characterizes the atmosphere and activities surrounding God's throne (Rev. 4–5), which will be the center of New Jerusalem (Rev. 21–22)?

6. To sit at the right hand of a king in antiquity was to occupy the place of highest power, honor, access (to the king) and privilege in one's kingdom, second only to the king himself (Gen. 41:40–41; Esther 10:3). Thus, Jesus sits today beside His Father (Rev. 3:21; 5:12–13). So Paul reminds us we shouldn't seek the "things on the earth" because they're too low for us as redeemed heavenly royals and regents. Since our Lord—in whom our lives are "hidden" (Col. 3:3)—already sits enthroned "at the right hand of God" (3:1), we're already there spiritually enthroned with Him "in heavenly places" (Eph. 2:5–6). Why, then, should we come down from our elevated, spiritual life and Lord to live for and love the vain pursuits and goals of this lower, temporal realm?

focus implies we must set our wills with firm resolve, since everything in this world works against a heavenly focus. And since we often fail and come short of God's perfect will, we will need to repent and reset our wills, whenever distracted, on heavenly things—daily, if necessary, hourly. One translation brings this out: "Set your minds and keep them set on what is above" (3:2, AMP). Every time we turn affectionately and believingly to God through prayer, worship, Bible meditation, or humble obedience, we're resetting our hearts and minds on heavenly things.

Warren Wiersbe writes:

> Our feet must be on earth, but our minds must be in heaven...[This] means that [in] the practical everyday affairs of life [we] get [our] direction from Christ in heaven. It means further that we look at earth from heaven's point of view...
>
> When the nation of Israel came to the border of the Promised Land, they refused to enter; and, because of their stubborn unbelief, they had to wander in the wilderness for forty years (see Num. 13–14). That whole generation, starting with the twenty year olds, died in the wilderness, except for Caleb and Joshua, the only two spies who believed God. How were Caleb and Joshua able to "get the victory" during those forty difficult years in the wilderness? *Their minds and hearts were in Canaan!* They knew they had an inheritance coming, and they lived in the light of that inheritance.
>
> The Queen of England exercises certain powers and privileges because she sits on the throne. The President of the United States has privileges and powers because he sits behind the desk in the oval office of the White House. The believer is seated on the throne with Christ.

> We must constantly keep our affection and our atten-
> tion fixed on the things of heaven, through the Word
> and prayer, as well as through worship and service. We
> can enjoy "days of heaven upon the earth" (Deut. 11:21)
> if we will keep our hearts and minds in the heavenlies.[7]

Paul's order to "seek" heavenly things was a demanding
one. Every Colossian was to launch a diligent, earnest, life-
long search to find, have ever more of, and increasingly delight
in Jesus (the greatest "thing above") and everything related
to his (her) new life-walk with Him. This meant questing
for spiritual riches, the enduring wealth of heavenly truth,
the "rich, eternal treasures that are above" (3:1, AMP), which
Jesus called "gold tried in the fire" and urged the Laodiceans
to seek (Rev. 3:18). It meant not partial but total commitment to new life goals. It also meant forging lasting relationships with other upward-bound, God-questing believers.
This order contained two implications.

First, they must no longer yearn for and seek after "the
passing things of earth" (3:2, PHILLIPS), what the apostle
John called "the things that are in the world" (1 John 2:15-
17). Their thoughts must not be captivated, nor their actions
motivated, by these worldly ends, which will mean nothing
when Jesus establishes His eternal kingdom. We may assume
most of the Colossians understood and complied. We must
also! We'll never seek heavenly goals until we stop longing
and living for worldly ones. Second, this radical disinterest in
worldly goals will separate us from some Christians. Or more
accurately, they'll leave us alone! Believers ardently seeking
things above are going in the opposite direction from those

---

7. Wiersbe, *The Bible Exposition Commentary*, Vol. 2, Col. 3:4b, note, 134.

still panting for things below (3:2). Sooner or later they pull apart.

THE LIFE BELOW. A visionary, yet also a realist, Paul didn't intend for us to devalue, despise, or ignore our life in this world. To the contrary, he knew well we're in this world now for a divine purpose: to honor God by knowing Him more, praising Him continually, pursuing our work or ministries faithfully, fulfilling our commissions (evangelizing, discipling, witnessing) to build His kingdom, and by doing "whatever" we do as unto Christ (3:23). We're also to stand firmly for eternal (biblical) truth and against sin and false doctrines and philosophies. Thus, we will be shining lights in this dark world and spiritual salt to disinfect from the corruption of sin all who turn to Jesus. So Paul first insisted, "Heaven matters most!" (3:1–4). Then he added, "But this life matters too!" (3:5–6:6). It's an addendum we mustn't miss. Why?

This life is a vital preparation for the next, an earthly means to our heavenly end. Everything we do in this life prepares us to better worship and serve our King in the next. And it's in this life, not the next, that we're working to bring souls into His kingdom and disciple them. So as we serve kingdom priorities in this world we're building heaven on Earth. This is why Paul readdressed the Colossians' practical living in his closing words (Col. 3:5–4:6), as he did when writing the Philippians (Phil. 4:1–19) and Ephesians (Eph. 4:17 – 6:9). They must realize, this life matters too!

THE HIDDEN LIFE. Paul further described the essential nature of the new life: "Your real life" (3:3, NLT). It is hidden, not visible; private, not public. Our new life-walk is "hidden with Christ in God" (3:3). While the Colossians had public responsibilities and duties, the core of their new life was very personal, a secret love relationship with Jesus (Ps. 83:3; 87:7; Ps. 91:1, 9, 14; Matt. 6:6; 11:28–30; Mark 3:14–15, 19; 6:46; Luke 5:16; Exod. 24:12; Song of Sol.; Gal. 1:17; 2 Cor. 12:1–5). Out of this central, intimate relationship known only to God, and cultivated only to please Him, they were to accept and discharge responsibilities and ministries in their families, churches, and communities. Just like the present aspect of God's kingdom is hidden within and among believers only (not a visible, political state), their individual lives also were hidden with Christ. Every kingdom grace, good work, or ministry they displayed openly sprang from their hidden life with the King (cf. Ps. 87:7).

Oswald Chambers called this hidden life a "workshop" where God prepares believers for intimate fellowship with Him and fruitful service for Him. Are we real, trusting, and obedient there, where only God sees, under our "fig tree" (John 1:48)? Or are we vainly imagining we can ignore our hidden life and still thrive in public usefulness for Christ? A master of the hidden life, Oswald Chambers wrote:

> "If God gives the call, of course I will rise to the occasion." You will not unless you have risen to the occasion in the workshop, unless you have been the real thing before God there. If you are not doing the thing that lies nearest, because God has engineered it, when the crisis comes instead of being revealed as fit, you will be revealed as unfit...
>
> The private relationship of worshipping God is the great essential of fitness. The time comes when there is no more "fig-tree" life possible, when it is out into the open, out into the glare and into the work...
>
> Worship aright in your private relationships, then

when God sets you free you will be ready because in the unseen life which no one saw but God you have become perfectly fit and when the strain comes you can be relied upon by God...

The workshop of missionary munitions is the hidden, personal, worshipping life of the saint.[8]

THE SECURE LIFE. Matthew Henry opens a second valid point concerning our "hidden" life (Col. 3:3). Since valuables are typically hidden for security against theft or loss, our new hidden life—our invaluable, eternal salvation—is safely laid up with Jesus. Whatever our present worldly needs, distresses, or failures, our salvation (life) is safely "hid with Christ in God."[9]

Shouldn't this eternal security spur us to unquenchably joyful obedience, sacrifice, and service in this world as an expression of our gratitude for "such a great salvation" (Heb. 2:3, ESV)? Shouldn't we be "strengthened with all might" by this hope "unto all patience and long-suffering with joyfulness, giving thanks," whatever thankless tasks are ours (1:11–12)?

THE END OF LIFE. Finally, Paul revealed the heavenly goal of their earthly walk: Jesus' heavenly appearing, which was the Colossians' portal to the "things which are above"! (3:4; Matt. 25:10; Rev. 4:1–2).[10] This was not coincidental. With

---

8. Chambers, *My Utmost for His Highest*, 254.

9. Henry, *Commentary in One Volume*, 1873.

10. No mere passing whim, Paul often described or alluded to Jesus' appearing, or as we call it, the Rapture. For instance, every chapter in 1 Thessalonians ends with a view to Christ's appearing and our gathering together unto Him (1 Thess. 1:9–10; 2:19; 3:11–13; 4:13–18; 5:23).

inspired concentration, Paul was still focused on their preparation for the "presentation" (1:22, 28) in "glory" (3:4)—heaven, where they will behold the glory of Jesus' splendor, share the glory of His honor, and live in the glory of their new immortal bodies (cf. 1 John 3:2). Thus, he really urged them to look in two directions: *upward* to all the spiritual things of heaven and *forward* to Christ's appearing to take them to "glory."[11] Why is this upward-forward focus important?

It will give them Rapture security—complete, restful confidence they'll be taken, not left behind, when Jesus appears. If they set their hearts and minds on seeking their heavenly life and hope "first" (Matt. 6:33), they'll have full assurance that whenever Jesus—who is their real, enduring "life"—appears, so will they! "Seek...set...then shall ye also appear with him in glory" (3:1–2, 4). Conversely, those whose hearts are set on passing things in this present order won't, they can't, be confident Jesus will take them when He appears—and if they don't recover themselves and get "ready" many may very well be left behind (Matt. 25:10–13).[12]

---

11. Walvoord and Zuck, *The Bible Knowledge Commentary: An Exposition of the Scriptures*, Vol. 2, Col. 3:3–4, note, 680.

12. At issue here is "Rapture security." It's highly unlikely Jesus will take in the Rapture Christians who are unconcerned with being spiritually prepared for that great, climactic event. Words mean something, and Jesus, God's living Word, didn't use them frivolously but rather with clear, precise intent. Whenever He spoke of His appearing, He exhorted not unbelievers but His own disciples to be sure they qualify by living "ready" (Matt. 24:44; 25:10; Rev. 19:7), "watching" (Matt. 24:42–43; 25:13), "worthy" (Luke 21:34–36), and "wise" (Matt. 25:2, 4, 8, 9). If these warnings don't matter, and Jesus will take all Christians regardless of their walk, why did He speak them? Wouldn't that view make Jesus' words irrelevant? And wouldn't He then be guilty of making misleading statements—something the utterly true and faithful One cannot do (Num. 23:19)? So the qualifications for the Rapture Jesus taught us have real meaning, and we should trust and obey them if

On reflection, we do well to remember Satan's strategy is to oppose Paul's! He wants us to keep trying to live in the old life, not the new. He wants us looking down, not up. He wants our hearts fixed on worldly desires and goals only so we'll be so distracted with personal, national, or world problems we don't even think about looking up to the "things which are above." Why? He knows if we live this way we won't be ready for Christ's appearing. Instead we'll be increasingly anxious, vexed, and fruitless in these last days as "distress of nations, with perplexity" increases (Luke 21:25). In such a condition, we'll neglect fellowship with Christ, ignore our divine gifts and callings, become apathetic about fellow believers and the church, and abandon our divine commissions (Matt. 24:44–51). How can you defeat his strategy?

Live in your new life!

3:1–4 The walking dead. A strange, macabre television series of recent origins is *The Walking Dead*. With blood and gore aplenty it depicts the departed rising to assault the living in a horrific, fictional, survivalist story straight from hell. Even stranger is this: The same title could be applied to this passage (3:1–4).

Paul reasoned, since the Colossians had died with Christ to their old, worldly existence they shouldn't try to walk in it anymore. Instead they should walk in their new, empowered, elevated, spiritual life in Christ. Then they would be "the walking live"—Christians who, walking ever steadily forward

---

we want to know beyond the shadow of a doubt that whenever He appears, wherever we are, whatever is happening in the world, we'll be taken.

in the Spirit, experience full spiritual vitality and revel daily in the wonderful "life more abundant" Jesus bequeathed us (John 10:10; Luke 12:15; John 14:6; Ps. 16:12). But they didn't have to. If they wished, they could opt to live life dead.

The Christians at Sardis did just that. Jesus reproved them, "People say that you are alive, but really you are dead" (Rev. 3:1, ncv). The Sardis believers had a reputation for spiritual vitality but were actually stone dead inside. There was no glory in their inner sanctums, no extraordinary divine life filling their ordinary human bodies. Though claiming to be Spirit-filled, they were Spirit-void, religious but empty vessels who hadn't experienced the Spirit's invigorating stirrings or refreshments in a long, long while. They were dry, dull, dead! The same choice is ours.

We can try to go back and live in, for, and by the things of our life BC (before Christ). But if we do, all we'll accomplish is rediscovering how true Paul's revelation is: "Ye are dead, and your [true, satisfying, spiritual] life is hidden with Christ in God" (3:3). We'll also grow increasingly like the church at Sardis. And that's not all. As long as we who are called to be spiritual in heart, mind, and lifestyle try to find fulfillment in the unspiritual things of this dead world, we are presenting a horrific specter to "the great cloud of witnesses" and angelic watchers who "surround" our lives (Heb. 12:1),[13] broadcasting heavenward the strangest TV series yet, *The Christian Walking Dead*. Let's review the gory details.

---

13. In expositing Hebrews 12:1, some insist the heroes of faith who've gone before us (Hebrews 11) and are described as "witnesses" are not aware of events on Earth. They take this position because in the Greek Paul used a word meaning "witness," not "spectator." But if these "witnesses" have finished their earthly races and now "surround" us as a "cloud" as we run ours, surely they are (to some degree) aware of our struggles in our trials of faith,

We're ambulatory, or walking around, busily working, monitoring politics, following business or financial news, watching sports or entertainment, and attending church. But inside too many of us are dead, spiritually unanimated, inactive, silent, purposeless, and secretly disappointed with Jesus. Inwardly lifeless, we're plodding along without Christ's sweet presence, opened Word, and reassuring touches. We're unresponsive to our ministers' teachings, warnings, and loving corrections, and the Spirit's quiet, internal conviction. Our Bible reading, which should be invigorating, is dull. Our prayers are lethargic and without expectation. Our worship is dutiful but without passion. We're apathetic about our divine callings, preferring and pursuing other interests. We're dead to fellowship, avoiding rather than enjoying time spent with other spiritually minded Christians. We're dead to hope, unexcited by the message of Jesus' return and trying to pump up excitement about other events. Our assemblies have become well-organized religious morgues, full of human programs without divine initiatives. We're dead to joy, void of sweet delight in living near Jesus. Our peace is dead—and our anxieties are alive and growing by the day. Our faith has flatlined, terminated by feeding insufficiently on God's Word, indulging sin, and holding offenses at other Christians or God for allowing hard tests or strange delays (John 11:21, 32). So there we are: unanimated, extinguished,

---

even though Paul chose to refer to them as witnesses rather than spectators. Though in heaven, Moses and Elijah were well aware of earthly events in Jesus' life (Luke 9:30–31). The angel who visited Daniel was well aware he had been fasting and praying for twenty-one days (Dan. 10:12). When Gabriel appeared to Mary, he informed her that her cousin Elisabeth was six months pregnant (Luke 1:36).

dry, dull, lukewarm, Christ's zombies, the Christian walking dead![14] And why?

We're still trying to go back and find rich satisfaction in our poor past. Sinful or self-centered living quenches the miraculous life Jesus, our "life" (John 14:6), wants to impart to us daily, hourly, every minute. Without that we're lifeless—bored, distracted, constantly discontent, insatiable, trying to find abundant life in a spiritual tomb! We already know that those who've never received Jesus are living in a state of spiritual death—sad, lonely separation from the life and fellowship of God. Why do we keep trying to join them in their plodding, purposeless, joyless, clumsy back-and-forth death march? Life doesn't have to imitate art.

Hollywood has given us the walking dead. Why don't we give them back! Instead of following television's descent into strangeness, let's go in the opposite direction. Our congregations already have the frozen chosen and rigid righteous. Let's not add the walking dead! Settle it: There's no life-joy in the old things, and there never will be. Our life is forever before us, not behind us, in Christ and the awesome love, biblical way of life, divinely assigned work, and kingdom destiny He has graciously given us.

So refocus and go forward: "Walk [onward] in the Spirit, and ye shall not fulfill the lusts of the flesh" (Gal. 5:16). Fix,

---

14. Like the aforementioned zombies, too many of us are also spiritually cannibalizing one another by contentiousness, slander, gossip, and bitter rivalries. Again Paul warned us against devouring ourselves by unloving attitudes and harsh words: "If ye bite and devour one another, take heed that ye be not consumed one of another" (Gal. 5:15). Who have you "bitten" lately by sharp-tongued, impatient, callous, or angry words? Or who has "bitten" you? See Ephesians 4:30–5:2; Philippians 2:3; 4:1–2; Colossians 3:12–14; 2 Timothy 2:14, 24–26.

and whenever necessary re-fix, your heart on "things above" (Col. 3:1–2). The living God will refill you daily with His living Spirit—and make you the walking live! That's a broadcast the witnesses and watchers are eager to see. And they're not alone.

This dying world desperately needs your living testimony. "They marveled, and they took knowledge of them, that they had been with Jesus" (Acts 4:13).

3:5–9 Putting off putting off? Paul's message in these verses was straightforward, no-nonsense, practical theology at its most practical. Paraphrasing, he ordered the Colossians, "Put off your old man (earthly nature) with all his sins."[15] Why? So they could "put on" the awesome new man in them, Christ (3:10–14)! It's the same with us.

As long as we let the old man and his ungodly ways continue, we can't "put on"—fully embrace and consistently demonstrate in thought and behavior—our new Christ life. Christ is in us, but not expressing Himself through us. He's present, but not seen or heard. We've received grace, but we're not showing graciousness. We're children of God, but not godly. We're loved by Christ, but not like Christ. We've received the Spirit, but we're not responding to Him. The reason?

---

15. Knowing our "old man" (sin nature, or "flesh") and its sins are still with us as Christians and they trouble us and our churches, Paul repeatedly urged that we "put off" or "mortify" them and "put on" Christian virtues (Rom. 8:12–13; Col. 3:5, 8, 9, 10; Gal. 5:19–21; Eph. 4:22; 5:3–7). That he commanded *us* to do so proves the Holy Spirit doesn't automatically do this for us. We must cooperate with the Spirit's convictions and prompts to obey scriptural righteousness if we hope to live consistently free from the domination of our old man.

We're putting off putting off our old man. Like Lot's wife, we know we've got to leave the popular values, ways, and corruptions of Sodom but don't really want to. So we're lingering when we should be leaving, flirting with sin when we should be fleeing it, looking back to worldly things when we should be looking away to Jesus (3:1–4), and delighting in our new, pure, joyful, spiritual walk with Him.

Specifically, Paul mentioned the following corruptions of the old nature and life:

- All illicit sexual activity and desire (3:5):[16]

    1. "FORNICATION": (Greek, *porneia*; "sexual immorality, often... [ways, acts of] prostitution"[17]) extramarital intercourse; in Paul's day, much pagan "worship" consisted of rites involving fornication with cult prostitutes. In our culture, cohabitation, or worse, random Internet sexual

---

16. The heretics troubling the Colossians taught the prevailing Greek and gnostic view that our bodies (like everything material) are corrupt, but our spirits are pure. Thus, one's body is insignificant and a hindrance to spirituality. Several reactions followed. Greeks didn't want to be resurrected, feeling death released them from the body's hindrances, so why should they desire to return to a body? Ascetic gnostics afflicted and punished their bodies, hoping thereby to become less adversely affected by them and therefore more spiritual (Col. 2:20–23). Indulgent gnostics believed they could practice fleshly sins at will without their actions affecting their relationship to God (Rom. 6:1–2; 1 Cor. 5:1–2). (Too many American Christians have quietly adopted this, in part due to the hyper-grace error.) Paul warned our bodily (esp. sexual) sins are important, impeding our spiritual growth, witness, and usefulness for God (Gal. 5:16–17) and provoking His wrathful chastisements (Col. 3:6; 1 Thess. 4:3–8, esp. v. 6).

17. Louw and Nida, *Greek–English Lexicon of the New Testament: Based on Semantic Domains*, electronic ed. of the 2nd edition, s.v. "*porneia*."

encounters, are becoming increasingly common. Fornication will increase in society (Rev. 9:21) but must not among Christians (1 Cor. 5:1–7).

2. "UNCLEANNESS": sexually impure actions; any illicit, deviant, unnatural, filthy, or biblically prohibited sexual activity, including such things as self-gratification (self-stimulation), homosexuality (Lev. 18:22; Rom. 1:24–28), bisexuality, incest, pedophilia, and bestiality (Lev. 18:23)

3. "INORDINATE AFFECTION": sexual lust; any exciting of inappropriate or excessive sexual desires

4. "EVIL DESIRE": base desires; desiring or fantasizing of perverted sexual activity that dishonors God and degrades ourselves and others (Rom. 1:24; Gal. 6:7)

- "COVETOUSNESS" (3:5): avarice or greed; excessive desire for money or material things, especially when we already have enough (1 Tim. 6:8–10; Luke 12:15–21); also, greed for non-material things. All coveting is idolatry, since it involves loving, seeking, serving, and trusting in something or someone more than God (Eph. 5:5; 1 Tim. 6:9–10). This breaks the first and last commandments (Exod. 20:3, 17).

- "ANGER" (3:8): holding irritation or indignation toward someone with or without cause (Ps. 37:1, 8)

- "WRATH" (3:8): rage, or great anger; sometimes deep and long held; also, offensive displays of reckless anger. Wrath can't erupt if we keep the lava of anger out of our spirits, quickly facing and "ceasing" from it (Ps. 37:1, 8; Eph. 4:26–27), so it doesn't "rest" (remain) in us and prompt us to speak or act foolishly (Eccles. 7:9).

- "MALICE" (3:8): harboring ill will toward others or even a desire to harm them; implies holding grudges due to past offenses or in some cases envy (Matt. 5:22; Gen. 37:4; Matt. 27:18; 1 Pet. 2:1)

- "BLASPHEMY" (3:8): slandering or defaming God or holy things, including characterizing the works or gifts of the Holy Spirit as demonic (Mark 3:22–29). Paul said before his conversion he was a "blasphemer" because he denounced Jesus of Nazareth as a false messiah (1 Tim. 1:12–13; Rev. 2:9; 13:5–6) and compelled many Jewish Christians to also (Acts 26:9–11).

- "FILTHY COMMUNICATION OUT OF YOUR MOUTH" (3:8): all ungodly, rude, profane, off-color, or indecent talk (Eph. 4:29–31; James 1:26; 1 Pet. 2:1)

- "LIE NOT ONE TO ANOTHER" (3:9): intention-
  ally using partial truths, twisted truths, or
  innuendos to create false impressions to deceive
  others and further our ends. Since this is a
  prime trait of the "father" of lies (John 8:44),
  Paul bids us no longer speak as his children:
  "Don't deceive each other with lies any more"
  (3:9, PHILLIPS; cf. Eph. 4:25).[18]

All these are root or fundamental sins of the old nature
and its carnal ways. There are numerous others described
elsewhere in Scripture.[19] Paul ordered the Colossians, and
us, to "mortify" them (3:5), or destroy them by steadily
neglecting them and replacing them with the thoughts and
ways of God. The more we mortify these old ways, the more
our new life will be energized and consistently manifested.
And, as Paul faithfully warned, the more we'll avoid the
"wrath of God" that visits those who continue practicing
them (3:6). It's time to get serious about obeying Paul—and
not displeasing the Father!

Let's lay our spiritual axes to the roots of these sins, as
John the Baptist exhorted us (Luke 3:9), by determinedly and

---

18. Warren Wiersbe wrote, "A lie is any misrepresentation of the truth, *even
if the words are accurate*. The tone of voice, the look on the face, or a gesture
of the hand can alter the meaning of a sentence. So can the motive of the
heart... An old proverb says, 'Half a fact is a whole lie.'" See Wiersbe, *The
Bible Exposition Commentary*, Vol. 2, Col. 3:5–9, note.

19. For instance: unbelief (Heb. 3:12–13), pride (Mark 7:22–23; 1 John 2:16),
envy (Gal. 5:21, 26; James 3:14–16), unforgiveness (Matt. 18:35), fear (2 Tim.
1:7; 1 John 4:18), unfaithfulness (Ps. 78:57; Prov. 25:19), bitterness (Heb.
12:15), prejudice (Acts 10:34–35; James 2:1), strife (contentiousness, Prov.
21:19; 26:21; 2 Tim. 2:24), indolence (Prov. 21:25; Rom. 12:11).

diligently putting them off.[20] If we don't, we'll keep putting off putting off—and hindering the manifestation of Christ in us from blessing others and drawing them to Him.

3:5 The ministry of mortification. As stated, Paul instructed the Colossians to "mortify" their old sinful ways and desires. To "mortify" is simply to kill: "Put to death...whatever belongs to your earthly nature" (3:5, NIV), "killing off everything connected with that way of life" (THE MESSAGE). The flesh's control must not be toyed with but terminated; not decreased, limited, or suppressed, but finished...kaput! Why this death warrant?

Two reasons stand out. First, as Matthew Henry wrote of the sins of our fleshly nature, "If we do not kill them, they will kill us"—more specifically, the fruit of Christ in us![21] So it's a matter of our spiritual survival and fulfilling our destinies in Christ's kingdom. Second, the spiritual and carnal ways of life are polar opposites. We can't grow in Christ's higher, spiritual lifestyle while indulging our old nature's lower, corrupt sins (Gal. 5:17; 1 Pet. 2:11). The next question then is: How do we mortify our fleshly nature with all its manifestations?[22]

---

20. "Rid yourselves of all such things" (Col. 3:8, NIV). One commentator notes, "The word 'rid' (Greek, *apothesthe*) means 'to put off' like a suit of clothes. In its ethical use here it means 'throw it off like a dirty shirt' (cf. Rom. 13:12; Eph. 4:22, 25; Heb. 12:1; James 1:21; 1 Peter 2:1). In the Bible, behavior is often likened to a garment (e.g., Job 29:14; Ps. 35:26; Isa. 11:5; Rom. 13:12; 1 Thess. 5:8)." See Walvoord and Zuck, *The Bible Knowledge Commentary: An Exposition of the Scriptures*, Col. 3:7–9, note.

21. Henry, *Commentary in One Volume*, 1873.

22. See my earlier entry, "Christian circumcision" (Col. 2:11–13), where the various manifestations of the fleshly nature are discussed: proud flesh, religious flesh, idealistic flesh, intellectual flesh, independent flesh, worldly

Some suggest vows will reverse our fleshly bent: "I will never do this again!" Others teach "reckoning" ourselves identified with Christ's death (Rom. 6:11; cf. 6:7–18)! Still others recommend new godly habits. Some are confident fasting will bring victory. Others suggest going ever onward spiritually leaves the flesh behind. Still others feel accountability is the answer. Some are convinced self-examination is the great key. Why choose between these methods? Aren't we free to employ them all to kill this "Fleshtine" giant, our Goliath, and keep him entombed?

Let's examine them closer:

1. Vows. Vowing isn't required, only obedience. But if ready to make a vow to God, pledge only what you're sure you can keep. Take your vow seriously, and remind yourself of it periodically so you won't forget. Why? God says it's better not to vow than to vow and not pay (Eccles. 5:4–5; cf. Ps. 50:14). And don't trust in your willpower alone. Ask the Holy Spirit—your personal, supernatural Helper—to give you sufficient grace to faithfully keep your vow. "Ask, and it shall be given" (Matt. 7:7).

2. Reckoning and yielding. Since your flesh died with Christ, "Reckon yourselves to be dead indeed unto sin" (Rom. 6:11) and "say so" aloud: "Let the redeemed of the Lord say so" (Ps. 107:2). This affirmation of faith releases fresh grace to deaden your sinful impulses and

---

flesh, and lustful flesh.

227

"save" you in your test: "With the mouth he confesses, resulting in salvation" (Rom. 10:10, NAS). Simultaneously, yield! In every temptation you will yield to God or Satan. So remember God's Word in the matter and "yield yourselves unto God" (Rom. 6:13). When temptation returns, reckon and yield again, and again, until Satan's thought-assault in your mind ends.

3. New habits. Changing your habits, or fixed ways of thinking and living, is imperative. Examine your experience to discover what habits are rendering you unspiritual, dull, weak, and thus susceptible to temptation. Then prayerfully seek ways to form new habits to reverse these trends. Start them and resolve to faithfully keep them; should you stumble, restart them with renewed resolve. Habit-building requires resilience. So be quick to rebound after every failure and determined never to give up.[23]

4. Fasting. Fasting is a powerful biblical method that sharpens our spiritual sensibilities and weakens our fleshly inclinations. While eating less, seek God more. Fasting helps fortify your

23. Regarding habits, Oswald Chambers said, "We must take care to launch ourselves with as strong and decided an initiative as possible...[and] never suffer an exception to occur till the new habit is securely rooted in your life," and added, "Seize the very first possible opportunity to act on every resolution you make." See Harry Verploegh, *Oswald Chambers: The Best From All His Books* (Nashville, TN: Thomas Nelson Publishers, 1987), 148.

will and lifts you above many pesky sinful urges.

5. FEED, AND GO FORWARD IN, THE SPIRITUAL. While disciplining your body, indulge your spirit. Feed your heart with feasts of God's Word, immerse your spirit in God's presence in prayer, let the Spirit rain on you abundantly as you praise and worship God in the secret place, and sharpen your soul in God-centered conversations with committed believers. Pursue whatever improves your spiritual life. Faithfully discharge the duties or ministries God has assigned you. Stay close to Christ by giving thanks and meditating on His Word through the day. Whatever happens, take the next step forward. Paul affirmed the best way to avoid sliding back is to always go forward: "Walk [on] in the Spirit, and ye shall not fulfill the lusts of the flesh" (Gal. 5:16).

6. BE ACCOUNTABLE. Accountability is another aid. Find another committed Christian in your circle of friends, preferably with similar weaknesses, who can be a "flesh buddy." Faithfully report to each other on a regular basis, especially when one of you is weak and needs extra prayer or exhortation. This small support can go a long way toward helping your spiritual house stand (Matt. 7:24–25).

7. SELF-EXAMINATION. Monitor your spiritual condition regularly, quickly confessing any

sinful thoughts or behavior to God (1 John 1:9). Never beat yourself up but instead receive forgiveness and quickly take the next step to resume your spiritual journey (1 John 1:5–9). And, of course, to examine ourselves efficiently we must stop examining everyone else obsessively, as Jesus so pointedly taught us (Matt. 7:1–5)!

⊷⊷

All these simple-but-proven methods further the ministry of mortification in us, strengthening our Christ life and weakening our fleshly nature. And they all check our enemy's relentless assaults.

By God's direct permission Satan knows every Christian's fleshly weaknesses, just as he knew Samson's, Balaam's, David's, and Peter's (Luke 22:31). Satan will tempt us with provocations, allurements, and suggestions, hoping we'll yield to them and fail. But God allows them, as in Job's case, to build our characters by testing our loyalty to Him and His Scriptural commands—in this case Paul's injunction to "mortify" our flesh. So check the tempter and please the Tester!

Remember the methods of mortification described above and practice them until your flesh's ability to spoil your walk and work with Jesus is, well, kaput!

3:5 A common—and hidden—idol. After ordering the Colossians to mortify all forms of sexual immorality, Paul ordered they should also mortify "covetousness" (3:5). Then he went further, affirming the latter is a form of "idolatry"

(3:5)—a sin that displeases God so much His first two commandments forbid it (Exod. 20:1–5; Matt. 6:19–21, 24), He sent Israel and Judah into exile for it, and, Paul warned, He will visit in anger Christians who practice it (Col. 3:6). No isolated statement, Paul also affirmed greed is idolatry in his letter to the Ephesians (Eph. 5:5).[24] Surprised?

We shouldn't be. Just look around! The ardent desire for more money and things is the most common god wooing and driving the whole world. Avarice has been quite evident in post–Second World War America, where we've experienced unprecedented economic prosperity, real (1950s, 1960s) and artificial (1980s to present).[25] Of course, prosperous American Christians didn't have to turn our blessings into idols. We could have worshiped the Blesser even more for His goodness and carefully kept Him and His kingdom work front and center. While many have done so, sadly, many others have not. And many who have not enjoyed material prosperity have served covetousness by making their prime life goal socioeconomic advancement. While many idols may lurk in our hearts, the sacred shrine of "mammon"—riches and property loved or trusted in more than God—is arguably the one most widely visited in our thoughts, conversa-

24. Additionally, Paul mentioned sexual immorality and covetousness in the same breath in several of his letters (Rom. 1:29; 1 Cor. 5:11; Eph. 5: 3, 5). His clearest link is in 1 Timothy 6:9: "They that will [desire to] be rich fall into temptation…and into many foolish and hurtful lusts." Sexual immorality and love of money are spiritually linked because both are soul-lusts, unreasonably impatient desires demanding instant gratification without any regard of the consequences for others, oneself, or ones' relationship to God.

25. Much of the personal wealth acquired in the last few decades in America has been artificial because it's been obtained with credit, not capital.

tions, life planning, and efforts. This is why Jesus, knowing and anticipating us so perfectly, forbade mammon worship in Matthew 6:19–21, 24, and Paul, writing by Christ's inspiration, did the same in 1 Timothy 6:6–11, 17.[26] But we've largely ignored their conspicuous and passionate warnings. While in our public discourse we fret loudly over more overt forms of sin (abortion, homosexuality, atheism, fornication, invalid divorce and remarriage, occultism, etc.), covetousness, alive and well, lurks in our hearts.

It's not uncommon for born-again Christians to ardently discuss money-making methods in many of their private conversations or study it in conferences on stewardship, investment training, family planning, estate planning, or other legitimate fields of financial interest. This is harmless, even beneficial—*if* our hearts aren't set on accruing wealth to trust in, love, or boast of. I wish this were always the case.

But the truth is, in such conversations or conferences gain is all too often the real motive, and idol, of our deceitful hearts—which reduces Christ to a mere religious hobby and our profession "Jesus is Lord" to a hypocritical mask hiding our real god. This covetousness remains largely hidden while semi-weekly we study the teachings of one who lived a possessionless life and warned, "Take heed, and beware of covetousness," and then dropped this philosophical bombshell: "A man's life consisteth not in the abundance of the things

---

26. J. B. Phillips translates "covetousness" as "the lust for other people's goods" (Col. 3:5, Phillips). Thus, besides feeding idolatrous greed, covetous also spawns envy. We are inclined to envy those who have the material things we covet (Exod. 20:17) and senselessly and unjustly hate them merely because they have them and we don't! This leads to harmful judging, contention, confusion, failed relationships, and needless divisions in homes, churches, and nations (James 3:14–16; Gen. 26:12–21; Matt. 5:21–22).

which he possesseth" (Luke 12:15); or, "Beware! Guard against every kind of greed. Life is not measured by how much you own" (NLT; cf. Ezek. 33:31). How can we know our true heart condition?

Three simple litmus tests reveal it. First, what excites us more, ways to make money or ways to walk closer with Jesus? Second, what holds our interest longer, talks on wealth creation or expositions of Jesus' teachings? Third, are we peacefully content with "whatever" material possessions we have (Phil. 4:11–12), even if only food and clothing (1 Tim. 6:8; Heb. 13:5), or do we always desire more, even when we have enough or have recently received increase?

If only half the time, thought, energy, and expense we spend on temporal wealth creation was spent instead on seeking the eternal spiritual wealth of God's truth, Spirit, and faith, we'd be rich in the things of God—and, ironically, very adequately provided for materially also, enjoying everything we need as we need it (Matt. 6:33; Phil. 4:19).[27] It's time we become serious self-iconoclasts, zealots earnestly discerning and destroying our own heart idols! Jeremiah had to "throw down" idols before God could build and plant in Judah (cf. Jer. 1:10). Willing to be a spiritual demolitionist?

---

27. As in all matters, we need balance here. While turning from avarice, we should turn to a stronger work ethic (Rom. 12:11; Col. 3:17, 23), greater financial responsibility, and increased charity, striving always to be excellent stewards of whatever material prosperity God entrusts to us. Having wealth is not sin, as Paul instructs (1 Tim. 6:17–19), but longing for it, and refusing to be content, is (1 Tim. 6:9–10; cf. 6:6–8; Heb. 13:5). We must also understand divine wealth creation. God grants extraordinary financial success to chosen believers so they may use their resources as "helps" (1 Cor. 12:28) to forward His kingdom work—which, however spiritual it may be, can't function without material support! See Deut. 8:18; 2 Chron. 31:4–10; Luke 8:1–3; 1 Cor. 9:14; 16:1–3; 2 Cor. 9:8; Phil. 4:10, 14–18.

In June 1987, President Ronald Reagan called upon then–Soviet leader Mikhail Gorbachev to remove the Berlin Wall, the iconic barrier between Communist East Berlin and free West Berlin: "Mr. Gorbachev, tear down this wall!" Just over two years later, jubilant German citizens began dismantling the wall and enjoying newfound freedoms. Who among us today hears Christ, His explicit warnings against mammon-worship long ignored, calling us to rid our hearts of every vestige of money-loving and materialism? "Christians, my chosen bride, tear down this idol!" If we don't respond, we'll prevent Him from dwelling in us in all His fullness, because He will not dwell with idols. If we do, He'll restore the fullness of His Spirit, favor, and joy. Full insight into His Word, a renewed sense of His presence and voice, and opportunities to serve Him will rush back into our lives, filling the void created by our departed idols, and we'll be reestablished in spiritual freedom. Ready to "tear down this idol"?

If we catch ourselves dreaming of more wealth we're still serving mammon, not Messiah, and chasing a mirage that will never satisfy our deepest soul needs (Eccles. 5:10). Ask the first-century Laodiceans. They said they were "rich and increased with goods," but Jesus said they were spiritually poor and unsatisfied (Rev. 3:18). Conversely, their poor, persecuted neighbors, the Smyrnans, were materially needy but Christ declared them "rich" in faithfulness and worthy to be crowned with more heavenly life and rewards (2:10). Which example are we following?

When Jesus returns He'll remove Antichrist's idol-image from the yet-to-be-constructed Jewish temple and take His rightful place there. Pure worship will ensue—and Christ's wide, powerful ministries throughout all nations. At the

Beautiful Gate, the idol-free apostles Peter and John testified they had no "silver and gold" (Acts 3:6), but they had spiritual power and used it freely to heal a lame man. Sadly, just a few centuries later, the Roman church, earnestly engaged in the idolatrous, headlong pursuit of worldly wealth and power, was in just the opposite condition: increased with silver and gold but void of spiritual power! Which condition do we want? Idolatrous impotency or holy power?

Let's "tear down this wall"—remove the anti-Christian mammon idol hidden in the temple of our hearts—so Jesus may revisit and refill us, and we may again offer pure worship and minister in divine power.

3:6 Our Father's anger. Paul warned the Colossians that their loving heavenly Father had "holy anger" (3:6, PHILLIPS) and listed specific sins (3:5) that not only blocked their fellowship with Him but also stirred His anger: "These things make God angry" (3:6, NCV; cf. Eph. 5:3–6). The Colossians no doubt believed and received this warning. Do we?

Today many don't. We believe the Bible's declarations of our Father's love yet doubt or deny its assertions that sin brings His anger and chastisement (clearly implied in Col. 3:6; Eph. 5:6). Paul didn't specify when, where, or how God's wrath "cometh" on His disobedient children but assured us it will (cf. Rom. 1:18). Though very forbearing, God isn't to be taken lightly as we would someone who repeatedly issued empty threats. Like a loving, earthly father, He never chastens unless He must, and when He must He defers as long as possible. But if we force His hand by persisting willful disobedience, He shows His displeasure by sending us troubling unnecessary adversities—our Jonah's storms (Jon. 1–3),

Asa's sickness (2 Chron. 16:10, 12), Samson's captivity (Jud. 16:1–22), or Jacob's Shechem disaster (Gen. 34:1–31). Yet even these shocking wake-up calls are motivated by His loving compassion. He loves us enough to do whatever it takes to drive home the most ancient and basic lessons of wisdom. For instance:

1. We should, "Fear God, and keep His commandments," because He examines and repays all our acts, good and bad (Eccles. 12:13–14).

2. We should remember even when God forgives He sometimes lets us pay for our misdeeds (Ps. 98:8; Matt. 5:25–26).[28]

3. We should realize we will reap whatever we persistently sow (Gal. 6:7–8).

So though grace saves us and sustains us throughout our earthly walk, it doesn't prevent God's measured punishments when we anger Him by stubbornly continuing to practice sin. Alarmed?

We should be. But this is a wake-up call, not a death knell, and we need it! Today many Christians have misunderstood God's love and fallen asleep spiritually with indifference to their besetting sins (Hos. 7:2; Heb. 12:1). But God's love is holy, not permissive; it forgives but never indulges sin. And because we know God's truth, He holds us to a higher standard than unbelievers (Luke 12:47–48). So whenever it

---

28. Some sins are committed, confessed, and washed away by the blood privately before God (1 John 1:9), while others involving or harming other people create lasting repercussions that, after forgiving us, our wise Father lets us endure and learn from (cf. 2 Sam. 12:9–12; Matt. 5:23–26).

becomes necessary, rather than prevent corrective punishment, God's love prompts it—to initiate our conviction, repentance, and restoration to a sanctified, loving walk with God (Heb. 12:5–6; Prov. 3:11–12; Rev. 3:19). What's our heavenly Father's objective in all this? Christlike character! He's training us to walk in not only the faith and forgiveness but also the integrity, righteousness, faithfulness, and consistent obedience of His Son (Rom. 8:29). Thus Paul's alarm to the Colossians and us. Awake yet?

Soon all believers will be. Father will see to it in these last days, the easy way or the hard way (1 Pet. 4:17). If lesser means fail our Father may send some "Ananias and Sapphira" shock treatments to stir us from our sleepy indifference to His holy anger and restore in us healthy respect for Him (Acts 5:1–11). I pray this isn't necessary.

But if it is, even so, come Lord Jesus. Better that we respect our Father's holy anger now than suffer its consequences at Christ's judgment seat (2 Cor. 5:10–11).

3:10–4:6 Pressing on with putting on? In the larger context (3:8–4:6), Paul urged the Colossians to "put off" their old attitudes and behavior and "put on" the new ways of thinking and living they had received in Christ. His "put offs" and "put ons" describe how we change clothes spiritually. Every sin forbidden or virtue ordered constitutes a separate piece of spiritual clothing to be discarded or donned as we progress toward spiritual maturity, or consistent Christlike behavior. Eventually we've completely changed "clothes," or our usual behavior visible to others. Our old "grave clothes" gone, we're now covered in new "grace clothes."[29]

We begin this wardrobe change by diligently discarding our old spiritual clothes, the sinful attitudes and behavior of our fleshly nature Paul outlined in 3:5–9.[30] As we lay them aside, we should increasingly focus on putting on each piece of our new clothing in Christ. In the verses that follow Paul informed the Colossians, and us, precisely how to do this.

Let's review his instructions in 3:10–4:6:

- 3:10 Renew the new man in you daily by seeking ever more knowledge of Him through studying the Scriptures,[31] meditating on them, spending devotional time with Christ, and observing how He deals with you and other believers. As it grows and becomes ever "fuller and more perfect" (AMP), this biblical and experiential knowledge of God helps gradually conform you to "the image of its Creator" (NIV).[32]

- 3:11 Fully accept God has no biases and freely adopt His attitude. Be a prejudice-free Christian, fellowshiping and worshiping with all believers regardless of their race, nationality,

---

29. Wiersbe, *The Bible Exposition Commentary*, Vol. 2, Col. 3:12–17, note.

30. See my note on Col. 3:5–9, "Putting off putting off?"

31. Prayerful immersion in the written Word feeds and strengthens our intimacy with the living Word (John 1:1–5, 14; cf. Ps. 1:1–3).

32. "This 'new self' needs constant renewal or refreshing—it is *being renewed* (pres. tense), in order to keep it victorious over sin (2 Cor. 4:16; Rom. 12:2; Eph. 4:23)." See Walvoord and Zuck, *The Bible Knowledge Commentary: An Exposition of the Scriptures*, Col. 3:10, note.

religious background, education, sophistica-
tion, crudeness, political views, or socioeconomic standing (Acts 10:34–35).[33] Though born
unequally, every Christian has been born again
equally (Gal. 3:27–28). "Christ is all" that matters now, and He is "in all" who receive Him.[34]

- 3:12–13 Consider how God has elected, consecrated, and kindly loved you, and continue
doing so until you're rapt in His love. Then
show the same mercies to others (cf. Phil.
2:1–5). Think, speak, and react with humble
kindness to everyone, especially "one another,"
"forbearing" with difficult people, and "forgiving" offenders quickly ("readily pardoning
each other," 3:13, AMP), remembering "Christ
forgave you" a debt you could never pay.[35]

---

33. The kingdom is, and forever will be, a classless society. Even the overcomers who will rule with Christ over others will consider themselves, and
be considered, first among equals. Are we practicing this mentality now, or
do worldly distinctions still cause us to think too highly or lowly of fellow
Christians? Do we realize that worldly measurements of importance—
wealth, office, achievements, academic distinctions, ancestry—mean nothing
in Christ's kingdom and that every soul is equally precious to Him? Only
continuing willful sin or erroneous salvation doctrine should prevent our fellowship with other professing Christians (1 Cor. 5:9–11; Gal. 1:6–9; 2 John
10–11).

34. Christ is in us all, ruling us all, teaching us all, forgiving us all, correcting us all, guiding us all, and His views are all that matter—overruling
all our former prejudices.

35. Jesus reminded us forgiveness is mandatory if we wish to live in the
Father's favor and fellowship (Matt. 18:21–35; Mark 11:25–26). It is also one
of the great keys to all relational unity. The refusal to forgive spoils friend-
ships, marriages, families, churches, and revivals. Be forgiving, not foolish;
obedient to your Forgiver, not obstinate.

- 3:14 Put on God's love as a cloak or mantle covering all your other Christ-clothes. His love is "shed abroad" in your heart if you've received His Spirit (Rom. 5:5), and your determination to release it by steadily walking in love marks you as truly Christlike or spiritually mature (Matt. 5:48). As "the bond of perfectness" it's a unique linking agent capable of creating and sustaining unity in even the most troubled human relationships and social units. This amazingly strong and patient understanding for others is willing to respond meekly to arrogance, forgive endlessly, and endure injustice or difficult people long seasons without becoming bitter (1 Cor. 13:4–8).[36]

- 3:15 Remember you're "called" by God to live in "the peace of God." So walk with Christ without doing anything that agitates your calm, quiet, inner fellowship with Him (or others, if possible; Rom. 12:18, NIV). Guard this priceless tranquility that "passeth all understanding" (Phil. 4:7). Let it be an impartial judge (lit. "umpire") evaluating your soul's condition and how you treat others (3:12–13).[37] When it

---

36. Long-suffering (endurance) is a core characteristic of God's love. The Amplified Bible describes "long-suffering" as "tireless," having "the power to endure whatever comes with good temper" (Col. 3:12). Warren Wiersbe calls it "long-temper," as contrasted with being short-tempered. Are we patiently enduring in prayer and kindness with mean-spirited adversaries and exasperating Christians or becoming argumentative or resentful? See Wiersbe, *The Bible Exposition Commentary*, Vol. 2, Col. 3:12–17, note.

37. We should also allow God's peace to judge all matters of guidance,

abides, all's well; when it goes, examine yourself to discover why. "And be thankful"—sinners
can't, many Christians won't, but you can be
clothed daily, if you will, in the very wondrous,
undisturbable calmness Jesus walked in!

- 3:16 Stay full of "the word of Christ"—all
  God's Word, but especially Christ's teachings. Filled "richly" with His Word—steadily
  remembering, studying, and meditating
  on it[38]—you'll increasingly thrive in "all
  wisdom."[39] (This also applies to churches: "Let
  the word of Christ dwell in [or 'among[40]] you";
  or, "in you [all]." Interpreting Scripture and

"deciding and settling with finality all questions that arise in your minds"
(3:15, AMP). When needing guidance, if we pray, make the best reasonable
and biblical choice, and maintain peace about it, we may safely act. If, however, we try but can't find inner peace about our choice, we should wait and
continue seeking God's guidance (Prov. 3:5–6; Rom. 8:14; Acts 16:6–10;
James 1:5).

38. One simple, practical way to grow "rich" in God's Word is to keep
it on or near your person—in a favorite devotional, a pocket testament
and psalms, a small book of Scripture quotes or pithy biblical teachings, smart phones, iPads or laptop computer—to aid your meditation on it.
Enrich your odd moments in the day by "withdrawing" God's Words from
such spiritual ATMs and meditating on them. Rich in the Word, you will
then find it easier to obey it when tests arise (James 1:22–25). Also, the best
way to enrichment in "the full richness of Christ's teaching" (3:16, PHIL-
LIPS) is simply to read and study the gospels. Paul's instruction here to stay
full of God's Word compliments his instruction to stay full of the Spirit in
Eph. 5:18–21 and reminds us we need to be as full of God's Word *and* Spirit
as possible.

39. Paul's reference to "all wisdom" is another reminder that "all the treasures of wisdom and knowledge" are in Christ (2:3)—and another rebuke to
the heretics who claimed to have exclusive access to wisdom!

40. Wiersbe, *The Bible Exposition Commentary*, Vol. 2, Col. 3:16, note.

applying it to our lives should be central in our meetings.) And thriving, you'll overflow, "teaching and admonishing one another" with God's Word daily (3:16; cf. Prov. 27:17; Heb. 3:13).[41]

- 3:16 Clothe your new life with God-songs! With "grace in your hearts," or with "thankful hearts" (NLT), sing "psalms and hymns and spiritual songs"[42] not merely about but "to" the Lord (cf. Acts 13:1–2; 16:25).[43] As you sing worshipful songs of adoration and exuberant praises to God, He gives fresh inspiration to power you through tough times and persisting temptations (Mark 14:26; Acts 16:25).

- 3:17, 23 Do "whatever" you do—at home or work, in private or public, in word or act— with excellence and enthusiasm (3:23), as

---

41. "Many have the word of Christ dwelling in them, but it dwells in them but *poorly*. The soul prospers when the word of God dwells in us *richly*." Henry, *Commentary in One Volume*, Col. 3:12–17, note, 1873.

42. God loves variety in our worship. Thus, Paul suggests: "psalms," the pure, biblical chants and worship songs of the psalter used by ancient Israel and the early church; "hymns," the lyrically and harmonically rich songs of traditional Protestant churches; and "spiritual songs," the fresh, new worship songs the Spirit releases to gifted modern songwriters, psalmists, and worship leaders every time He refills and revives the body of Christ. He suggests the same in Ephesians 5:19. Are you willing to try this varied or blended worship Paul by inspiration recommends?

43. In the early church individual believers sometimes stood and sang spontaneous solos—not for performance but as worship, testimonials, or teachings in song—expressing in their own unique way and voice their love or praise to Christ. See *Life Application Study Bible*, Col. 3:16, note, 2035.

representing Christ, as being authorized by
Him,[44] as if He ask you personally to do it
(3:23), and for His pleasure and honor (3:17).
And be "giving thanks," not complaints, as you
do it (cf. Phil. 2:14)!

- 3:18–4:1 Faithfully fulfill your marital, family,
  and vocational obligations as Paul described
  them here. Your motive should be one: to
  please Christ! Why? At the judgment He
  will without "respect of persons" evaluate and
  reward you for your conduct in these areas.

- 4:2–4 Continue praying persistently and
  with thanksgiving for everyone around you,
  including Christians (Eph. 6:18). Also ask
  God to give your ministers divinely inspired
  speaking opportunities, inspiring messages, and
  the inspiration to deliver them as they should
  be delivered—fearlessly.

- 4:5 Redeem your time, buying back through
  spiritually disciplined living after your conversion all the time you wasted before your
  conversion.

- 4:5–6 Behave wisely, not naively or argumen-
  tatively, toward unbelievers, remembering they
  are spiritually hostile but also pitiable captives

---

44. By authorizing us to pray, minister, and even remove spiritual mountains (obstacles) in His Name, Jesus gave us His power of attorney to conduct His kingdom work till He returns (John 16:23; Mark 11:23; Acts 3:6;
16:18). See Finnis J. Dake, *Dake's Annotated Reference Bible* (Lawrenceville,
GA: Dake Bible Sales, 1963), John 16:23, note "h," 115.

of Satan (2 Cor. 4:3–4; 2 Tim. 2:24–26). Let your words always be "salted" with God's graciousness, and ask His gracious assistance "that ye may know how ye ought to answer every man" in a manner that pleases Him and does not stumble them.

By practicing these things again and again you "put on" more and more of the New Man until one day you're entirely clothed in consistently Christlike thinking and behavior. The regular manifestation of these righteous ways constitutes our special wedding garment that ensures our participation in the joyful, heavenly "marriage supper of the Lamb" (Rev. 19:7–9; cf. Matt. 22:11–13). Knowing how serious this is, Paul urged the Colossians to diligently pursue their spiritual clothing process. Considering what excellent believers they were (Col. 1:3–8; 2:5–7), I'm sure they responded. Are you responding?

Are you donning new grace clothes daily or content with your old grave clothes? Not yet serious about acquiring the life changes Paul ordered or focused on cultivating them? Christ is coming soon. It's time we press on with putting on.

3:17 Paul's thanksgiving trilogies. This is the second of Paul's three primary commands in the New Testament to give God thanks, the others being Ephesians 5:20 and 1 Thessalonians 5:18.

In Thessalonians he ordered thanksgiving "in" every circumstance or situation (5:18). In Ephesians he urged us to give thanks "for" all things (5:20). In Colossians he counseled thanksgiving in whatever we "do" (Col. 3:17). Every situation, every circumstance, every action—that pretty much covers our whole existence, every waking moment! And note in each reference Paul used specially crafted all-inclusive language: "everything" (1 Thess. 5:18), "all things" (Eph. 5:20), "whatever" (Col. 3:17). Thus, there are no situations and no actions excluded from these thanksgiving commands. We should, therefore, offer thanks as continually as we breathe.[45] But Paul wasn't finished.

He inscribed a second "mini-trilogy" in this context in Colossians: verses 15, 16, and 17 each exhort us to give God thanks.[46]

> And let the peace of God rule in your hearts...and be ye thankful.
>
> —COLOSSIANS 3:15

> Let the word of Christ dwell in you richly...singing with grace ["thankfulness," ESV[47]] in your hearts to the Lord.
>
> —COLOSSIANS 3:16

> And whatever you do, in word or deed, do all...giving thanks to God and the Father by him.
>
> —COLOSSIANS 3:17

---

45. We breathe in good times and bad. So we should offer God thanks in prosperity and adversity, the latter being especially pleasing to Him (Ps. 69:30–32; Acts 16:24–25).

46. Carson, France, Motyer, and Wenham, *New Bible Commentary: 21st Century Edition*, 4th ed., Col. 3:17, note.

47. "Grace" (Col. 3:16) is translated from the Greek *charis*, which may refer to thankfulness, goodwill, gratitude, or joyfulness. Numerous translations (ESV, NAS, NLT, NCV, ISV, MLB, MOFFATT) feel "thankfulness" is the meaning best suited to Paul's context of worshipful singing. For definition, see Spicq and Ernest, *Theological Lexicon of the New Testament*, s.v. "*charis*."

Combining and paraphrasing these three verses, Paul said:

> Live in God's peace, and thank Him you can! Sing to
> Him regularly with a heartful of heartfelt thankful-
> ness. And whatever you do, give Him thanks while
> doing it.
>
> —AUTHOR'S PARAPHRASE

Often the Bible emphasizes truths or subjects merely by repeating them. Thus, by not one but two inspired thanksgiving trilogies, Colossians' author and His heavenly Inspirer heavily emphasized this subject: Not just Paul but Christ wants us being thankful to God and giving Him thanks always—every waking moment! Without constantly inhaling oxygen and exhaling carbon dioxide we can't live. Without steadily breathing in and out thankfulness to God our new man won't grow properly, endure trials successfully, and glorify Christ fully! Nor will we be exemplary New Testament believer-priests offering the "sacrifice of praise to God continually, that is, the fruit of our lips giving thanks to his name" (Heb. 13:15).

This explains why the Spirit of God prompted Paul's repetition. Yes, to God thanksgiving is that important.[48] Grasping this, the Colossians abounded with thanksgiving in their lives and meetings. Are we also "abounding with thanksgiving" (2:7)?

3:18–4:1 Commands and comments for home and work. As in Ephesians (Eph. 5:22–6:9), Paul addressed key home

---

48. Paul refers to himself or others giving thanks thirty-five times in the New Testament, seven of which are in this Colossian epistle alone (Col. 1:3, 12; 2:7; 3:15, 16, 17; 4:2).

and work duties in this Colossian letter.[49] While behavior codes were well known to Paul's Colossian readers, he gave them a new perspective on, or an inspired "revised version" of, familiar conventions. In Paul's behavioral guidebook he made pleasing Christ the central motive for all good conduct and Christ's judgment, not man's, its ultimate evaluator.[50] But there's something else here we should study.

Repeatedly Paul's commands are accompanied by comments that motivate compliance by offering clarifications, encouragements, or warnings. First he tells us what we should do and then explains why we should do it. Not exclusively a Pauline trait, this command–comment pattern is seen throughout the Bible and is a mark of God's great love. In His omnipotent sovereignty, God could simply command, "Do this!" or, "Don't do that!" After all, He's the only real God and fearfully omnipotent! Couldn't He just tell us what we should do, and if we comply, bless; or if we don't, punish? And if we're obstinate, couldn't He just remove us and create others to serve Him?[51] Certainly the capricious mythological Greek and Roman gods would have done so in a heartbeat. Why? They didn't care about their worshipers.

But the true God does. He's a compassionate, not a callous, deity who not only seeks "true worshipers" but helps us

---

49. This passage (Col. 3:18–4:1) is paraphrased excellently in *The Message*. (Please never use a paraphrase as your primary Bible or accept its version of biblical texts without comparing it with excellent literal Bible translations.)

50. Hayford, *The Spirt-Filled Life Bible*, Col. 3:18–4:1, note, 1818.

51. God almost did this to the nation of Israel twice (Exod. 32:10; Num. 14:12). It seems the Laodiceans were for one precarious moment in danger of a similar extinctive judgment (Rev. 3:16)—until Christ subsequently offered them mercy (3:18–22).

serve and worship Him (John 4:23–24). Knowing our compliance is best for us, our families, our churches, and His worldwide plan, He mercifully follows His commands with comments wisely crafted to motivate obedience. When we obey, everyone wins: God is honored for His wise and loving commands and His gracious extra efforts to motive obedience, we are honored for our submissive compliance, and everyone around us is blessed as well.

Let's examine more closely Paul's use of this command–comment pattern:

- Colossians 3:18

    COMMAND: "Wives, submit to your own husbands"—addresses not all "women," but "wives" only,[52] who should submit to "your own husbands," not all husbands or all men! To "submit" is to graciously yield to another's leadership decisions; to cooperate, assist, or support; or to "subordinate and adapt" (3:18, AMP; cf. 1 Pet. 3:1–6). Submission doesn't imply inferiority or worthlessness but simply establishes lines of authority so there may be order, peace, and progress. (This assumes husbands' willingness to lead their wives and families in love, integrity, and wisdom.)

    COMMENT: "As it is fit in the Lord"—means in the Lord's sight a wife's submission is "fit" (proper or good). Conversely it hints

---

52. These guidelines are not for single women in society, business, government, organizations, or even the church (Gal. 3:28) but specifically address wives' relations to their own husbands in the context of marriage.

some husbands' wishes may not be "fit," proper, or "in the Lord's" will. Thus, wives must use discretion and in rare instances not comply—though remain respectful.[53] Domestically, every husband is head of his household and family matters. But he's his wife's spiritual authority only if he's "in the Lord," or trusting and obeying Christ.

• Colossians 3:19

COMMAND: "Husbands love your wives"— daily, not sporadically; sacrificially, not selfishly, "as [deeply and perseveringly as] Christ also loved the church" (Eph. 5:25; 1 Pet. 3:7)! Love—seeking another's highest good—should motivate every decision and act. And every prayer. As Christ interceded for His "wife" on Earth (Mark 6:46–47; Luke 22:32; John 17:1–26), and still does in heaven (Heb. 7:25), so should every husband. Heartless headship fails, but loving leadership lasts![54]

---

53. This is the same discretion we exercise toward all authorities. If the leaders of any entity—governments, businesses, organizations, churches— ask us to do what is plainly contrary to God's Word and righteousness, we are duty bound to obey the higher authority of God, while remaining respectful toward such authorities though noncompliant with their unbiblical requests (Acts 4:19; 5:29). Thus, even in apparent rebellion we are still submissive to God.

54. "Headship is not dictatorship," and a good and wise husband will consider his wife's needs and preferences as keenly as his own. On quote, see Wiersbe, *The Bible Exposition Commentary*, Vol. 2, Col. 3:18–19, note.

COMMENT: "And be not bitter against them"—warns husbands of the danger of becoming "harsh" or "resentful" (AMP) at their wives' persisting weaknesses or resistance, especially their contentiousness, complaints, disrespectfulness, conjugal coldness, slander, or other ways they express dissatisfaction with their husband's authority (Exod. 4:25–26; Prov. 19:13; 27:15). Human love may fail this test, but God's "love never faileth" and can "suffer long" and yet still be "kind" (1 Cor. 13:4–8). Husband, stay close to Jesus, and, refilled with His love, don't let your kindness become curtness.

• Colossians 3:20

COMMAND: "Children obey your parents in all things"—not just when you agree! Humbly acknowledge your parents' greater experiences and wisdom (gleaned from successes... and failures!) and natural desire to see their children succeed, and do as they say.[55]

---

55. Parents are our first authority figures. Obeying them trains children to respect not just their parents but all authorities. But it should also be noted, especially today, children may be faced with unreasonable, morally wrong commands by very sinful, irresponsible, or criminal parents and thus have to use prayerful discretion and the counsel of spiritually minded adults in deciding when *not* to obey such parents. This is underscored by the many instances in which our courts justifiably step in to remove children from abusive, addicted, perverted, or emotionally unstable parents. Thus, by willful irresponsibility, criminal or abusive behavior, or other ways in which parents demonstrate total indifference to their children's welfare, they undermine their natural moral authority and forfeit their right to raise their children.

COMMENT: "For [because] this is well-pleasing unto the Lord"—Jesus is pleased with obedient children because they (1) follow His example (Luke 2:51–52) and (2) help maintain order, peace, and progress their homes. If your parents are unaffectionate, selfish, or too strict, obey them anyway, to please Christ and convert your parent![56] Many a hardened parent has been melted in conviction by a loving, obedient child.[57]

- Colossians 3:21

    COMMAND: "Fathers, provoke not your children to anger"—or, "Do not be hard on them or harass them...do not break their spirit" (AMP). How? By shouting, arguing, nagging, showing contempt over their failures, deriding them as inferior to their siblings, or merely by withholding expressions of the loving approval they need. All these fatherly failures crush the children God has

---

56. Ephesians 6:1–3 instructs children to (1) obey and (2) honor their parents. Craig Keener notes, "Throughout the ancient world (including under Old Testament law, Deut. 21:18–21), minor children were expected to obey their parents; although Roman law allowed the father to demand obedience even of adult children, adults no longer living with their parents were normally expected only to honor their parents." See Keener, *IVP Bible Background Commentary*, Col. 3:20, note.

57. This is the same principle as when the consistent godly behavior of a humble, loving wife convicts and converts her unsaved, and sometimes unsavory, husband (1 Pet. 3:1)!

given us to nourish and build up in His ways (cf. Eph. 6:4).[58]

COMMENT: "Lest they be discouraged"—dispirited or depressed due to suppressed anger (Eph. 4:26–27) and a sense of worth-lessness or hopelessness; or emotionally troubled by their parents' implacableness. Our consistent disposition and words make or break our children—and us at the judg-ment (3:25)!

• Colossians 3:22

COMMAND: "Servants, obey in all things your masters according to the flesh"—This orders compliance in "all things," not just requests we like (ct. 1 Sam. 15:1–26). "Ser-vants" in Paul's day were Roman slaves.[59]

---

58. This applies to mothers too. "Fathers" (Col. 3:21) is translated from the Greek, *patēr*, meaning "male parent." But *patēr* is also once translated "par-ents" in the New Testament (Heb. 11:23). This aside, common sense con-firms that coldhearted, contentious, or abusive mothers may also "provoke" their children to vexation and discouragement. Thus, we may amplify this text to read, "*Parents*, provoke not your children..."

59. The New Testament's teaching concerning slavery begs explanation. Unlike the racially driven American slavery, Roman slavery was a non-racially-based, long-established fixture in the empire (comprising roughly 30–40 percent of Italy's population; much less in the larger empire). When the New Testament was written the Christians were few and politically impotent, and slaves came from all races and ethnic groups (defeated com-batants, subjugated peoples). Some slaves were well-educated and held influ-ential positions (in various professions, trades; and in estates as stewards, pedagogues, trusted emissaries, etc.), making their day-to-day life surpris-ingly *better* than that of many free Roman laborers or peasants (and convicts suffering the unimaginable brutalities of Roman mines or galleys!). By nei-ther ordering slave owners to free their slaves nor slaves to rise and establish

Today, however, this command speaks to any subordinate accountable to superiors in any employment setting (Eph. 6:5–8; 1 Tim. 6:1–2; Titus 2:9–10; 1 Pet. 2:18–20).

---

democratic freedom by force, Scripture permits the institution of Roman slavery—but never justifies or promotes it. Instead it calls us all to a new, higher perspective. Free or slave, we should all see ourselves as *Christ's love-slaves*, relish our spiritual freedom (1 Cor. 7:22; Rom. 1:1), enjoy the perfect equality we (ideally) have now in the churches (Gal. 3:28; James 1:9; ct. James 2:1–9), and be content with our legal and social status even if disadvantaged (1 Cor. 7:20, 24) since all of us can now enjoy the highest human joy—the incomparable blessing of daily fellowship with Christ by His Spirit and Word (John 14:21–23; Heb. 13:5–6). Chiefly Scripture applies Christian truths and principles to both slaves' and owners' attitudes and actions toward the other (as discussed above, Col. 3:22–4:1), thus making the best of a bad institution early Christians were powerless to change. It also encourages slaves to seek legal freedom whenever opportunities present themselves (1 Cor. 7:21). Furthermore, Paul's command for slave owners to treat their slaves fairly and kindly (Col. 4:1) is supplemented by Jesus' standing commands to (1) walk in love toward all (Matt. 22:39) and (2) treat others as we want to be treated (Matt. 7:12). Anecdotally, after writing the Colossians Paul sent a recently converted runaway slave, Onesimus, (with the Colossian and Philemon epistles in hand) back to his Christian master and Paul's close friend, Philemon, instructing him to forgive Onesimus for abandoning him (and possibly stealing from him! Philem. 18–19) and resume fellowship with him now as a servant and faithful spiritual brother (Col. 4:9)—and, some expositors believe, perhaps free him (Philem. 21). While Roman law ordered the return of slaves with severe penalties for noncompliance, Paul's actions here represent something more than compliance with Roman legal code. By counseling Onesimus to return and submit and Philemon not to punish but forgive and reinstate him, Paul applied his own slave-master teaching in Colossians to the "Onesimus problem" at hand (Philem. 10–21; Col. 3:22–4:1). Thus, while neither justifying Roman slavery nor calling for its immediate eradication, the New Testament directed Christians how to behave if, for the time, their culture practiced slavery. Notably it does *not* forbid Christians, when numerically or politically able to do so, from throwing off this heinous and degrading institution, which is precisely what British and American abolitionist movements did centuries later in England and America—due largely through the enlightening influence of the Scriptures!

COMMENT: "Not with eyeservice...[but] in singleness of heart, fearing God"—Thus, Paul clarifies the Christian worker's goal— not merely to gratify our human employers but, aiming higher, to please our heavenly Employer. Thus motivated we should be the best employees in the work force. Our honest, willing, faithful, thorough labor makes our Lord and faith appealing to others (Titus 2:9–10). Thus, our excellent work becomes excellent evangelism (Matt. 5:16).

- Colossians 3:23–25

COMMAND: "Whatever ye do, do it heartily, as to the Lord"—addresses not only (then) slaves and (today) subordinates but all Christians in all our activities. Working "heartily" means with our entire animated soul and body fully engaged;[60] or with heart; wholeheartedly, not halfheartedly; spiritedly, not indifferently. "As to the Lord" means as if He (not your superiors) personally asked you to do it; or as an act of worship or service rendered personally to Him.[61]

---

60. "Heartily" is taken from the Greek *psychē*, meaning "breath, soul, life, personality, conscious self," as distinct from the body (*soma*). See Strong, *A Concise Dictionary of the Words in the Greek Testament and The Hebrew Bible*, s. v. "*psychē*." Also see Lust, Eynikel, and Hauspie, *A Greek–English Lexicon of the Septuagint: Revised Edition*, s.v. "*psychē*."

61. Not just our tithes and offerings, not just our songs of praise and worship, not just our gifts or acts of charity to the poor, not just our service in Christian ministry but everything we do every day is an offering of worship to our life-giving Redeemer. Are you worthily worshiping Him this

COMMENT: "Knowing that of the Lord ye shall receive the reward of the inheritance; for ye serve the Lord Christ"—reveals two key facts: (1) we're really serving Jesus, not people, and (2) at issue is not our advancement in this temporal world but our rewards in Christ's eternal kingdom (2 Cor. 5:10–11; Matt. 25:14–30). If remembering this doesn't put some spirit in our service, nothing will!

But sometimes only a stern warning gets our attention. So Paul adds: "He that doeth wrong shall receive for the wrong which he hath done." It's sobering to not only slaves and subordinates but all Christ's servants to remember there are always adverse consequences for spurning God's lovingly designed commands. "And there is no respect of persons" means regardless of any privileged status we may enjoy in this life, God judges us all equally (Gal. 6:7–9).

• Colossians 4:1

COMMAND: "Masters, give unto your servants that which is just and equal"—orders slave masters (then) and employers (today) not to neglect but rather attend to the needs of their slaves or employees. Paul asserted this is only fair, or "just and equal." "Serve them as they do you," or, "Seek to satisfy their needs and interests as they do yours"

---

moment by doing whatever you're doing "heartily, as to the Lord"?

(author's paraphrase). This is Jesus' golden rule (Matt. 7:12).

COMMENT: "Knowing that ye also have a Master in heaven"—reminds Christian masters (then) and employers (today) they are not above accountability (cf. Eph. 6:9). Though in authority they're also under it and will account to Christ for how they treat their subordinates, in heaven and in this life (Prov. 11:31; Ps. 58:11). Unchecked authority often breeds unmerciful leadership, but a mastered master is a merciful master.

In each of these relationships Paul addressed (husband–wife, parents–children, masters–slaves) there is a "mutual responsibility to submit and love."[62] Every authority is commanded to be loving and fair with their subordinates, and every subordinate is reminded to be submissive and respectful toward their superiors—and all to please Jesus, who will reward us individually with perfect fairness![63] My, how our marriages, families, churches, businesses, and every other social unit would thrive if all parties complied with this simple-but-inspired counsel!

---

62. *Life Application Study Bible*, Col. 3:18 – 4:1, note, 2036.

63. As Romans, Christian men had absolute authority in their households. Thus, Paul's instruction tempered their power with humility and love. Roman women who became Christians enjoyed a new, freer, elevated status in Christ and their churches (Gal. 3:28, as did slaves), and some were apparently too assertive in their marriages or talkative in their churches (1 Cor. 14:33–35, 40). So Paul's instruction tempered their Christian liberty with a reminder to respect their God-ordained authorities by cooperating with their husbands and being orderly in church meetings. For more, see *Life Application Study Bible*, Col. 3:18, 19, note, 2036.

Sometimes when this command–comment pattern appears in God's Word, the comment precedes the command, informing us first why God wants us to do something and then what He wants us to do (cf. 1 Sam. 15:2–3). But in every case the comment is motivational, explaining, warning, or urging in order to induce obedience. For more examples of this command–comment pattern, see Gen. 2:16–17; 6:14–17; 9:5–6; Deut. 8:1; 28:1–2; Eccles. 7:9; 12:13–14; Ps. 107:1; 118:1; 150:1–2; Prov. 3:9–10, 21–24; Isa. 41:10; 54:1–3; Ezek. 3:22; Dan. 4:27; Luke 21:36; John 5:14; Rom. 12:19; 1 Cor. 5:6–7; 2 Cor. 6:17–18; 1 Thess. 5:18; 2 Tim. 2:24–26; Eph. 6:2–3; James 3:1; 1 Pet. 5:6, 7, 8; Rev. 2:5; 3:11–12. Here is cause for new praise and practices.

Shouldn't we thank and worship the Lord profusely for being so kind as to add motivational comments to His sovereign commands? And shouldn't we follow His example by clarifying to others why they should comply with biblical requirements, divine guidance, or, when we're in positions of authority, our requests, by pointing out the disadvantages of noncompliance and the advantages of compliance? Isn't that better than just dictating, "Do this because I'm your boss," or "I'm your pastor," or "I'm your husband," or "I'm your parent," and so forth?

3:24 The reward of the inheritance. Paul reminded Colossians presently held in slavery that as believers in Jesus Christ they could take comfort in knowing they were heirs to a heavenly inheritance. This "reward of the inheritance" (3:24), or "an inheritance from the Lord as a reward" (NLT), was their due for simply being believers—God's adopted children, in Christ's mystical body, in God's family, and younger siblings of His chief Son and Heir, Jesus.

An inheritance consists of benefits received from fathers, as directed by their legal wills. God our Father authored our inheritance, His Son's death activated it, and its benefits are described in His will, primarily the New Testament. The Father originally granted this eternal inheritance to Jesus (Heb. 1:2; Ps. 2:7–8; Mark 12:7; Heb. 1:4; Matt. 28:18), and we partake of it by virtue of being in Him (Acts 20:32; 26:18). As God's adopted children by redemption (Gal. 4:4–7) we are joint-heirs with Christ—"if" we continue faithfully trusting and obeying Him and, when necessary, "suffer with Him" (Rom. 8:16–17).

Our eternal inheritance has present and future aspects. Beginning in time and extending throughout eternity, it consists of three major divisions:

1. COVENANT BENEFITS. Every believer enjoys various natural and spiritual covenant blessings now in this life. "Forget not all his benefits," the psalmist urges (Ps. 103:2). One rich benefit is the right to claim the promises of God (Gal. 3:28; 4:29; Eph. 3:6; Heb. 6:12). Another is the bodily aspect of our salvation, including divine healing (Matt. 8:17; James 5:14–16; 1 Pet. 2:24), blessed health (Ps. 91:16; Prov. 4:20–22), and ultimately translation to heaven in an incorruptible body (1 Cor. 15:50–54; 2 Cor. 5:1–5; Eph. 1:14).[64] Our greatest benefit,

---

64. God's promises of healing, health, and long life referenced above do not imply He will never let us be tried, proven, purified, and deepened by experiences of sickness, weariness, or, if our earthly work is finished, an early passing. The Bible plainly shows He does this also (2 Kings 13:14; Job 2:1–8; Phil. 2:25–27; 2 Tim. 4:20).

the down payment (or "earnest," Eph. 1:13–14) of our eternal inheritance, is the Holy Spirit, who enters us at salvation but whose fullness we receive subsequently by request (John 4:10; 2 Cor. 1:21–22). He in turn leads us into the priceless spiritual enrichment of an earthly life lived in heavenly, intimate fellowship with Christ daily (Eph. 1:3–5; John 14:26; 16:13; 17:3; Rom. 8:28; 1 Cor. 10:13; 12:1–31; Eph. 2:6; 3:14–19; Col. 2:3, 9–10; 3:16; Heb. 6:4–5; 10:19–22).

2. ADMISSION TO THE KINGDOM. Every believer receives the right to live in God's kingdom, with all its indescribable blessings, beauties, and joys—forever (1 Cor. 2:9–10; Rev. 21–22)! That divinely ruled realm, which now exists only spiritually in and among those who believe in Christ, will manifest openly in a visible political state in two stages: (a) the thousand-year reign of Christ on this Earth after His bodily return in glory (Matt. 25:34–40; Rev. 20:1–6), and (b) the eternal kingdom of God on the new Earth with New Jerusalem as its capital (Rev. 21–22). The sweetest privilege in the eternal kingdom will be full, direct access to God, as we behold the ineffable glory of the Father and Son and interact with and worship them and the seven-fold Spirit forever (Rom. 8:17–18). It will be unending, unprecedented, unimaginable delight as we enjoy not only the fullness of God but also the fullness of His

new heavens and Earth, with all its natural
wonders on land, in the seas, and in the skies
(Matt. 5:5; Ps. 37:29).[65]

3. PERSONAL REWARDS. Every believer receives
by grace the opportunity to receive additional eternal blessings, gifts, offices, ministries, and privileges by works. While the first
two parts of our inheritance described above
apply equally to us all, our personal rewards
will be based solely on our individual works in
this life (Rom. 14:10–12; 2 Cor. 5:10–11; Col.
3:25). While Paul's phrase "the reward of the
inheritance" points to our inheritance itself as a
redemptive reward, his use of the term *reward*
further suggests our *awards* for personal righteousness or service post conversion (as earthly
inheritances are sometimes altered due to heirs'
good or bad behavior). If referring only to our
common grace-given inheritance, he would
have called it "the *gift* of the inheritance." But
his use of the term *reward* is suggestive of not
just common grace-given benefits (e.g., covenant benefits, admission to the kingdom) but
also special awards for personal merit.

---

65. John asserted we will inherit "all things" in the eternal world (Rev. 21:7).
Does this also imply the ability to freely traverse, explore, study, and fully
understand the incalculable, enormous wonders of deep space (cf. Gen. 1:28;
Ps. 19:1; 1 Cor. 13:12b)?

This wonderful, inspiring, incorruptible inheritance is "reserved" for us on Earth and in heaven (1 Pet. 1:3–4). But there's more we should understand.

All the future aspects of our inheritance are encapsulated in the term "eternal life," which, ironically, we begin in time (Luke 18:18; John 17:3). Of all the great present aspects of our legacy, the greatest is God Himself! The special inheritance of Israel's priestly tribe (Levi) was not land but God (Lev. 18:1–2; Num. 18:20). Similarly, as New Testament believer-priests, our special inheritance is not material things but the immortal, immaterial God himself. No benefit can match worshiping and walking and working closely with our Benefactor in this life (cf. Ps. 84:10). Spiritually minded, David realized this and rejoiced in it: "The LORD is the portion of mine inheritance…I have a goodly heritage.…In thy presence is fullness of joy" (Ps. 16:5–6, 11; cf. Ps. 73:26; 119:57; Lam. 3:24).

Our Christian inheritance is also a great equalizer. Some Christians inherit substantial worldly estates, while others receive little or nothing. But our Christian legacy renders us all wealthier than all earthly heirs combined. Whatever our socioeconomic standing, we now possess a fabulous, rich spiritual and material legacy…forever (cf. Rev. 2:9)! This checks pride, envy, or discouragement. We can't be proud because our inheritance isn't superior to other Christians'; needy and affluent believers are equal in Christ (cf. James 1:9–11). We can't envy because our legacy isn't inferior to any other Christian's. And because our faithful Father cannot fail to deliver our inheritance as promised, we can't be discouraged. But neither should we be presumptuous!

As with natural inheritances, we may lose part or all of our Christian inheritance. The New Testament emphatically and repeatedly warns that by willfully practicing the sins of the flesh we forfeit our blessings (or presence!) in God's eternal kingdom (1 Cor. 6:9–10; Eph. 5:3–7; Gal. 5:19–21), as Esau disrespected his inheritance and lost it (Heb. 12:16–17). Our personal rewards may also be lost by continuing any disobedient behavior (2 John 2:8), neglecting our "so great salvation [close walk with the Savior]" (Heb. 2:3), or by disloyalty or apostasy in trial (Rev. 3:12; cf. 2 Tim. 4:10).

Finally, let's remember we are God's eternal inheritance (Eph. 1:18, NLT; Ps. 28:9; Deut. 32:9). This explains why He's ceaselessly working in us—teaching, warning, testing, correcting, challenging, convicting, forgiving, restoring, encouraging—to conform us to Christ's character image (Rom. 8:28–29). This constant, gracious divine attention proves we are His eternal legacy, the special portion He will receive and enjoy for endless ages. So let's accept, not reject, the rigors of our character-building challenges so after Jesus raptures us He'll be rapt with us.

Distracted or discouraged by your earthly inheritance? Don't be! Whatever your worldly lot, if you believe in Jesus you're a joint-heir to history's most fabulous estate. Covenant benefits, the kingdom, personal rewards, and God himself—all these enviable benefits are yours in Christ now and forever! Let your otherworldly inheritance inspire your worldly pilgrimage.

Chapter Four

PAUL'S FAITHFUL FINAL WORDS

Paul's last words to the Colossians were no passing thoughts, no mere addendum full of interesting but useless biblical information.

To the contrary they instruct, reveal, warn, and remind. Incessantly teaching, Paul gave additional practical instruction. Always candid, he issued sweet personal greetings that reveal much about his ministry associates and typical first-century church life. Ever the watchful apostle, he warned us to fulfill, not fail, our ministries. A timely reminder, his last verse leaves the key topic of Christian sufferings lingering in our minds. This is no rhetorically correct but empty farewell.

It's an inspired closing, faithful final words from above for us to faithfully ponder and practice here below.

4:1 Masters mastered by the Master. Paul charged Colossian slave owners (earlier) and employers (today) to treat their earthly subordinates with fairness, mindful they will one day give account to their heavenly Master, Christ. I've covered this verse in the previous chapter, since it is part of the preceding context. See my note, "Commands and comments for home and work," Col. 3:18–4:1.[1]

4:2–4 Continue praying! Paul urged the Colossians to "continue in" the divinely appointed, always effective, often neglected, typically underappreciated kingdom work of "prayer" (4:2). He knew well God has arranged things so that prayer makes Christians, churches, and ministries go, enabling His eternal will and works to be accomplished.[2] Prayer links us to our lone Source of unfailing strength, wisdom, grace, guidance, and favor. So it is not a hobby to be doodled with but a habit to be diligently observed: "Always maintain the habit of prayer" (4:2, PHILLIPS).[3] One source states:

---

1. Remember, there are no chapter divisions in the original New Testament manuscripts.

2. So vital is intercession to Christ's plan for His people that it is His current heavenly ministry. At the Father's right hand, "He ever liveth to make intercession" for us (Heb. 7:25). Isn't it entirely proper, then, for us to see intercession as a legitimate vocation, spiritual profession, and chief ministry? Medieval Benedictine monks certainly considered prayer a work, making their motto *ora et labora* (pray and work). Should we do less?

3. This explains why Paul so often reminded his readers of his constant prayers for them (Eph. 1:15–19; Col. 1:9–12; 1 Thess. 1:2; 3:9–10), requested their prayers for him and his coworkers (Eph. 6:19; Col. 4:3; 1 Thess. 5:25; 2 Thess. 3:1–2), and urged them to "pray always" (Eph. 6:18), "pray without ceasing" (1 Thess. 5:17), and "in everything by prayer" address all their needs and problems (Phil. 4:6–7).

Prayer is not a spiritual luxury; it is essential for growth. Prayer—as vital to one's spiritual health as breathing is to one's physical health—should be continual (1 Thess. 5:17), not casual.[4]

Paul credited the Colossians for already being a praying church with praying leaders (4:12; cf. 1:7) and here reminded them to keep up the good work: "Continue steadfastly in prayer" (4:2, ESV). His words allude to several key aspects of excellent prayer.

- PRAY WITH DEVOTION. "Devote yourselves to prayer" (4:2, NAS), or dedicate yourselves to pray regularly with devoted hearts (heartfelt zeal and loyalty to the chief Intercessor), seeing prayer as Christ's chosen way of facilitating His heavenly will on Earth.[5]

- PRAY WITH PERSISTENCE. We should "continue in prayer" (4:2), "unwearied and steadfast" (4:2, AMP) in our perseverance, "praying always" (Eph. 6:18) and "without ceasing" (1 Thess. 5:17)—that is, with importunity (cf. Luke 11:5–10; 18:1–8). This requires determination not to stop seeking God's help until it arrives on the

---

4. Geisler, Walvoord, and Zuck, *The Bible Knowledge Commentary: An Exposition of the Scriptures*, Vol. 2, Col. 4:2, note, 685.

5. Paul charged, "Pray without ceasing" (1 Thess. 5:17). This implies talking to God should be as natural and constant an act as talking to others with whom we live and work, not something limited to special times, places, or conditions of need.

shores of our lives (1 Kings 18:41–45; Matt.
15:21–28; Mark 8:23–25; Acts 1:14–2:1; 12:5).[6]

PRAY WITH WATCHFULNESS. "And watch in the
same" (4:2), or "being on alert" (WEY). Thus,
Paul ordered a prayer vigil of expectant anticipation (Heb. 9:28). We should look daily to
see not if but when, where, and how God's
answers appear. Intercession is kingdom "business" (Rom. 12:11), and if we're serious about it,
we'll be watchful. Gracious as He is, our Father
often answers prayer even when this vigilant
expectation is lacking (Acts 12:5, 15–16), but He
always does so when it's present (James 5:16).

This "watching and praying" also means
watching: (1) over our own souls in self-
examination (1 Cor. 11:28, 31; 1 John 1:9);
(2) for Satan's retaliatory attacks on us, our
family, or friends (Eph. 6:10–17); (3) for detrimental changes in our fellow believers' attitudes or behavior;[7] (4) for other people, issues,

---

6. "Our persistence is an expression of our faith that God answers our
prayers. Faith shouldn't die if the answers come slowly, for the delay may be
God's way of working his will in our life. When you feel tired of praying,
know that God is present, always listening, always answering—maybe not
in ways you had hoped, but in ways that he knows are best." *Life Application
Study Bible*, Col. 4:2, note, 2036.

7. Far from a superior-minded, unloving, judgmental preoccupation, this
vigilance is a loving readiness to notice when Christian friends begin slip-
ping in their walk with God and quickly pray and, as far as possible, exhort
them to return to God's ways and their former good condition before sin
hardens and turns their heart (Heb. 3:14).

or problems we should pray for (Matt. 26:41; Mark 13:33; 14:38; Eph. 6:18).

• PRAY WITH THANKSGIVING. "Watch...with thanksgiving" (4:2). We should thank the Lord before (John 11:41), during (Dan. 6:10; Phil. 1:3–5), and after our prayers (Phil. 4:6–7), and again when His answers manifest (Phil. 4:6–7; Col. 3:15).

As in his living and ministry, Paul was unselfish in prayer. He asked prayer not for himself only but also for his ministry staff: "praying also for us...open unto us" (4:3). In this and other epistles he requested aid for Timothy, Epaphroditus, Mark, Onesimus, and others who were assisting him (1 Cor. 16:10–11; Phil. 2:29–30; Col. 4:10; Philem. 10–18). Thus, he followed the instructions of Christ, who taught us to pray primarily from a plural, not a singular, viewpoint: "give us...forgive us...lead us not...deliver us" (Matt. 6:11–13).

By requesting prayers for himself, a suffering minister ("I am...in bonds," 4:3), Paul reminds us to pray for all ministers, especially those suffering for the gospel. Ministers are prolific light-bearers sent with exceptional gifts to help the church in exceptional ways (Eph. 4:11–13) and are therefore special targets for Satan's malicious agents, the "rulers of the darkness of this world" (Eph. 6:12). In seasons of suffering ministers need even more prayers for grace to rise above their distresses, griefs, and hindrances to continue releasing the light of Jesus' truth.[8] Plentiful in ministry works and suffer-

---

8. The persistent prayers of the Jerusalem church saved Peter from an appointment with Herod Agrippa I's executioner and released him to finish his course of light-bearing ministry to the church (Acts 12:5–11, 17c).

ings, Paul requested the saints' prayers regularly (Rom. 15:30; Eph. 6:19; 1 Thess. 5:25; 2 Thess. 3:1–2) and persisted in his prayers for them also (Col. 1:9).

Specifically Paul asked the Colossians to ask God to open "door[s] of utterance" (4:3), or divinely led speaking opportunities, and (implicitly) for the courage and words to speak the gospel boldly and effectively (4:4; cf. Eph. 6:19).[9] Besides these requests, we should ask God to give our ministers Spirit-led biblical texts and topics, life-changing biblical insights, excellent illustrations, and Spirit-empowered, soul-moving words. Neither evidence of timidity nor of insufficient public speaking skills, Paul's request was a frank admission that, like all ministers, he needed the Spirit's leading and empowerment in his sermon preparation and delivery (Zech. 4:6).

Warren Wiersbe writes:

> The proclamation of the Gospel is empowered by prayer. The Spirit of God uses the Word of God as we come to the throne of grace and ask God for His blessing. We must never separate the Word of God from prayer because God has joined them together (Acts 6:4).
>
> A visitor at Spurgeon's Tabernacle in London was being shown around the building by the pastor, Charles Spurgeon. "Would you like to see the powerhouse of this ministry?" Spurgeon asked, as he showed the man into a lower auditorium. "It is here that we get our power, for while I am preaching upstairs, hundreds of my people are in this room praying." Is it any wonder that God blessed Spurgeon's preaching of the Word?

---

9. On God opening speaking opportunities for His servants, see Gen. 41:14–15, 37–41; 1 Sam. 3:17–18; 1 Kings 17:24; Dan. 5:10–16; Acts 8:30–31; 10:33; 13:7, 44; 16:14, 29–30; 17:18–19; 1 Cor. 16:8–9; Rev. 3:7–8.

> Never say to your pastor, "Well, the least I can do is
> to pray for you." The *most* you can do is to pray![10]

Specifically, Paul requested God's help presenting "the mystery of Christ" (4:3). This is "the open secret of Christ" (MOFFATT), or the previously hidden but now revealed divine plan of the gospel—that Jesus of Nazareth is the Jewish Messiah, and through Him God is reconciling Jews and Gentiles unto Himself on equal ground in one body by grace through faith (Col. 1:26–28; Rom. 16:25–26; Eph. 1:9–10; 3:3–6, 9; 6:19–20). Paul said as Christ's minister it was his duty to present this mystery: "as I ought to speak" (4:4). It's our duty too every time God opens a "door of utterance" (Acts 1:8; 3:15; 10:39).

"The mystery . . . for which I am also in bonds" (4:3, 18) is yet another reference to Paul's unusual condition as a prisoner detained without cause on false charges trumped up by his enemies (cf. Eph. 6:19–20; Phil. 1:7, 13–14, 16; 2 Tim. 2:8–9; Philem. 10, 13). These words explain his implicit request for courage. Paul realized all too well that presenting the "mystery"—a religion not authorized by Roman law, therefore making its proponents and adherents subject to severe penalties[11]—in the Roman capital risked even further rejec-

---

10. Also, let's pray for our pastors, teachers, and counselors to have grace to consistently obey God in their numerous trials, since this fully authorizes God's Word in their lips (James 1:22–25; connect Jesus' full obedience, Luke 2:51–52 and 4:1–13, with His powerful utterance (speaking) ministry, Matt. 7:28–29; Mark 1:22; cf. Phil. 2:12–16). For the quote above, see Wiersbe, *The Bible Exposition Commentary*, Vol. 2, Col. 4:3b–4, note, 147.

11. Christianity was not legalized until the fourth century. At the time Paul wrote Colossians it was seen by the Romans as a sect of Judaism and thus was presumably protected by the Jewish exception. Due to its great antiquity Judaism, which predated Rome's inception, was given a religious exemption

tion or persecution. Thus, he asked continued prayer and prayed continually.

Are we doing the same? Are we continuing in the privilege and habit of prayer? With devotion, persistence, watchfulness, and thanksgiving? Asking God to give us and our ministers open doors and the Spirit's aide in proclaiming who Jesus is and what He's done for us? Asking special grace and strength for Christians "in bonds"? We continue in Paul's teaching; let's also continue in his praying!

4:5–6 Walking in wisdom. These verses reveal four ways we interact wisely with unbelievers and believers in our daily living. We do so by:

1. Behaving wisely (4:5)

2. Redeeming our time (4:5)

3. Speaking with grace (4:6)

4. Answering others well (4:6)

BEHAVING WISELY. "Walk in wisdom toward them that are outside" (4:5), or "Live wisely among those who are not believers" (NLT). How? In this context, by redeeming our time (4:5), speaking graciously (4:6), and answering others, especially inquiring unbelievers, well (4:6). But there's more here.

---

under Roman law, thus protecting Jews from religious persecution for non-compliance with Roman religious practices. But the Jews had already begun to publicly argue that Christianity was not a Jewish sect (Acts 18:12–15), thus exposing its followers to Roman persecution (Acts 16:19–21)—which began under Nero in AD 64, shortly after Paul's writing.

Walking wisely toward those "outside" also means not casting our "pearls [precious biblical truths and spiritual practices] before swine" (hostile unbelievers; also the general unbelieving public), as Jesus instructed (Matt. 7:6).[12] Why? Unenlightened by the Spirit, they can't understand and appreciate them (1 Cor. 2:14) and are therefore inclined to ridicule them and abuse us (Matt. 7:6; 1 Cor. 14:23)! Also, we must learn not to resist evil done to us by unbelievers but to overcome it Christ's way, the Scripture's way—by nonresistance, gentle responses to angry words (Prov. 15:1), and by praying for and when possible doing good to the very ones who despise us (Prov. 26:4; Matt. 5:38–48; Acts 6:9–10; Rom. 12:17–21; Gal. 5:15). If we give our adversaries what they give us (resisting "evil with evil"), we unwisely make bad situations worse, overwhelm ourselves emotionally, damage the gospel message, disillusion bystanders, and disappoint the Lord, who inspired Paul's call to "behave wisely toward outsiders" (Col. 4:5, ISV). But we can't walk in wisdom—divinely inspired good judgment as revealed in the Bible—if we've never studied it.

So seeking wisdom is the first prerequisite. Wise Christians diligently study their Bibles, especially the wisdom books and wisdom sayings of Jesus. Prayerfulness is implied too. A prayerless life is a foolish one, as God's wise guidance comes through prayer. Patience is also required. Impatience, however we justify it, always leads to folly. Trust and obedience

---

12. Some of our precious "pearls" are prophecy, dreams or visions, praying in our prayer language, gifts or operations of the Spirit, and the sweet, personal ways Christ guides us, confirms His nearness and care, and by His Spirit's witness causes us to sense certain scriptures have an immediate application to our lives.

impart wisdom. The apex of human wisdom is to trust God's wisdom.[13] His wisdom inspired all His Word and every guiding prompt or check He gives us. Thus, trustful obedience is wise and disobedience foolish. The wise also obey the counsel of wise ministers, scholars, and thinkers, gleaning their factual research, good judgments, experiential insights, and testimonies from the past and present. Wise ones fear God and avoid sin, since practicing sin stirs God's wrath, induces self-deception, brings divine chastisements, dishonors God, and disqualifies us for higher use. They also walk in love, realizing love is God's greatest desire for us, the foundation of all His commands, Jesus' new commandment, the perfect unifier, and our greatest need. So the wise forgive, give, abandon judgmentalism, and, while opposing sin, never condemn sinners. These are the ways of the wise to those outside and inside Christ's church.

REDEEMING OUR TIME. "Redeeming the time" (4:5), or "make the best possible use of your time" (PHILLIPS). How? In this context, we do so by using well every opportunity to speak for Christ, particularly by answering unbelievers' questions about the faith graciously and satisfactorily (4:6). Thus, when God gives such opportunities, you "redeem" or "buy" them for Him by using them for His purposes.

Redeeming time begins by realizing it's fleeting, irrecoverable, and therefore precious. The psalmist prayed for a revelation of the brevity of life so he would live well daily (Ps.

---

13. The Book of Daniel showcases the superiority of the Spirit's wisdom perhaps more than any other biblical book. Time and again when the most astute, experienced, and trusted human counselors failed to solve urgent state problems or enigmas, Daniel, "a man" in whom was "the spirit of the holy gods" (Dan. 5:11), stepped in to give the Spirit's perfectly accurate solutions to pagan kings (Dan. 1:20; 2:27–28, 46–47; 4:4–8, 19–27; 5:8–17).

90:12). Paul's charge here agrees. Each new day affords us a wondrous opportunity to live for Christ's pleasure, purposes, people, kingdom, and honor. By day's end that opportunity is gone...forever. Redeeming time, therefore, means using every day Christ gives as He wills. Periodic rest and relaxation are necessary and productive, because without them we work poorly, but never idleness or excessive time spent on trivial or selfish pursuits. Thus, being redeemed—bought out of sin-slavery by Christ—we redeem every day for our Redeemer, buying up every opportunity, open door, mission, ministry, divine appointment, and task He puts before us.

SPEAKING WITH GRACE. Paul instructed the Colossians to speak "with grace," adding this seasons our speech "with salt" (4:6). As salt makes food tastier and thus more desirable, so "grace" makes our words more tasteful and thus appealing. So grace is the "salt" of our communications: "The salt of grace" (WEY).

"Grace," the universal Christian enabler, refers to God's divine gifts, strength, or ability imparted to believers by the Spirit without merit through Christ (2 Cor. 12:9). Most obviously, God's grace enables us to speak graciously—or gracefully, pleasantly, sensitively, discreetly, and opportunely. It also refers to the Spirit's spontaneous assistance when we're suddenly thrust into challenging opportunities to share the gospel or testify (Mark 13:11; Acts 4:8). According to some ancient sources speaking "with salt" also means speaking with wit.[14] A touch of humor has diffused many a touchy situation (cf. Prov. 17:22). Since Christ used salt as a meta-

---

14. See A. T. Robertson, *Word Pictures in the New Testament* (Broadman Press: Nashville, TN, 1933), Col. 4:6, note.

phor for spiritual potency (Matt. 5:13), it further alludes to believers speaking strong or undiluted truths, yet, as Paul elsewhere attributes to mature Christians, also speaking with utmost politeness: "speaking the truth in love" (Eph. 4:15). So speaking potentially offensive truths in a nonoffensive manner is a mark of spiritual maturity—or Christlikeness (John 1:14, 16; 4:16–18; 7:46; 8:10–11; Ps. 45:2)—specifically, that one is learning to consistently master his (or her) own tongue (James 3:2).[15] Why should we speak with grace?

Ministering God's truth graciously "minister[s] grace unto the hearers" (Eph. 4:29). Christ's gracious peace will calm their troubled hearts and, if unconverted, lead them to receive saving grace, or God's gracious gift of salvation, Christ. "Let your talk always have a saving salt of grace about it" (4:6, MOFFATT). Since winning souls is wise (Prov. 11:30), speaking truth graciously is also a mark of wisdom.[16] The wise recognize not only what but how we speak is important (Isa. 50:4), that speaking biblical truth *without* grace drives others from the very truths (and the Truth) we wish to draw them to (Prov. 12:18)! It exacerbates our critics' antagonism, gives them fresh cause to accuse us of wrongdoing, and thereby "increases their prejudice against religion."[17] But sometimes that's unavoidable anyway.

---

15. "Speaking the truth in love" (Eph. 4:15), however, doesn't mean using euphemisms so vague the truth itself is veiled and indiscernible. The full force of the truth must never be blunted or hidden yet ever be stated with a courteous respect for others and without angrily or arrogantly disparaging them.

16. "Rabbis sometimes used 'salt' to mean 'wisdom.'" See Carson, France, Motyer, and Wenham, *New Bible Commentary: 21st Century Edition*, 4th ed., Col. 4:5–6, note.

17. Henry, *Commentary in One Volume*, Col. 4:5, note, 1874.

Remember, salt was antiquity's prime antiseptic and pre-
servative. Newborns were rubbed in it to prevent infections,
and all meats were salted to preserve them from spoiling.
So the "salt," or potent holiness or righteousness of our
words of biblical warning, correction, or exhortation, even
when spoken kindly, may sting their sin-wounded hearts and
evoke a bitter response. Surprisingly, they may later thank us
for the stinging: "Faithful are the wounds [and stings] of a
friend" (Prov. 27:6; cf. Ps. 141:5).

In Paul's day Christians were grossly misrepresented and
disparaged by the Roman public. Many Romans believed
Christians were unpatriotic, atheistic, unsociable, ignorant, anti-family, incestuous, even cannibalistic! Thus, Paul
wanted the Colossians' wise and gracious speech to expose
the falseness of such base rumors and draw Romans and
Jews to Christ despite the widespread slander. Peter and
other leaders shared this hope (1 Pet. 3:15–16), which, due in
part to Paul's call for believers to speak with grace, eventually was realized as Christianity gradually became known for
what it was, not what it was reported to be.

ANSWERING OTHERS WELL. "That ye may know how ye
ought to answer every man" (4:6). Were the Colossians ready
to answer their clever gnostic antagonists? Are we ready to
answer questions posed by "every man" (4:6), whether a sin-
cerely curious unbeliever, hostile secularist, spiritually hungry
Christian, or one with differing opinions?

For this tall task we mustn't be short on love, knowledge,
attentiveness, patience, or discretion. It's easy to love those we
converse with if we remember how much Jesus loves them—
so much He was brutally beaten and staked to a tree so they
might know and love God. Besides the right spirit we need

the right substance: Facts matter! To answer a wide range of spiritual questions we need a broad field of biblical knowledge, something only those who seriously study, ponder, and analyze God's Word possess (2 Tim. 2:15; cf. 1 Tim. 4:15–16). To answer well we must listen well. Do we give those questioning us undivided or unfocused attention? When politicians don't answer a question, that's usually their intention. When we don't, it's sometimes due to our inattention; we never really heard the question because we didn't bother to listen well. Are we cultivating the ministry of listening? Patience too is required. To answer someone thoroughly—till their curiosity is satisfied, doubts are quelled, confusion is dispelled, and reason is convinced—we may have to explain, illustrate, and reiterate various points repeatedly over several conversations. Will we patiently lead them into full understanding, being "gentle unto all men, apt to teach, patient" (2 Tim. 2:24), or, annoyed, selfishly brush them off? Finally, discretion is needed. Some questioners want answers, others arguments. Some are open-, others close-minded. One calls for our attention, the other our avoidance—and we must pray to discern which is which (2 Tim. 2:14, 16, 23; Prov. 26:4; James 1:5). By practicing these things we learn to consistently answer sincere questioners well. And "walk in wisdom" (4:5).

Thus, Paul set before the Colossians, and us, the basics of a life wisely lived. Are we behaving wisely, making the best use of our time, salting our talk with grace, and preparing to "answer every man" adequately? Unwise Christian speech and conduct has turned many away from Christ. May God help us walk and talk in His gracious wisdom so consistently that they are turned back to Him.

4:7–17 Paul's revealing valedictory. Paul's farewell to the Colossians reveals more about Paul, his associates, early Christianity, and the typical first-century worship experience.

Followers of an illegal religion, few in number, widely misunderstood and despised, and generally uneducated and poor, Christians met not in public temples but private homes,[18] as is seen in Paul's reference to Nymphas and "the church which is in his [or her] house" in Laodicea (4:15).[19] Besides praying, singing psalms a cappella,[20] fellowshiping, celebrating Communion, sharing meals, and listening to recitations of Jesus' teachings and works, early Christians read

---

18. While the exception rather than the rule in America today, house churches were the *only* way Gentile Christians worshiped for nearly three centuries. Even today, millions of Christians worship informally in homes around the world. Is our view of Christian worship so narrowly focused on our culture's norm that we forget, devalue, or despise those who choose to worship humbly in a home setting? We've long valued home schools; why not house churches also? Is it not the spirit and truth of our assemblies, not their settings, that counts (John 4:21, 23–24)?

19. Nymphas was "a Christian in Laodicea to whom Paul sends his greetings (Col. 4:15) and who owned the house in which the congregation met. The name occurs in the Greek text in a form that makes it impossible to determine whether it is Nympha (feminine; so RSV) or Nymphas (masculine; so KJV)." See A. C. Myers, *The Eerdmans Bible Dictionary* (Grand Rapids, MI: Eerdmans, 1987), s.v. "Nympha."

20. Churches didn't use instruments in their worship for over a thousand years, and then only organs on a limited bases for several more centuries. Early Christians associated instruments with the pagan festivals and parades of their idolatrous culture and concluded wrongly instruments were inappropriate for worship, ignoring David's instrumental worship and the Psalter's repeated exhortations to use various instruments (Ps. 33:2–3; 43:4; 57:8–9; 81:1–3; 98:4–6; 147:7; 150:3–5). This is not to diminish the sweet, pure beauty of our voices raised to God in a cappella worship but rather to assert the legitimacy of both instrumental and non-instrumental worship (which we blend with delight in our church's worship). As noted earlier, individual believers would sometimes sing spontaneous songs of thanksgiving or praise to God in their assemblies (1 Cor. 14:26, NLT, NIV, NCV).

aloud the Jewish Scriptures (Law, Prophets, Writings) and apostolically authored letters, as we may infer from Paul's request that the Colossians read this letter aloud in their assembly: "When this epistle is read among you" (4:16).

Such letters of apostolic instruction were considered so valuable they were hand-copied and circulated from church to church. This practice explains Paul's request for this letter to be shared with the nearby Laodicean Christians: "Cause that it be read also in the church of the Laodiceans" (4:16).[21] It also explains his request for another letter he sent to the Laodiceans (or from Laodicea) to be shared with the Colossians: "That ye also read the epistle from [or to] Laodicea" (4:16).[22] And Peter alluded to this practice when endorsing Paul's letters as being unquestionably full of inspired wisdom and thus Scripture (2 Pet. 3:15–16).

Paul's letters characteristically exuded warm Christian love, as seen in not only the firsthand but also the numerous secondhand greetings they contain. In this letter he conveys kind hellos from his companions Aristarchus, Mark, Justus, Epaphras, Luke, and Demas (4:10–14). This confirms that first-century Christians were very serious about keeping Christ's new command (John 13:34–35) and, contrary to public opinion, were highly social (not withdrawn, secretive, antisocial types) despite their socially marginalized standing in Roman society. Such messages were sent not only in letters but also by the messengers carrying them. Paul here sent Tychicus and Onesimus to give a full report on his

---

21. For more on the Laodicean church, see my entry, "Laodicea, a privileged church," Col. 2:1.

22. This epistle is not extant. Whether sent to or from Laodicea, the point is that it was Paul's apostolic message and therefore inspired instruction.

circumstances and activities to the Colossians (4:7–9). These couriers, then, not only authenticated Paul's letters but also offered the recipients a double dose of Paul's text, audibly elaborating on the profound truths written in his letter (4:18; cf. Acts 15:25–27).[23]

Paul sometimes recognized Christians of outstanding spiritual zeal or ministry labors. In this passage he commended several outstanding ministry associates (Tychicus, Onesimus, Aristarchus, Mark, Justus), but especially Epaphras, whose incessant intercessions were exemplary (4:12–13). By referring to a Colossian Christian named Jesus as "Justus" ("the just or fair one"[24]), Paul hints early Christians liked to assign each other nicknames highlighting their endearing qualities (4:11). If so, they were continuing a practice begun by no less than Jesus himself and carried on by His first disciples (cf. Mark 3:16–17; John 21:2; Acts 1:23; 4:36; 13:1).

Incidentally, Paul's valedictory confirms the existence of the Laodicean church, which Christ addressed some thirty years later in John's Revelation (Rev. 3:14–22). Though it seems sure Paul never personally visited Laodicea (or Colossae or Hierapolis, Col. 2:1), the Laodiceans surely received his ministry indirectly through (a) the Colossian and Laodicean

---

23. Authentication was an important issue in the first-century church. Even though letters were typically sealed to secure them from tampering, Paul's theological enemies were not above forging letters in his name (2 Thess. 2:1–2). Thus, it was helpful for Paul's known associates to hand-deliver his epistles whenever possible. It also seems Paul's signature, which he usually personally inscribed to close his letters otherwise dictated to and handwritten by his secretaries, was widely known (2 Thess. 3:17)—though this, too, could be forged.

24. Literally *Justus* means "Upright; just; righteous." See Smith and Cornwall, *The Exhaustive Dictionary of Bible Names*, s.v. "Justus."

epistles (4:16); (b) Nymphas and Epaphras, whom Paul taught and counseled; and (c) numerous others Paul evangelized, discipled, and commissioned during his three-year ministry in Ephesus and sent to minister throughout Asia, who likely founded its churches, including those at Colosse, Laodicea, and Hierapolis (4:15; cf. Acts 19:9–10, 26). Since Paul offered no doctrinal or behavioral correction for the Laodiceans in this epistle (4:15–16), it appears they had not yet sunk into the proud, materialistic, lukewarm condition for which Christ later so memorably rebuked them (Rev. 3:15–17). If they had, Paul, the church's foremost spiritual examiner and apostle of correction,[25] would surely have taken them to task.

Finally, Paul addressed Archippus: "Say to Archippus, Take heed to the ministry which thou hast received in the Lord, that thou fulfill it" (4:17). Archippus was likely Philemon's son or a member of his house church in Colosse (Philem. 1–2). It's unclear whether Paul's charge was a rebuke for ministerial negligence or a spirited encouragement to press on through an unspecified adversity to complete his ministry. Some feel the context suggests Archippus was called to minister not in nearby Laodicea (Col. 4:15–17). Whatever the case Paul felt impressed to spur him on.

Do we need a spur—to remember and emulate the beautiful simplicity of first-century house church worship? To practice the warm love shared among early Christians? To share with other believers and churches the excellent, edifying writings of our inspired teachers and scholars? To

---

25. Paul's ministry of correction is overwhelmingly evident throughout his New Testament writings (cf. 1 Cor. 5:1–13; 2 Cor. 13:2; Gal. 1:6–7; 2:11–14; 3:1–3; Phil. 4:2; 2 Tim. 4:2; Titus 2:15) and Acts (Acts 15:1–2).

exhort discouraged, flagging ministers to press on and finish their courses of ministry?

4:7–14 Paul's holy club. In these verses Paul listed his "fellow workers" in Rome whose presence, prayers, and assistance were a "comfort unto me" (4:11). They constituted his unofficial Holy Club.

Centuries later, disdainful Oxford scholars gave the same title to a small group of scholars led by Charles and John Wesley who met regularly to seek a holy life (1729–1738). The members of Oxford's "Holy Club"[26] devoted themselves rigorously to a fixed routine of Bible study, prayer, Communion, fasting, plain food, self-examination, and charitable works, including giving to the poor, helping orphans, and ministering in the dangerous and filthy prisons of eighteenth-century England. Observing their methodical religious regimen, their fellow Oxford scholars jokingly dubbed them "Methodists." During the later Wesleyan revival the moniker resurfaced and stuck. Eventually a humble young student and former bartender named George Whitefield, who after leaving Oxford became the eighteenth century's greatest evangelist, joined this serious-minded but small union. John Wesley, Charles Wesley, George Whitefield, and other subsequently influential ministers—sounds like an elect bunch!

So were those who gathered with Paul in Rome as he wrote Colossians. In a much less distinguished setting (house arrest) they distinguished themselves by surrounding and supporting God's humble apostle as he ministered God's

---

26. For further reading on the Wesleys' Oxford Holy Club, see http://wesley.nnu.edu/john-wesley/john-wesley-the-methodist/chapter-v-the-holy-club/ (accessed April 12, 2016).

holy Word to His holy people through holy epistles. Paul's spiritual regimen was probably not too different from John Wesley's—except for his "chains" (Acts 28:20). Though bound to an imperial (Praetorian) guard day and night, Paul managed to fill his days with prayer, preaching, teaching, testimony, counseling, writing, giving to the poor, eating plain food, self-examination (1 Cor. 11:28–31), fasting (2 Cor. 11:27), ministering to Rome's poor (Gal. 2:10) and its prisoners whenever possible, and probably some tent-making in his spare time (Acts 28:30–31). All while in Roman custody. All while falsely accused. All while having no human prospect of release. All while facing a hearing before that inimitable psychopath, Nero! However else they differed, Paul and Wesley were each masters of spiritual methodology and assisted by holy clubs.

The biblically distinguished roll of Paul's holy club reads as follows:

- TIMOTHY (1:1): Paul's prime ministerial protégé, spiritual son, trusted messenger, travel companion, surrogate observer, and substitute minister, Timothy was by his side in Rome (1:1). His outstanding character is well-attested in Paul's New Testament writings (1 Cor. 4:17; 16:10; Phil. 2:19–22; 1 Thess. 3:1–2; 2 Tim. 1:1–5).

- TYCHICUS (4:7): Tychicus was a "beloved brother" (true friend "born for" Paul's "adversity," Prov. 17:17), a "faithful minister and fellow servant" of Christ, and one Paul trusted to examine and exhort the Colossians in his stead and report back to him, thus his selection to deliver this epistle (4:8). Paul's glowing praise for his fellow ministers (Tychicus, Epaphras; 4:7, 12–13) showed his humility and promoted loving unity in his holy club and among ministers everywhere.[27]

- ONESIMUS (4:9): A former slave from Colosse ("one of you," 4:9), Onesimus was now "a faithful and beloved brother" to Paul (4:9) and the central figure in the Book of Philemon. That epistle reveals after running away from his master, Onesimus became Paul's convert (Philem. 10), valued ministry associate[28] (vv. 11, 13), and precious friend (v. 16). Thus, Paul chose him (with Tychicus) to bear this epistle to his former city—and master, Philemon.

- ARISTARCHUS (4:10): Not literally but figuratively Paul's "fellow prisoner" due to his constant presence with the incarcerated apostle, Aristarchus was an extraordinarily faithful

---

27. When rather than proudly compete ministers humbly appreciate each other's devotion, gifts, knowledge, and ministries, we increase in love and effectiveness together. Conversely when ministers pettily and needlessly snipe at each other the opposite occurs: their pride is exposed, church unity is weakened, and ministers are generally less esteemed. See Henry, *Commentary in One Volume*, Col. 4:7–18, note, 1875.

28. As stated earlier, many slaves in this period were not only manual laborers but also highly skilled and well-educated professionals: teachers, tutors, musicians, craftsmen, stewards, doctors, tailors, scribes, salesmen, purchasing agents, and so forth. Whatever Onesimus' natural skills, spiritual gifts, or ministries, his fellowship and assistance greatly helped Paul in a most challenging time.

friend and assistant to Paul through many great adversities: an Ephesian riot (Acts 19:29); long, arduous travels (20:4; 27:2); a great hurricane at sea (27:2, 14–44); and now imprisonment (Col. 4:10; Philem. 24).

- MARK (4:10): John Mark was Barnabas' "sister's son" (lit., "cousin"), formerly out of Paul's favor due to unfaithfulness in ministry (Acts 15:37–40) but now, having proved himself, back in his fellowship, ministry (2 Tim. 4:11), and fatherly favor (Col. 4:10).

- JUSTUS (4:11): Paul's Jewish companion Jesus[29] was nicknamed Justus ("the just one," or "the fair"). This hints this believer, whom Paul probably met in Rome (Acts 28:17–24), was known for being fair-minded and upright in character.

- EPAPHRAS (1:7–8; 4:12–13): Colossians and Philemon jointly reveal Epaphras was the Colossian church's elder, messenger, and perhaps founding pastor (Col. 1:7), and also Paul's dear friend, faithful coworker (1:7), and "fellow prisoner" (Philem. 23).[30] He was also

---

29. Jesus was a familiar first-century name. *Yeshua* in Hebrew (*Iesous* in Greek, Matt. 1:21), it means, "Yahweh is salvation"; or "Yahweh saves."

30. Like Aristarchus, Epaphras became a *de facto* prisoner due to his constant companionship with Paul—though apparently willing to be an actual prisoner, if necessary, to serve Christ's will that he assist Paul! Pray for more Epaphrases: *"Lord, send us more Christians like Epaphras!"* Better yet, be one: *"Lord, make me Your Epaphras, willing to endure confinements, restrictions, and other adversities, if necessary, to help Your chosen ministers and ministries bless Your people!"*

an extraordinary intercessor (Col. 4:12–13),
thus becoming increasingly like Him who
"ever liveth to make intercession" for the saints
(Heb. 7:25; cf. Luke 5:16; Mark 6:45–46; John
17:1–26).

• LUKE (4:14): A man of many hats and gifts,
Luke was Paul's Gentile "beloved physician"
(4:14),[31] ministry associate, travel companion
(Acts 16:10, 13, 16; 20:6; 21:1; 27:1–5; 28:10–
11, 16), ministry historian, and, as author of
his Gospel and Acts, the most prolific New
Testament writer (in words, not books, the

---

31. Luke was a physician, but nothing like our superbly educated, board-
certified, scientific doctors and other health care professionals today (PAs,
RNs, etc.). In antiquity, disease was believed to be caused not by physical
factors (contact with germs, which weren't widely understood till the nineteenth century) but by spirits and gods. Healing arts, therefore, were practiced in conjunction with magic, astrology, religion, and superstition, and
physicians were more likely to be magicians or cult priests (e.g., of Asclepius,
say, in Pergamum) than scientists dealing with bacteria and pathologies.
Rational medicine began largely with Hippocrates in the medical school on
the Greek island of Cos in the late fifth and early fourth centuries BC. By
Luke's day (first century) the body of medical knowledge was built upon the
extensive works of Hippocrates and Herophilus of Chalcedon and others of
the Alexandrian medical school (and later, Galen). Proper physicians were
from all classes (including slaves) and both sexes and gained their knowledge by serving as apprentices to other established senior physicians. Though
likely trained in this manner, yet as Paul's associate also fully oriented to the
spiritual and divine factors in illness and healing, Luke was able to describe
with considerable specificity the physical and spiritual conditions (and sometimes causes) of many people divinely healed by Christ or His followers in
his Gospel and Acts (Luke 5:18–25; 13:11–13; Acts 3:2–11; 4:21–22). Incidentally, Luke's presence with Paul was as a friend, ministerial aide, and
divinely called historian. If he rendered any medical assistance to Paul while
injured or sick (cf. Acts 14:19–22; Gal. 4:13–15), we have no biblical record of
it. To teach such, therefore, is pure conjecture, however plausible.

latter distinction belonging to Paul). "Beloved" hints Luke was very pleasant company to Paul and to others who worked with him or received his caring, prayerful medical assistance. It's very likely Luke wrote Acts during this time in Rome with Paul (Acts 28:30–31). He remained faithfully by the apostle to the end (2 Tim. 4:6–8, 11).

- DEMAS (4:14): Currently Demas was one of Paul's valued "fellow workers" (Philem. 23–24, NIV), but he later apostatized, as Paul sadly noted to Timothy (2 Tim. 4:10). Demas' story warns every ministry assistant: "Don't forsake your 'Paul,' whatever your challenges or temptations!" And it soberly reminds ministers: "Never put absolute trust in coworkers—who, still human, are subject to the follies and foibles of their old nature!"

These Jewish and Gentile individuals constituted Paul's holy club, a union of consecrated believers gathered around Paul for fellowship and assistance in his vital kingdom work. I wonder how they interacted in things profound and shallow.

Did they pray together? That's certain, since we know Paul and Epaphras were constant intercessors.[32] Did they share meals and Communion together? Undoubtedly! Oh, what conversations they must have enjoyed on a variety of key subjects—theological, ideological, historical, philosophical,

---

32. Matthew Henry suggests Paul taught Epaphras to be "much in prayer for his friends." Henry, *Commentary in One Volume*, Col. 4:7–17, note, 1875.

social, spiritual, and practical![33] Perhaps they briefly discussed Rome's news, the Senate's recent actions, Caesar's decrees, the Legions' latest conquests, recent winners at the Circus Maximus,[34] and so forth. One thing is sure: Their most oft-visited topic was *Jesus*—His life, works, sufferings, and teachings. Considering Paul's end-time interest (1 and 2 Thessalonians), they probably often discussed Christ's appearing, return, and glorious kingdom. Considering the growing anti-Christian sentiments in Rome, they likely discussed how, in light of Jesus' teachings, believers should react to public bias and abuse or imperial persecution (cf. Matt. 5:38–48; Rom. 12:17–21). Luke undoubtedly spent considerable time writing his Acts. Did he receive editorial help from Paul, himself a scholar, on the characters, events, or word choices he used to describe early church history? Or did Paul seek Luke's prayerful rhetorical input on Colossians or the other three epistles he authored during this period? Was Mark Paul's amanuensis (male secretary) during this time (cf. Rom. 16:22)?[35] Did Paul's holy club, Roman guards in tow, stroll to the Tiber occasionally to watch its waters, boats, and peoples flow by? Was Paul's "hired house" (Acts

---

33. Remember Paul taught the Philippians and us to "think on" not just biblical topics but also "whatever" subjects are worthy, virtuous, and instructive (Phil. 4:8). He must therefore have been a knowledgeable and engaging conversationalist in things biblical and (in the healthy sense) worldly.

34. Paul's use of multiple athletic metaphors (1 Cor. 9:24–26; Phil. 3:13–14; 2 Tim. 4:6–8; Heb. 12:1) reveals he was at least familiar with Greco-Roman sporting events, though not preoccupied with sports, as too many American Christians are today (cf. Col. 3:1–4).

35. Paul's usual method was to dictate his letters to a secretary and then, as previously stated, affix his distinctive signature to the completed document to authenticate his authorship. See Keener, *The IVP Bible Background Commentary: New Testament*, Col. 4:18, note.

28:30) situated so it offered a view of a major thoroughfare, public square, the Forum, or Coliseum? Wherever Paul and friends gathered, theirs was a rare fellowship indeed. While we can only speculate, Tychicus and Onesimus fully shared these juicy details in their "missions report" to the Colossians: "They shall make known unto you all things which are done here" (4:9b).[36]

Paul's language confirms his holy club was small: "These [few] only are my fellow workers..." (4:11).[37] But they were faithful and by God's grace provided everything the worn and weary apostle needed: "These...have been a comfort unto me" (4:11). The lesson? It's better to have a few holy, faithful friends than many unholy, unfaithful ones! Ready to start a holy club?

Begin by honestly examining your Christian companions. Are they serious or casual Christians? Our friends influence us more than we know (Prov. 13:20). Then follow Paul's and the Wesleys' examples by choosing holy friends—a circle of ministers, fellow university students, your prayer group, Bible

---

36. Along with Barnabas, Paul had shared a captivating missionary report when they returned from their first apostolic mission (Acts 14:26–27). To learn more about God's past and present work in other cultures and continents I suggest two excellent "Tychicus and Onesimus" periodicals. (1) *Christian History* Magazine (see https://www.christianhistoryinstitute.org/magazine/ [accessed April 14, 2016] or write Christian History Institute, P.O. Box 540, Worcester, PA 19490); and (2) *The Voice of the Martyrs* Magazine (see http://www.persecution.com/ [accessed April 14, 2016] or write The Voice of the Martyrs, P.O. Box 443, Bartlesville, OK 74005-0443). Perusing and supporting such resources will stimulate your faith, broaden your perspective of God's work, and increase your praise of His wondrous grace and power.

37. Though "these only" refers immediately to his Jewish brothers present, Aristarchus, Mark, and Justus, it also applies to his Gentile associates.

study fellowship, or committed church members—to boost your walk and work with the holy One. Get close, candid, unified, focused. Share prayer, good works, and thought-provoking conversations. Share biblical insights, spiritual experiences, and ministry visions. Experience life's deeps and shallows together. Freely give and receive help, and thank God for your associates often, as Paul did. If your holy club is small, don't worry. So were Paul's and Wesley's. Just stay committed to the holy One, remembering what amazing things He's done through their holy unions and stands ready to do again through yours!

4:10 Commanding mercy. Paul reminded the Colossians to warmly "receive" John Mark if he visited them (4:10).[38] Apparently he had had concerns they might not freely do so. Why this apostolic concern and prodding?

While the text offers no explanation, Acts suggests one. It describes how John Mark failed the Lord—and Paul and Barnabas—on his first known ministry assignment, returning home well before his mission was completed (Acts 13:4–13). It also shows for this reason Paul disqualified Mark from assisting him on his second mission and how Barnabas (Mark's cousin), sharply disagreeing, broke with Paul over his decision (15:36–40). Now, over ten years later,[39] clearly Paul

---

38. Since many ministers were itinerants, Paul was urging the Colossians to fully "receive" Mark—personally, by lovingly fellowshiping with him; ministerially, by receiving whatever messages, teachings, or insights he may share; and hospitably, by seeing to all his needs and sending him on his way sufficiently supplied in food, funds, and, if possible, travel companions (cf. Acts 17:14–15; 3 John 5–8).

39. This estimate is based upon Paul's first mission trip (and Mark's failure) beginning in AD 46–47 and his writing of Colossians, occurring

has changed his mind about Mark, perhaps due to the latter having proven himself faithful in the Lord's work during the interim. But all this didn't happen in a vacuum.

As in our day, news of all this would have spread throughout the ecclesiastical rumor mill, and some, perhaps many, believers would have heard of Mark's failure and Paul's consequent falling out with Barnabas. Some may have internally taken Paul's side and thus been disinclined to befriend one they felt had failed their beloved apostle. Such pettiness had occurred before when the Corinthians divided into three camps, jealously supporting their favorite teacher, Paul, Peter, or Apollos, but not the other two (1 Cor. 1:10–13; 3:1–8)! Was Paul's prod his way of reminding the Colossians to be large-hearted, not petty; spiritually minded, not carnally minded, specifically to show Mark mercy and not condemn him today for yesterday's failures? It wasn't Paul's first plea for Christians to show mercy.

As stated earlier, he was simultaneously writing Philemon to ask him to show mercy on his former runaway slave, Onesimus, who was now converted to the faith, committed to Christ, and a valuable ministerial aide (Philem. 8–21). He had warned the Corinthians to not hold an unforgiving attitude toward a man they had earlier (at Paul's urging) expelled from their church for practicing incestuous adultery, since he had repented and was seeking reconciliation (2 Cor. 2:6–11). And it's likely Paul made other requests not included in the New Testament.

---

in AD 60.

But one key request was. Paul summarized his teaching on restoring fallen Christians in his instructions to the Galatians:

> Brethren, if a man be overtaken in a fault, ye who are spiritual restore such an one in the spirit of meekness, considering thyself, lest thou also be tempted. Bear one another's burdens, and so fulfill the law of Christ. For if a man think himself to be something, when he is nothing, he deceiveth himself.
> —GALATIANS 6:1–3

Or paraphrasing:

> Brothers, if a believer sins or fails, react spiritually (and maturely). (Instead of rejecting him,) restore him in a humble attitude prompted by the realization that you too (have sinned or failed before and) may be tempted and fall even now. Then you will help each other bear (or get over) your failures whenever they occur, and simultaneously fulfill Jesus' prime command to love each other. But if you proudly conclude you're too good (and your brother too undeserving) for that, your pride is already deceiving you (and causing you to fall from Christ's approval).
> —AUTHOR'S PARAPHRASE

Paul's summation plainly proves pride motivates us to condemn others—and implies the opposite attitude, humble love, prompts us to restore them! But let's go higher.

Above Paul's summary stands Christ's command to show mercy. Jesus cited condemnation of others as a manifestation of unmercifulness and ordered us, "Be ye therefore, merciful, as your Father also is merciful...condemn not" (Luke 6:36–38). To condemn someone is to reject them as contemptible, worthless, and unhelpable, and therefore hopeless, beneath God's grace, undeserving of our attention, and fit only for scorn and punishment. While we may not consciously think these things, they are the underlying sentiments driving us when we dismiss and spurn someone. Why did Jesus insist we never condemn others, however sinful or foolish their actions? Instead of lifting them, condemnation crushes them. Instead of restoring, it ruins. Instead of releasing Christ's compassion, it vents Satan's hatred. Instead of producing fruit, it spoils it. Instead of reviving the Christ-life, it suffocates it. Instead of helping God's will, it hinders it. Why is this topic so important?

We all occasionally fail or come short of God's will. Our reaction to others' failures either helps or hinders not only them but also Christ's will for loving, productive, gospel-advancing unity to prevail in His church (John 17:21–23). By restoring other Christians we help reestablish their fruitfulness and unity in the body and delight Christ's heart. Our thinking therefore must always be redemptive, constructive, positive, ever seeking to lift and repair troubled or broken believers. We must never harbor a scornful attitude (Ps. 1:1) because, whatever a Christian has done (including condemning us![40]), he's (she's) still beloved by Christ—and indwelt by Him! With your steady, gracious assistance and

---

40. After learning not to condemn sinners, we must learn not to condemn scorners. Never condemn with cause those who condemn you without cause! Make your one "cause" obedience to your merciful Master (Luke 6:36–37). If David could forgive his Shimei, you can forgive yours...and walk on peacefully and fruitfully with Christ (2 Sam. 16:5–14; 19:16–23)!

intercession, he can still make a turn and contribute significantly to Christ, His church, and His kingdom plan. Mark proves this.

After restoration, Mark made an outstanding contribution to the early church.[41] He became Barnabas' assistant (Acts 15:39b), more famously Peter's, and finally Paul's. Peter lauded Mark as a valued "son" (1 Pet. 5:13), and Paul added he was "profitable to me for the ministry" (2 Tim. 4:11). But Mark's greatest contribution was his Gospel, which has blessed the entire church age! Thus, his example proves restoring fallen Christians is not only obedience to Christ but also potentially the means of producing significant kingdom fruit!

Even the Old Testament ordered brotherly mercy. God instructed the Jews that when a wicked person (including a Jew) turned from their wickedness to Him, all their past wickedness was not to be mentioned again (Ezek. 33:14–16). Should Christians show less mercy in this age of grace? If we're eager for unbelievers' sins to be cleansed and forgotten, how much more those of believers!

Another argument against condemnation is perhaps the simplest: How do you like it? Ever been condemned by someone who, no matter what you said or did subsequently, refused to readmit you into their circle of friends? How did it make you feel? Then Jesus' golden rule compels you not to do that to another (cf. Matt. 7:12).

---

41. Mark's remarkable turnabout probably resulted from the balanced application of apostolic mercy and discipline. The discipline Paul administered by disqualifying Mark for his second mission trip paid huge dividends in causing Mark to ponder his previous failure and determine "not again!" Have we learned there is a time for mercy and a time for discipline—but never condemnation? If so, we're becoming more like our Lord (cf. Ps. 99:8; Matt. 18:15–17; 1 Cor. 5:13; 2 Cor. 2:6–7).

If still unmotivated, consider Jesus' somber warning against stumbling "little ones" (Matt. 18:5–6). Every Christian, regardless of age, is by virtue of their childlike faith one of Christ's "little ones." Condemning them may so discourage them that, stumbled spiritually, they fall away from Christ. You don't want a "millstone" around your neck, do you? Thus, for many reasons Paul commanded mercy.

Are you complying? After remembering Paul's repeated pleas, Mark's wonderful restoration, his subsequent fruitfulness, Paul's summation in Galatians 6:1–3, Jesus' towering command in Luke 6:36–37, and the other points above, there are only two things left to do: Stop condemning, and start being merciful. And today's the day for both!

4:12–13 Epaphras, an incessant intercessor. Interestingly Paul chose to openly showcase Epaphras' hidden prayer life. Why? Perhaps he was rejoicing to see his own intercessory zeal, and that of the great Intercessor, Christ, being replicated in his committed student.[42] It's more likely he recognized Epaphras' intercessions were a great example for us. Let's examine their spirit, steadfastness, strenuousness, substance, and scope.

Their spirit was not apathetic but zealous or fervent: "Laboring fervently for you in prayers...he hath a great zeal for you" (4:12–13; cf. 1 Kings 18:42; James 5:16b). They were strenuous, as if Epaphras was "wrestling" with powers of darkness opposing the Colossians' spiritual growth: "He is...wrestling in prayer for you" (4:12, NIV).[43] They were

---

42. See my entry, "The incessant Intercessor," Col. 1:9.

43. Epaphras' "wrestling" was not with God but with demons. Steadfast, fervent intercessors are always opposed by demonic forces, as are their

steadfast, as Epaphras was praying "always"—daily, if not several times a day (4:12; cf. Ps. 55:17; Dan. 6:10). Their substance was inspired by the Holy Spirit, as Epaphras prayed that his fellow Christians would stand firm in spiritual maturity in all circumstances, unmoved in their faith, devotion, and service: "That ye may stand perfect and complete in all the will of God" (4:12); or, "stand mature and fully assured in all the will of God" (ESV); or, "stand firm like mature and convinced Christians, whatever be the will of God for you" (MOFFATT). (Here's another inspired, New Testament model prayer we should pray often for Christians and churches, like those we find in Ephesians 1:15–21; 3:14–19; Philippians 1:9–11; Colossians 1:9–12.) Their scope was wide, as he prayed for not just his home church in Colossae but also other congregations in nearby Laodicea and Hierapolis, where he apparently ministered and fellowshiped: "And for them that are in Laodicea, and...in Hierapolis" (4:13).[44] In every way, then, Epaphras' prayer life is compelling.

Will it compel you to move? To abandon any apathy or unbelief that, lingering in your spirit, may be keeping

---

answers (cf. Dan. 10:12–14). Thus, the faithful intercessor ("praying always with all prayer and supplication in the Spirit," Eph. 6:18) will find himself (or herself) often in a spiritual conflict, wrestling against "the [demonic] rulers of the darkness of this world" (Eph. 6:12). This grappling may take the form of spiritual resistance while we're praying or more likely counter-attacks of satanically prompted adversities striking our lives to offend us and thereby reduce the frequency or fervency of our intercessions. Make no mistake, this is the price we must pay to bring spiritual blessings—conversions, deliverances, healings, biblical insights, divine correction, divine guidance, spiritual growth—to those for whom we pray "without ceasing" (1 Thess. 5:17). Are we willing to wrestle against demonic forces to bless others through prayer?

44. See my entry, "Prayer-driven growth," Col. 1:4–7.

you from prayer? To henceforth pray with the same spirit, steadfastness, strenuousness, substance, and scope seen in Epaphras?

4:18 Paul's faithful final word: Remember! Paul's final word to the Colossians was simply "Remember."[45] Specifically what should they, and we, recall?

"Remember my chains" (4:18, NIV). That is, "Remember I'm suffering for Christ." Says one commentator, "The chain clanked afresh as Paul took the pen to sign the salutation. He was not likely to forget it himself."[46] But Paul's goading suggests more.

For instance, he would have us also remember:

- Other believers are also suffering for Christ (Heb. 13:3), and we should pray for their protection and deliverance.[47]

- We too will in some way suffer for our faith if we remain committed to Christ, His gospel, and His call (Phil. 1:29; Matt. 5:10–12; Acts 14:22).

---

45. The following, and technically last statement, "Grace be with you" (4:18), is Paul's standard farewell used with alternate wordings to close all his epistles. Therefore "Remember my bonds" is the last word he addressed personally to the Colossians, and us.

46. See Robertson, *Word Pictures in the New Testament*, Col. 4:18, note.

47. Every day Christians all over the world—especially in Muslim or communist nations or other repressive regimes—are suffering a variety of "chains," from economic disadvantages, legal oppressions, and social ostracism to violent attacks, destruction of property, and imprisonment. Let's "remember" and support them by prayer, missionary ventures, economic assistance, and other encouragements (Heb. 13:3).

- If while suffering Paul could continue ministering by writing the epistle he was then signing (Col. 4:18a), we too can minister while suffering. Paul's example challenges us to rise above our "chains"—limitations, weights, pains, or other unyielding or entangling hardships—and share Jesus, His Word, and His hope with others![48]

- Our sufferings will likely be less numerous and severe than Paul's (2 Cor. 11:23–12:10), so we should give thanks and endure our chains and crosses with grace and contentment (1 Cor. 13:13; Phil. 4:11–12).

- The secret to Paul's victory over great adversity was God's wondrous grace—divine favor giving him wisdom and power to endure without merit, simply for the asking! Without God's grace we can do "nothing" (John 15:5); with it, "all things" (Phil. 4:13)! So Paul prayed for the Colossians, as we should for each other, "Grace be with you" (4:18).

Since Paul's prod closed not just this context but his entire letter, "remember" suggests another larger review.

---

48. Joseph, Moses, David, Jeremiah, Ezekiel, Stephen, John, and Jesus rose above their physical and figurative chains and crosses to minister while suffering. Look to their examples and rise with them (Gen. 40:1–19; Exod. 2:16–19; 1 Sam. 23:1–5; 25:14–16, 21; Jer. 1:17–19; 20:1–2; 37:15–16; Ezek. 3:22–27; Mark 15:34; Luke 23:33–34, 39–43; John 19:25–27; Acts 8:3–8; Rev. 1:9–10)!

We should remember all the vital subjects Paul opened in this letter, such as: Christ's preeminence and fullness, our coming presentation, our great Philosopher, the errors of gnosticism and legalism, Paul's call to focus on heavenly things, his practical commands concerning earthly relationships, continuance in prayer, walking in wisdom, holy clubs, completing our ministries, never condemning others, and so forth. That's Paul's faithful final word to the Colossians, and to us, from above.[49] There's but one thing left to do.

"Remember" it, and live it here below.

---

49. No isolated occurrence, Paul's charge here was characteristic of his apostolic ministry everywhere. For instance, in his final talk with the Ephesian elders he charged them to "remember" all the instructions and warnings he had given them during their three years together (Acts 20:25–32, esp. vv. 27, 31).

SELECT BIBLIOGRAPHY
OF SOURCES CITED

Books

Brand, C., C. Draper, A. England, S. Bond, E. R. Clendenen, T. C. Butler, and B. Latta, editors. *Holman Illustrated Bible Dictionary*. Nashville, TN: Holman Bible Publishers, 2003.

Bunyan, John. *The Pilgrim's Progress*. Old Tappan, NJ: Fleming H. Revell, 1979.

Carson, D. A., R. T. France, J. A. Motyer, and G. J. Wenham, editors. *New Bible Commentary: 21ˢᵗ Century Edition*, 4th edition. Leicester, England; Downers Grove, IL: Inter-Varsity Press, 1994.

Chambers, Oswald. *My Utmost for His Highest*. New York: Dodd, Mead, & Company, 1935.

Cowman, Mrs. Charles E. *Streams in the Desert*. Grand Rapids, MI: Zondervan Publishing House, 1965.

Dake, Finnis Jennings. *Dake's Annotated Reference Bible*. Lawrenceville, GA: Dake Bible Sales, Inc., 1963.

Eckman, J. P. *Exploring Church History.* Wheaton, IL: Crossway, 2002.

Elwell, W. A., and P. W. Comfort. *Tyndale Bible Dictionary.* Wheaton, IL: Tyndale House Publishers, 2001.

Graham, Billy. *Hope for Each Day: Words of Wisdom and Faith.* Nashville, TN: Thomas Nelson Publishers, 2002.

Hayford, Jack W., general editor. *The Spirit-Filled Life Bible.* Nashville: Thomas Nelson Publishers, 1991.

Henry, Matthew. *Commentary in One Volume.* Grand Rapids, MI; Zondervan Publishing, 1961.

Hyatt, Eddie. *The Azusa Street Revival.* Lake Mary, FL: Charisma House, 2006.

Keener, C. S. *The IVP Bible Background Commentary: New Testament.* Downers Grove, IL: InterVarsity Press, 1993.

_____. *Miracles: The Credibility of the New Testament Accounts,* Vol. I. Grand Rapids, MI: Baker Academic, 2011.

Kittel, G., G. Friedrich, and G. W. Bromiley. *Theological Dictionary of the New Testament,* electronic edition. Grand Rapids, MI: W. B. Eerdmans, 1985.

Liddell, H. *A Lexicon: Abridged From Liddell and Scott's Greek–English Lexicon.* Oak Harbor, WA: Logos Research Systems, Inc., 1996.

Life Application Study Bible. Wheaton, IL: Tyndale House, 2004.

Louw, J. P. and E. A. Nida. *Greek–English Lexicon of the New Testament: Based on Semantic Domains*, electronic edition of the second edition. New York: United Bible Societies, 1996.

Lust, J., E. Eynikel, and K. Hauspie. *A Greek–English Lexicon of the Septuagint: Revised Edition.* Stuttgart: Deutsche Bibelgesellschaft, 2003.

Marsden, George. "The Born-Again Mind." *Christian History Magazine*, Issue 92: A New Evangelical Awakening. Worchester, PA: Christian History Institute, 2006.

Mueller, George. *Answers to Prayer.* Chicago: Moody Press, 1984.

Myers, A. C. *The Eerdmans Bible Dictionary.* Grand Rapids, MI: Eerdmans, 1987.

Robertson, A. *Word Pictures in the New Testament.* Nashville: Broadman Press, 1933.

Scofield, C. I. *The New Scofield Study Bible.* New York, NY: Oxford University Press, 1967.

Smith, S. and J. Cornwall. *The Exhaustive Dictionary of Bible Names.* North Brunswick, NJ: Bridge Logos Publishers, 1998.

Spicq, C. and J. D. Ernest. *Theological Lexicon of the New Testament*. Peabody, MA: Hendrickson Publishers, 1994.

Strong, J. *A Concise Dictionary of the Words in the Greek Testament and The Hebrew Bible*. Bellingham, WA: Logos Bible Software, 2009.

———. *Enhanced Strong's Lexicon*. Bellingham, WA: Logos Bible Software, 2001.

Swanson, J. *Dictionary of Biblical Languages With Semantic Domains: Greek (New Testament)*, electronic edition. Oak Harbor: Logos Research Systems, Inc., 1997.

Tenny, Merrill C. and Moises Silva, editors. *The Zondervan Encyclopedia of the Bible, Vol. 1, A–C*. Grand Rapids, MI: Zondervan, 2009.

Thomas, R. L. *New American Standard Hebrew–Aramaic and Greek Dictionaries*, updated edition. Anaheim: Foundation Publications, Inc., 1998.

Tozer, A. W. *The Best of A.W. Tozer*. Harrisonburg, PA: Christian Publications, 1978.

Verploegh, Harry. *Oswald Chambers: The Best From All His Books*. Nashville: Thomas Nelson Publishers, 1987.

Walvoord, J. F., R. B. Zuck, and Dallas Theological Seminary. *The Bible Knowledge Commentary: An Exposition of the Scriptures*. Wheaton, IL: Victor Books, 1985.

Weymouth, Richard F. *New Testament in Modern Speech.* Grand Rapids, MI: Kregel Publications, 1978.

Wiersbe, W. W. *The Bible Exposition Commentary.* Wheaton, IL: Victor Books, 1996.

Wuest, K. S. *The New Testament: An Expanded Translation.* Grand Rapids, MI: Eerdmans, 1961.

Web sites

- www.brainyquote.com: The official Web site of BrainyQuote, the world's largest quotation Web site, "On a mission to share our knowledge with the world."

- www.britannica.com: The official Web site of Encyclopedia Britannica

- www.christianhistoryinstitute.org: The official Web site of the Christian History Institute and *Christian History* Magazine

- www.christianity.com: A Web site produced by a group of writers and editors with a passion for giving people access to what is enduringly Christian

- www.cslewisinstitute.org: The official Web site of the C. S. Lewis Institute, which, in the legacy of C. S. Lewis, endeavors to develop disciples who will articulate, defend, and live their faith in Christ in personal and public life

- http://gracequotes.org: Grace Quotes, the largest topically organized collection of Christian quotations available on the Internet, with over 10,000 Christian quotations, is intended to edify and equip the worldwide Christian community.

- http://hebrew4christians.com: The official Web site of Hebrew for Christians ministry, a resource for the church regarding its rich Hebraic heritage that promotes Jewish literacy among all those who claim Jesus Christ as their Lord

- www.ligonier.org: The official Web site of Ligonier Ministries, the teaching fellowship of the Reformed theologian R. C. Sproul

- http://www.myjewishlearning.com: A leading transdenominational Web site of Jewish information and education

- www.persecution.com: The official Web site of Voice of the Martyrs ministry

- www.stephenmansfield.tv: The official Web site of Christian author, historian, speaker, and commentator Stephen Mansfield

- http://wesley.nnu.edu: The official Web site of the Wesley Center for Applied Theology at Northwest Nazarene University. The Wesley Center Online is a collection of historical and scholarly resources about the Wesleyan tradition, theology, Christianity, and the Church of the Nazarene.

- https://en.wikipedia.org: Three times in this work I have cited Wikipedia. Since it is an open source online encyclopedia (subject to public editing), I have also cited alternate sources to corroborate the information noted.

CONTACT THE AUTHOR

Greg Hinnant Ministries
P. O. Box 788
High Point, NC 27261

Telephone:
(336) 882-1645

E-mail:
rghministries@aol.com

Website:
greghinnantministries.org

Also visit Greg Hinnant
on Facebook and LinkedIn.

OTHER BOOKS BY
THE AUTHOR

Walking in His Ways

Walking on Water

*DanielNotes: An Inspirational Commentary
on the Book of Daniel*

*PhilippianNotes: An Inspirational Commentary
on Paul's Epistle to the Philippians*

Precious Pearls From the Proverbs

Word Portraits: Five Illustrations of the Mature Christian

Gold Tried in the Fire: Tested Truths for Trying Times

*Spiritual Truths for Overcoming Adversity: Life-
Changing Biblical Insights on Christian Difficulties*

Not by Bread Alone: Daily Devotions for Disciples, Volume One

*Sweeter Than Honey: Daily Devotions
for Disciples, Volume Two*

*Water From the Rock: Daily Devotions
for Disciples, Volume Three*

Key New Testament Passages on Divorce and Remarriage